THE LURE

OF

SAILING

The
Lure
of
Sailing

BY EVERETT A. PEARSON

A HARPER INTERNATIONAL EDITION

JOINTLY PUBLISHED BY

Harper & Row, NEW YORK, EVANSTON & LONDON

AND *John Weatherhill, Inc.,* TOKYO

To my wife

Contents

FOREWORD, vii

1. *The New Age of the Sail,* 1

A Look at the Fleet . . . Sailboat Styles . . . Hull Construction . . . Modern-Day Sails . . . Engines for Sailboats . . . Necessary Safety Equipment . . . A Home for Your Boat . . . Marine Insurance . . . Before You Get Under Way

2. *Reviewing the Art of Sailing,* 33

Aerodynamics of Sailing . . . Know Your Sails . . . Know Your Rigging . . . The Points of Sailing . . . Bending and Hoisting Sail . . . Sailing to Windward . . . Sailing Before the Wind . . . Reaching . . . Handling the Spinnaker

3. *Reviewing Sailing Seamanship,* 69

Leaving the Mooring . . . Getting Under Way from a Dock . . . Helmsmanship and Trim . . . Right-of-Way Rules . . . Anchoring and Leaving an Anchorage . . . Laying To . . . Approaching and Picking Up the Mooring . . . Rafting . . . Docking Procedure . . . Leaving Her Shipshape . . . Marlinspike Seamanship

4. *Weather Wisdom and Sailing,* 102

Radio Weather Reports . . . Storm Signals . . . Weather Maps . . . Visual Weather Indications . . . Weather Instruments . . . Reefing . . . Tactics in Bad Weather . . . Tides and Their Effects

5. *Getting Where You Want to Go,* 134
Nautical Charts and Pilot Aids . . . The Mariner's Compass . . . Plotting a Course . . . Aids to Navigation . . . Finding Your Position . . . Night Navigation

6. *The Lure of Cruising,* 162
Types of Cruising . . . Planning a Cruise . . . Cruising Gear . . . Fall Cruising . . . Group Cruising

7. *Living Afloat,* 186
Cruising Routine . . . Cruising Records . . . Eating Afloat . . . Boatkeeping Afloat . . . Children on a Cruise . . . Cruising Activities . . . Emergency Procedures at Sea

8. *The Lure of Racing,* 212
Racing Courses . . . Sailing Instructions . . . Racing Rules . . . Races Are Won at the Start . . . Racing Pitfalls . . . Class Association

9. *The Lure of Ocean Racing,* 231
Handicap Systems . . . Measurement Rules and Time Allowance . . . Midget Ocean Racing Club . . . Tips on Distance Racing

10. *Yachting Etiquette and You,* 249
Good Manners Afloat . . . Flag and Yachting Routine . . . Clothing for Yachtsmen

11. *The Care of Your Sailboat,* 265
Lay-up Time . . . Spring Fitting-out . . . Sail Care . . . First Aid for Your Yacht . . . Midseason Care

GLOSSARY, 307

INDEX, 321

Foreword

It has been my aim in writing this book to explain the lure of sailing to the novice as well as to those familiar with this great sport. For the latter sailors, there are two refresher chapters on refinements of the fundamentals that should add polish to otherwise casual seamanship and sailing techniques. These same chapters will also serve the beginner with the necessary information needed to "get off on the right foot." Except for the last chapter which is devoted to the maintenance of your craft, the rest of the book is dedicated to having fun with your sailboat, whether cruising, racing—inshore or offshore—or just loafing around out on the water. And there is advice for emergencies—should they arise. While it is impossible to give all the lures of sailing in one book, or even give a complete word picture of our great sport, I have attempted to supply enough to whet your appetite. But let me make one point clear right away—you can't have this fun only by reading this book or any other. You have to go out on the water in a sailboat of your own.

The success of any cruise or sail depends on the help of your crew. And when writing a book, the author needs the cooperation of many people and organizations. I would like to thank the following for their help in this book: Columbian Rope Company, United States Coast Guard, United States Department of Commerce, Yacht Racing Association of Long Island Sound, Cruising Club of America, Inc., Midget Ocean Racing Club, Rohm & Haas Company, Owens-Corning Fiberglass Corporation, Ferro Corporation, Ratsey & Lapthorn, Inc., Raritan Engineering Company, Curtis Publishing Company, Plymouth Cordage Company, and the various boating publications: *Popular Boating, Motor Boating, Rudder, Yachting,* and *Sea and Pacific Motor Boat.* I am genuinely indebted to these firms and their employees as I am to the people of my own firm. All their help is appreciated. But I am sure that we all hope this book will open new vistas of pleasure for you and your family.

Everett A. Pearson

Bristol, Rhode Island

1

The New Age
of the Sail

What lures the sailor? If you must ask, he'll rarely tell you. He may say, "Oh, it's quiet out there." Or, "I like my traffic lights on lighthouses." Or, "No telephones!" Or he may quote, half wryly, half reverently, Sir Thomas Lipton's phrase, "the glorious and health-giving sport of yachting." In my mind, however, I believe the reason why Americans the length and breadth of the land have revived the old tradition of a great maritime nation and made sailing the country's newest mass sport is stated in the marvelous opening paragraphs of *Moby Dick,* where Herman Melville says that all mankind, even inland away from the sea, feels the lure of sailing. "There is magic in it."

An old magic, inherent in man. Today's playtime sailor shares it with a long past. His weekend sea legs roll with the ages and his small dacron jib-headed sails are the survival of clouds of historic canvas. The tennis racket and the golf club were always toys. Sail and spar and keel and tiller are old gear, rich in significance and years. Actually, no one knows exactly who invented the sail, for its origins lie far beyond the dawn of history. The Egyptians were running down the Nile under square sail of papyrus fiber in 6000 B.C. From that time until the steam engine was hooked up to drive a ship, sailing was exploration and discovery and the transportation of sea-borne commerce. It helped build empires, stretch frontiers. Save for the tedium of voyages that were too long or too hard, or those voyages harassed with hunger, crossing the Trades, the long drives across the date line in the China trade, even the tempestuous passages of the Western Ocean, the North Atlantic, were all part of what the sailing man gloried in, as countless logs and diaries testify.

While sailboats are no longer used commercially, the popularity of sailing as a sport is increasing yearly in North American waters. But why this great interest in sailing? The answer is that the average man (or woman) has found gratification in the sense of swift motion under sail. He has felt kinship with nature in connection with the free-flowing wind. Even before the age of telephones and ulcers, there was vitality and healing peace for him under sail, free of the feverish, wheel-rumbling, profit-grabbing land. And more deeply emotional and splendid than all the rest, there was a vain, fine pride in being a part of a thing of beauty, a sailing ship. She was and is a creature of man's making, but so vibrant and aware and temperamental and lovely that she is always "she," a feminine personality, alive and sprightly.

Our modern pleasure sailor has the same sensations, no matter where or in what sort of boat he may sail, no matter what sort of sailor he is. There are many sorts: rich sailors and poor ones, old ones and lisping tots, male and female, big-boat and little-boat sailors, cruising sailors and those who live only to race all day long around a small triangle of water. There are sailors who have only an academic interest in how a boat reaches across the wind or runs off broad before it, but glory in her ability to slice to windward. There are sailors who are happiest in one-design boats made as exactly similar to many others as craftsmanship can contrive. There are others who consider such craft as so many wind-driven flivvers, and who want all of the comforts of the larger, more expensive sloops and yawls.

To the pleasure sailor, the sport of sailing can satisfy nearly all the senses and stir all the emotions. The sea and the wind are seldom the same on two consecutive days. One day you'll get a feeling of complete peace and serenity, with no sound except a gentle chuckle under the bow; another day, the wind is strong and one achieves a feeling of exhilaration and power as the craft surges through the water.

Maybe the reason why it's so hard to describe the feeling of sailing is because of its "creative" aspect. It is most difficult to explain how your touch upon the tiller is like the stroke of an artist, fashioning from the raw materials of water and wind something that is self-expressive, graceful, and powerful. While most of us rarely stop to think of this quality in sailing, it is certainly present. If you analyze it for a minute, you're working in a medium that is very much alive, brighter than any paint, broader than any canvas, and punctuated with the musical sounds of wind and water. You're making of these things something that is very personal—that gives you a feeling of accomplishment during the summer days and becomes a vivid memory in winter. If this isn't creative, I don't know what is.

There are many further rewards than these; for instance, resourcefulness, self-discipline, and confidence develop not from arduous cultivation, but as natural complements to the adventure of sailing. As a matter of fact, there are so many rewards that sailors like you and I get from our sport that to describe them would completely fill this book. But, rather than go on, let's answer the opening question by saying that sailing is a thousand lures. It is nothing but lure and beauty.

A Look at the Fleet

One of the great pleasures of sailing is merely to look at, and perhaps covet, the infinite variety of vessels found afloat. Of the sailing craft that you'll most likely spot, there are six basic types: catboat, sloop, cutter, yawl, ketch, and schooner. The catboat, sloop, and cutter all have a single mast, but the catboat can be distinguished by her single sail set abaft the mast. The sloop's single mast supports a mainsail and one or more other sails, either abaft or forward. The difference between the cutter's and sloop's mast is its position. On the sloop the mast is set forward of amidships, while on the cutter it is set amidships. This amidships setting of the mast allows for more headsail area, and the cutter usually carries two or three jibs or small sails forward. The yawl, the ketch, and the schooner are two-masted boats. The yawl differs from the ketch in that the smaller mast (the mizzenmast) is set abaft the tiller or wheel. If the mizzenmast were missing from either the yawl or ketch, these sailboats would look like a sloop. (Several of the cruising-racing sailboats that we build are rigged as either sloops or yawls.) The schooner might be described as a large ketch with her masts reversed. The mainmast of the schooner is behind the smaller mast. But of all the sailboat types, the sloop is by far the most popular. As a matter of fact, the cutter, ketch, and schooner are seldom seen afloat any more.

Sailboat Styles

Two basic styles of sailboats are popular today: one-design racer–day-sailer and one-design cruiser-racer. The term "one-design" for all

Figure 1-1: Popular types of sail rigs (left to right): cat, sloop, and yawl.

sailboat styles means that all boats of that class (for example, the Ensign Class) have been constructed to the same set of plans, specifications, and measurements. In other words, each boat in a class is as similar to her sister ships in sailing characteristics and dimensions as possible. This means that, within a class, success in racing depends upon the skill of the skipper rather than upon his ability to pay for expensive refinements built into his craft. It also means you may race in competition on an even basis—no handicap system required—almost anywhere that you find boats of your class.

Many of the more popular one-design classes are represented by associations. These have been founded by owners joining together for mutual protection and exchange of ideas. The association then draws bylaws and racing rules, and conducts sanctioned class events. These may include local, regional, national, and in some cases, world-championship regattas. A few associations are large, formal affairs, administered by a paid executive secretary, but the majority are smaller and more informally run by a devoted group of owners of a particular class. Most of them publish either or both newsletters and yearbooks that are of great interest and value to the owners.

Ownership of a class boat and membership in a class association have many advantages. In addition to the way in which these associations enforce their class rules and promote well-run, well-organized racing, they also serve to bring sailors with common interests together socially at class meetings and regattas, and they protect the value of any boat in the class. By strict enforcement of the rules, by maintaining standards, by registering boats and keeping a record of them, the association protects the buyer and seller when a class boat changes hands, and this tends to keep the value of boats up over the years. Actually, unless radical changes occur in the sailboat market, you should be able, when you decide to sell, to get back most of, and sometimes more than, the amount you invested—considering, of course, that the craft was well-maintained. Remember

Figure 1-2: One-design racer-cruiser (left) and racer–day-sailer (right) that are both 23 feet. Note that the bracket on the transom of the racer–day-sailer is equipped for an outboard motor.

that sailing boats—especially those built of fiberglass—are long-lived and therefore don't rapidly depreciate in value. At one time it was a generally accepted rule of thumb that a five-year-old one-design sailboat would sell for approximately 75 percent of what she cost when new. (Powerboats depreciate much more rapidly in value and in relative performance than do sailboats. Their depreciation scale is similar to that of automobiles.) Under this old formula about half of this depreciation was prorated over the first two years. With the increased interest in sailing and the rise in the cost of building new boats, however, the market value of well-kept used boats has soared. Actually, some owners who purchased new boats ten or twenty years ago have had the pleasant experience of selling their craft for more than they originally paid. Thus, there's always a distinct possibility that a one-design class sailboat *may* even prove to be a financially profitable investment.

Getting back to the styles themselves, the racer–day-sailer offers the pleasure of an easy day-sail with your family, plus the fun of racing against other boats of the same class. But, if you want to go day sailing comfortably, or if you're a beginner in racing, or especially if you want your family to learn to like sailing, don't pick too extreme a racing type of boat. Buy a one-design boat of the day-sailer type with a comfortable cockpit to sit in, not one in which you have to hang out over the rail and make with the acrobatics to keep it right side up. A boat on the heavy and beamy side is better for the afternoon-sailing family, or for the beginner, than the ultrafast types. Even though you don't want to race at first, you may later. In other words, with a one-design class sailboat, you can sail for fun and still race in competition if you wish.

Some of the larger racer–day-sailers have a cuddy-cabin arrangement that will permit two or more persons to sleep overnight. The previously mentioned Ensign, for example, is a very active class boat with one-design racing fleets from coast to coast. But her deep, large, nine-foot cockpit, convenient head, and two bunks in the cuddy cabin make her an ideal family day-sailer between races.

The cruiser-racer or cruising auxiliary—the boat with sails, engine, and cabin—is a great favorite all over the world. The cabin provides shelter for the youngsters on day sails, and longshore accommodations for periods ranging from a weekend in the small sizes to more extended voyages in thirty-footers and up. They are stiff, able, and seaworthy, and can negotiate a lot of rough water in safety. While many auxiliary and cruising sailboats are considered one-design boats and do have associations, quite often—unlike boats of smaller class—there are not sufficient numbers in a given area for even-up racing. To overcome this, most yacht clubs have a program of handicapped racing for cruising sailboats, so the cruiser or auxiliary isn't excluded from active competition (see Chapter 8 for details). If the skipper and crew are experienced enough, and your boat can pass the race-committee requirements, you can participate in the classic offshore races such as the Bermuda, Nassau, Mackinac, Ensenada, and Honolulu events.

Of all the cruiser-racers, the group of so-called midget ocean racers is most popular. These are cruisers that are under thirty feet and meet special requirements (see Chapter 9), and the class holds frequent offshore races under the sponsorship of the Midget Ocean Racing Club. We are proud of the part our company has played in the development of one of the most successful MORC sailing auxiliaries. During a casual meeting in 1958, Carl A. Alberg, naval architect, and Thomas A. Potter, a lifelong yacht salesman, discussed the postwar boom in pleasure boating, especially the fact that it had become a family sport rather than a recreation for males only. Their conversation turned to the sailing auxiliary, by definition a sailboat with a small inboard engine for auxiliary power, big enough to shelter a family in relative comfort for a cruise of three days or more. It must also have cooking and toilet facilities, people-size bunks and adequate storage space. Until that time, the sailing auxiliary (the cruiser-racer) was out of the financial reach of most Americans. The depression and war decades weren't opportune for its growth, and technology had not broken through the hand-crafted wooden construction that made this style of craft so costly. But Alberg and Potter were convinced that such a boat of fiberglass with full headroom in the cabin would be popular if it could be built for about $10,000. They brought their idea and design to us, and after a great deal of work by our company the Triton Class was born.

This class reflects three trends: the family sailing boom, the popularity of fiberglass, and the relatively low price of mass-produced boats. But it also reflects others; according to my friend Mr. Alberg: In the old days, sailboats tended to be narrow. They had little freeboard and the crew were apt to be soaked in any kind of a blow. Now, in boats like the Triton Class, they are beamier and have more freeboard, stability, and seaworthiness. We got tired of nestling down into the waves every time we went off shore. The new auxiliaries will take seas in stride we would have considered too rough in the old days.

Hull Construction

As previously mentioned, one of the most startling developments of the new age of the sail has been the introduction of fiberglass reinforced plastic boat construction. We feel especially proud of the general acceptance by the sailing public of this material since we were one of the first manufacturers to use it for various styles of sailboats. Actually, today we make over twenty-one one-design sailboats ranging from eight feet to forty-four. We are also proud of the fact that we now construct our boats in the same yards where Captain Nat Herreshoff, the "Wizard of Bristol," and his craftsmen created so many successful America's Cup defenders.

Our continuing research and development in mold design, plastic materials, and construction methods have resulted in many breakthroughs in design, quality, and price. We are often asked why we consider fiberglass construction so superior to wood—the most popular boatbuilding material since the dawn of history—in the building of cruiser-racer sailboats. Here are the two major advantages we have found over the years:

1. The naval architect has a great deal more freedom in the design of shapes and styles. Compound curves in the hull are no problem, nor are rounded corners. Fiberglass lends itself to integral, monocoque construction that has the rigidity of more traditional wood construction of light planking over ribs. Perhaps this heavy strength accounts for the growth in "glass" auxiliary construction. After all, most keel sailboats carry lead keels. The slight gain in weight at deck level is offset by the design factor that the tanks are placed down low. If he uses aluminum for the spars, he saves a little more weight high up, where it counts the most. One other factor may become important in the future: as naval architects get more experience with the engineering of fiberglass boats, they may find they have made them overstrong and therefore somewhat heavy.

2. The problems of repair and maintenance are greatly simpli-

Figure 1-3: The construction of a hull. The fiberglass is built up in layers over a wood form (left), while at the right we see a completed hull. The hull is then smoothed up (left) and the bottom given a coat of antifouling paint (right).

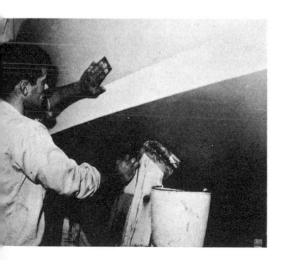

fied with fiberglass construction. But, as for claims beyond these, which some proponents of fiberglass boats have made: A fiberglass boat will not be damaged by teredos drilling holes into the hull, as a wooden boat in southern waters may be—but a barnacle can still attach itself to fiberglass and slow the boat down. A deck leak is unlikely, easy to repair, and if it should go undetected will not lead to rot of the main structure. But if water gets under the wooden trim on the cabin top or the toe rail, the wood can still rot. Fortunately it is no harder to replace than on any other boat, and this kind of rot doesn't spread to the main structure. "Never needs painting"? That depends. It doesn't need painting to protect the surface, but it will need it for looks after a few years. "Unbreakable"? Like anything else, fiber glass can be gouged, cracked, and broken. It is tremendously strong. Actually, integrally molded hull, deck, and cabin gives amazing strength, pound for pound offering more impact tensile strength than other known marine construction materials, including steel. Glass-reinforced plastic construction bends; it resists abrasion. It is easy to repair. So you must put your own interpretation on phrases like "permanent, maintenance-free."

Let's take a slightly closer look at a well-made boat of fiberglass, woven cloth, and polyester. Let's take as an example the hull of a 32-foot cruiser-racer, the *Vanguard,* a single molded fiberglass—reinforced plastic unit. It consists of a pigmented outer layer (gel coat) which is sprayed into the polished inner surface of the mold. A layer of 1 ½-ounce fiberglass mat is then spread out on top of the gel coat and completely saturated with polyester resin. Next a layer of 10-ounce cloth is spread over the mat and saturated with resin. Alternate layers of mat and 24-ounce woven fiberglass roving are laid up and saturated in this manner until the hull is completed. To insure uniformity in the shape of the hull, all structural members and bulkheads are bonded into the hull before it leaves the mold. This process, called "hand laying-up," eliminates the possibility of "voids" or "dry spots" within the laminate. The combination of woven roving and mat fiberglass creates the strongest bond between laminates and thereby gives greater strength against shear. A completed hull carefully constructed in this manner has an inherent strength and resilience which can be found in no other material. Furthermore, any shock or stress is transferred in all directions simultaneously, thus minimizing the effect of the shock at any one point of contact.

Like the hull, the deck, cabin, and cockpit form a single molded fiberglass—reinforced plastic unit. The pigmented gel coat is sprayed into the polished inner surface of the deck mold. A nonskid pattern, part of the mold itself, becomes superimposed on the deck; this pattern is not a material that is added later. The method of laying up the deck is similar to that of making the hull; however, a balsa-wood core is incorporated between two layers of fiberglass laminate to achieve the necessary strength and stiffness as well as the light weight which is desirable in a deck structure. Although the balsa wood itself adds some strength to the deck, the real strength lies in the separation of the laminate, just as a steel I beam is stronger than a steel bar of the same weight. The balsa core also acts as an insulator against heat. The smooth interior of the cabin is accomplished by means of a separate molded fiberglass unit designed to fit snugly inside the cabin trunk with the smooth side exposed. This unit is called a headliner and serves the purpose of giving the interior a clean, finished appearance. After much of the interior work is done on the hull, and fittings installed on the deck, the deck is bonded to the hull with fiberglass cloth and mat all along the inside at the shear line. All structural bulkheads, which were bonded to the hull while it was still in the mold, are at this point bonded to the underside of the deck. The seam between the deck and hull is then filled from the outside with a silicon compound to insure its watertightness, and the teak cap-rail is installed. A stainless steel rub-rail is installed over the seam between the deck and hull.

All deck and cockpit scuppers drain out just below the waterline through rugged fiberglass tubes molded into the hull. This arrangement allows water to drain off the decks and out of the cockpit without leaving stains on the topsides. Both seat hatches in the cockpit have deep angled gutters to keep water out of these compartments. Two ventilators are molded in the deck with baffles to allow air but not water to enter. These ventilators, known as "Dorade" type ventilators, exhaust into the head area.

The mast is stepped on top of the cabin trunk. There are many reasons for this arrangement aside from the obvious advantage of a clear unobstructed passage from the main cabin, through the head, and into the forward cabin. Lack of a mast aperture in the deck eliminates the possibility of leaks around the mast. Stepping and unstepping the mast is greatly facilitated since the mast doesn't have to be lifted an extra six or seven feet and fed in through a small aperture. Tuning the rigging is easily done because the mast can be raked either forward or aft without adjusting a mast step on the keel. In the event of an accident in which a supporting shroud is severed, the mast will ordinarily fall over the lee side with little damage. The mast is stepped in a steel bridge which spans both of the structural bulkheads that form the "head" compartment. The bulkheads are reinforced further by crossbeams and upright stanchions which are bolted to the marine plywood. This entire structure is designed to withstand a downward thrust of the mast much greater than the breaking strength of the shrouds will allow.

In smaller fiberglass sailboats—especially the racer–day-sailer style —the cockpit is generally self-bailing. If the cockpit is too large and deep to be self-bailing, it is made absolutely safe by having enough foam flotation to support the hull and passengers on an even keel with the entire hull filled with water. This flotation is usually located in the bow compartment, the stern compartment, and under the seats in the cabin. In any case, the present development of fiberglass boats is not the last word. Boatbuilders are still experimenting to bring the very best boats to the sailing public.

Modern-Day Sails

The art of the sailmaker is complex and demanding. The unskilled or semiskilled boatmen of centuries ago created sails to meet personal needs. Sailmaking, however, has become for us one of the most skilled trades, one which demands virtual perfection to satisfy the many requirements of the owner, the type of boat, and the locale in which she is sailed. But, whereas the boatman of 6000 B.C. was forced to be content with a form of papyrus for a sail, the sailmaker of today is practically unlimited in his choice of fabric. This is merely an indication of the complexity that has come about in the sailmaker's art.

From the early 1800's to the beginning of the 1950's, cotton sailcloth, first made famous by the Yankee clipper ships and by yachts like the *America,* ruled as the standard medium for propelling ships and yachts by wind power. But, in the new age of sailing, cotton is no longer king. After World War II various synthetic fibers were tested for their potential as a sailcloth. Because they possessed certain obvious advantages over cotton, such as the ability to resist mildew, they were quickly put to use. Few of these materials actually had all of the attributes required of a satisfactory sailcloth. Some were too elastic, others stretched when wet, and still others were simply not sufficiently durable. Eventually, however, dacron and nylon emerged as the two nearly perfect materials for the purpose, and today almost all mains, jibs, genoas, staysails, and other working and racing sails are made of dacron, while nylon is used almost exclusively for spinnakers.

As a modern sailcloth, dacron fabric, when properly made and finished, has the following desirable properties:

1. It doesn't swell when wet or damp.
2. It stretches very little under tension.
3. It is mildewproof.
4. It is highly durable.

Most sailboats, especially the larger ones, are sold *without* sails; this permits the owner to purchase them from a sailmaker of his own choosing. The boatbuilder furnishes plans for a typical suit of sails, but the sailmaker can make any changes he thinks best for the area where the boat is to be sailed. The owner also may have some special design or custom features he wishes to incorporate into his sails. We, like most builders, do have suits of standard sails available, but I usually recommend that the owner buy them from a local sailmaker. For this reason, sails are not included in the price of a boat.

Engines for Sailboats

Yachtsmen used to scorn the lowly "gasoline breeze," but today, in the new age of the sail, there probably aren't very many sailing cruiser-racers (except the smaller ones) in the country without some type of auxiliary power.

As a rule, when one buys a class boat of 25 feet or more in length, she usually comes with the engine installed, and one must pretty much assume that the engine is well put in. There has been a tendency among several boatbuilders to make small cruiser-racers available with the power optional. This, in many cases, reduces the cost as much as two thousand dollars. Then the engine may be installed at a later date should the owner wish. In any case, if you wish to add power, check her original builder for his recommendations. Should these not be available, try to find a yard or mechanic that's familiar with sailboat installations. Mechanics used only to working on power cruisers just can't be trusted with the planning or installing of an exhaust system or line at all complicated. Nor is the average engine dealer likely to be up on the finer points of sailboat installations. You can, however, get worthwhile advice from the engine's manufacturer. I've found that the average manufacturer will plan the entire layout for you, if you'll supply him with the hull plan and particulars of the boat. Many have booklets on sailboat installation. Regardless of the circumstances, here are two rules to be sure to follow: 1) Select your engine intelligently, but be a real stickler as to how it is installed; and 2) follow through by giving your engine every chance to do its best. Don't baby it or hesitate to use it, for it's disuse rather than actual running that's responsible for so many engine ailments. Just see that your way of using it and of looking after its needs offset those disadvantages inherent to a sailboat installation.

Some smaller cruiser-racers and the larger racer–day-sailers have facilities for outboard motor power (1½ to 10 horsepower in size). An outboard well, ballast-compensated, is designed into the hull of some of these boats, while others have motor brackets available.

Necessary Safety Equipment

It is wise to check the builder's list of standard equipment before you set out to purchase any gear for your boat; in most cases, safety items are left for the owner to furnish. The United States Coast Guard has set up specifications for the equipment that must be carried on motorboats (if your sailboat has auxiliary power on board, you *must* comply with motorboat regulations) on Federal waters, while the Pilot Rules indicate items that must be available on boats of any kind, no matter what the method of propulsion. On waters not under the jurisdiction of the Coast Guard, other agencies, such as states or Federal bureaus, prescribe minimum requirements. Common sense calls for safety equipment even in instances where there is no official regulation.

It's not too difficult to follow an equipment list laid out by law, but it takes a little planning to be sure that you have aboard all of

SAFETY EQUIPMENT REQUIRED ABOARD*

Class*	Life Preserver	Fire Ex- tinguisher†	Horn or Whistle	Bell	Bilge Ventilators	Flame Arrestors
A (boats less than 16 feet long)	For each person on board: 1 Coast Guard approved life preserver, ring buoy, buoyant vest, or buoyant cushion	One	None	None	Bilge, fuel tank, and engine compartment ventilators	Every engine must have a carburetor flame arrestor
1 (16–25 ft.)	Same as Class A	One	One, Audible ½ mile	None	Same as Class A	Same as Class A
2 (26–39 ft.)	Same as Class A	Two	One, Audible 1 mile	One	Same as Class A	Same as Class A
3 (40–64 ft.)	Same as Class A, but life preserver or ring buoy only	Three	Same as 2	One	Same as Class A	Same as Class A

* Applies to sailboats with auxiliary power; all sailboats, however, must carry life preservers as noted above, plus a signaling device such as a horn or whistle.

† Carbon tetrachloride extinguishers are no longer approved.

the additional gear you may need. Here, prudence, and not jurisprudence, should be the guide. There are necessary items which don't appear on the required minimum list; for example, ground tackle.

Anchor and Anchor Lines. The anchor itself is still the key to your ground tackle even in this new age of the sail. It is necessary, therefore, to know what to expect from various anchors. The "patent" or "stockless" anchor holds 2 to 3 times its weight in small sizes, and about 5 times its weight in ship sizes. The "old-fashioned" or "yachtsman's" anchor holds 3 to 8 times its weight in small sizes, and about 5 times its weight in large sizes. The mushroom anchor, used for moorings, holds about twice its weight, although it is more effective if it has silted-in over a period of months. Concrete or granite blocks hold about one-half or two-thirds their weight in air, or an amount just about equal to their weight in water. Various modern patent anchors hold many times their weight, with the Danforth being the most effective. It holds 17 to 1000 times its weight in smaller sizes, and 8 to 30 times its weight in larger sizes. Actually your yacht should carry two anchors—one light-duty one for short stops such as for lunch, swimming, fishing; and a heavy-duty one for overnight stops—and a cruising boat may even carry a third or spare anchor.

Displacement alone won't determine the size of your ground tackle. For instance, sailboats strain more at anchor than power-boats because they have more rigging aloft. For this reason, it's

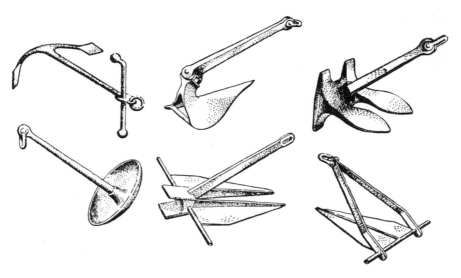

Figure 1-4: The more popular anchors (top, left to right): yachtsman's anchor, CQR plow, the navy stockless or patent; (bottom, left to right) mushroom, Dan-forth, and wishbone.

rather difficult to give a hard-and-fast rule on the size of anchors that your craft should carry. Anchor manufacturers, with their long ex-perience, and good marine dealers, with their knowledge of local "bottom" conditions, can usually make a good "educated" guess as to the size best for both light- and heavy-duty work aboard your yacht. The following table gives recommended anchor-line sizes, as well as amounts of line to have on board. Remember that, for maxi-mum holding power, it is important to have a length of anchor line (called "scope") out that is equal to many times the depth of the water—seven times is a safe minimum. It is a good idea to mark your line so that you can be sure that you will anchor with enough scope. Every fathom (six feet) paint a mark on the line. Anchor-line markers are also available commercially. When you lower the anchor to the bottom, note the depth by the number of marks you paid out, then continue until you have the desired length of line out. The effectiveness of an anchor at different scopes is as follows:

2 to 1—13%	5 to 1—65%	8 to 1—77%
3 to 1—46%	6 to 1—72%	9 to 1—82%
4 to 1—54%	7 to 1—75%	10 to 1—85%

Over-all Length of Boat (in feet)	*Anchor Used*	*Length of Anchor Lines (in feet)*	*Manila Rope Diameter (in inches)*	*Nylon Rope Diameter (in inches)*
Under 20	Light	100	½	
	Heavy			
				⅜
20–25	Light	125	½	½
	Heavy	200	⅝	
				9/16
25–30	Light	150	¾	9/16
	Heavy	200	¾	
				¾
30–40	Light	150	1	13/16
	Heavy	250	1⅛	
40–50	Light	200	1¼	⅞
	Heavy	300	1½	1⅛

The best method of attaching the anchor to the line or rode is a splice over a galvanized thimble (stainless steel if your anchor is stainless) fastened with a galvanized (or stainless) shackle. Next in order of preference is the fisherman's bend—two round turns and two half hitches, with the first hitch passed through the loop of the turns. (See Chapter 4 for complete information on tying knots.) The minimum "approved" hitch is the anchor bowline—two round turns and a regular bowline. Anything less will brand you as a novice. At the boat end of the line, a tight hitch is essential. Use a conventional hitch on a cleat (it should be simple, secure, and easy to cast off). For a bit, two round turns and two half hitches, or a clove hitch with a stopping hitch or two are excellent. Beware of the clove hitch without stoppers; it may slip under strain.

Chafe must be considered at the boat end as well. Chocks, bobstays, bow pulpit supports, even the boat's stem may chafe through a rode in short order. Areas of possible chafe should be protected with rubber hose, servings, canvas sleeves, or even old rags in an emergency. Don't forget that the rode will stretch under tension, and allow for this when applying chafe gear. Secure the chafe protectors to the line so they don't work away from the point they protect.

Permanent Moorings. What constitutes a proper mooring is as

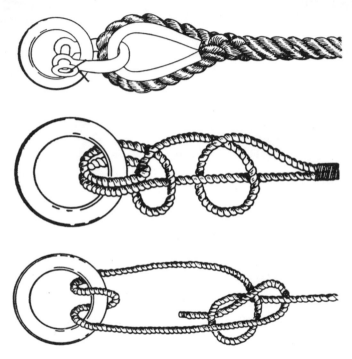

Figure 1-5: Method of attaching anchor to anchor (top to bottom): the eye splice, timble and shackle; the fisherman's bend; and the anchor bowline. (Courtesy of Columbian Rope Company)

controversial as the weather. Some say, "Use an old railroad wheel" or "Give me a cement block with an eyebolt in the middle." Some even prefer to use a special anchor. It's not possible to give specific recommendations as to the mooring itself, for much depends on local conditions. However, a mushroom anchor is thoroughly dependable for general use, easy to rig, and fairly easy to handle. When a mushroom anchor has dug itself in, it can resist tremendous force so long as the pull is steady and in one direction. But when the pull is sharp and hard and at short intervals, as often is the case during a severe storm, a mushroom anchor is liable to creep. To counteract this another anchor can be put out and the scope of the mooring line further increased.

The preferable method is to use a length of heavy chain between the mushroom anchor and the mooring line. This chain keeps the angle of pull on the anchor low and is especially useful in a crowded yacht basin where mooring lines have short scope. The weight of the chain, plus the cushioning effect of the water in controlling its up-and-down movement, builds up appreciable resistance. The mushroom is relieved of much of the strain because the chain acts as an anchor itself. When chain is used, it is better to provide a heavy rather than a light one to obtain the desired spring and strength. Also, be sure there is enough chain so that the end can be pulled up to the waterline at low tide without disturbing the mooring. Use a good strong shackle to attach the end link of the chain to the eye of the mooring.

RECOMMENDATIONS FOR PERMANENT MOORINGS
FOR WIND VELOCITIES UP TO 75 MPH

Over-all Sailboat Length in Feet	Mush-room Anchor (min. wt. in lbs.)	Chain		Length in ft. (min.)	Mooring Line		Total Scope in Ft. (Chocks to mushroom)
		Length (ft.)	Diameter (in.)		Diameter, in. (if manila)	Diameter, in. (if nylon)	
Up to 25	150	30	¾	40	1	⅞	70
25 to 35	250	30	1	40	1¼	1	70
35 to 45	350	40	1	40	1½	1¼	80

Lights. If you cruise after dark, you must have the proper lights as required by law. This, of course, is a must for the safety of yourself and other people you will meet while afloat. Lights must be displayed from sunset to sunrise. There are two sets of regulations regarding lights, International Rules and Inland Rules. Briefly:

Inland Rules. Correct lighting for inland waters, the Great Lakes, and western rivers.

International Rules. These rules meet the requirements of both inland rules and the high seas; thus, if you plan to sail on inland waterways and open seas, equip your boat according to these rules.

Before studying the table of lights required on boats under way between sunset and sunrise, let me explain the meaning of the word "point," which appears in all these lighting regulations. You will see it abbreviated as "pt." In marine lighting, a light that can be seen from every angle is said to be a 32-pt. light. Imagine a circle, the circumference being divided into thirty-two equal parts. This circle could be the globe of a lamp. Requirements say that lights should be visible so many points. Draw radii out from the center the required number of points, and you will see the area in which that particular light will be visible. (The vertical line, from top to bottom, can be assumed to be the keel, or parallel to the keel, of your boat.)

Other Safety Gear. Every skipper in this new age of the sail should have aboard equipment besides that required by law. In recent years a lot of safety requirements have been written into the circulars of ocean and longshore races, and they are equally good if you're cruising. The Cruising Club of America requires that no boat be permitted to start one of their sponsored events until every last one of the following equipment requirements has been met:

Necessary charts and navigating equipment.

Two compasses, one of which must be strongly mounted.

Set of International Code flags, and code book H. O. 87 (see page 258).

Radar reflector. (A multisurface folding metal box hung high in the rigging or mast makes a good reflector.)

Rigid dinghy, supplemented by additional dinghy or rafts of any type desired so that the entire crew can be carried in rough water in safety. (Inflatable rafts or boats should be tested.)

Two bilge pumps, at least one of which is hand operated.

Foghorn.

Fixed bow pulpit and double lifelines with stanchions with through-bolted sockets. The upper lifeline must be wire and permanently installed.

First-aid kit including instruction book and sufficient supplies to cover all ordinary contingencies on an emergency basis.

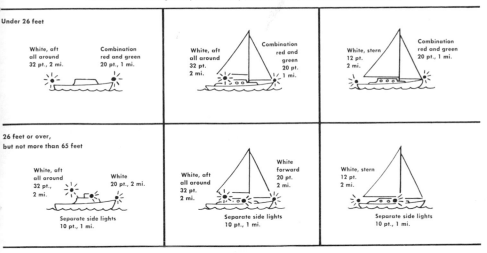

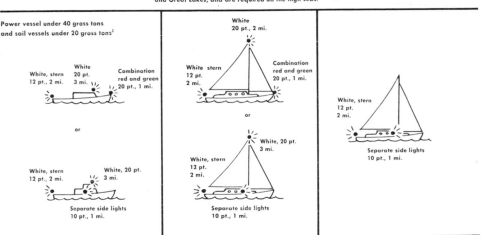

Figure 1-6: Lights required on sailboats, auxiliaries and power boats under way from between sunset and sunrise. (Courtesy of United States Coast Guard)

* Under International Rules powerboats of 40 gross tons or over must carry separate side lights, visible for two miles, and a 20-point white light visible five miles. Sailing vessels of 20 gross tons or over must carry separate side lights, visible two miles. Under sail, only boats of less than 20 tons may use a combination lantern. (Note: A vessel under sail alone on the Great Lakes is not required to display a stern light. Such boats should also carry a flashlight or spotlight to throw a white light on a sail when being overtaken.)

Twelve red parachute-type distress signals readily accessible.

Three white flares for signaling at the finish.

Safety belt for each member of the crew.

Rigging cutter (for use if a mast goes overside).

Yacht's name clearly painted on such equipment as dinghy, oars, life rings, rafts, life jackets, ballasted flag float, etc. This identifying

Figure 1-7: A wheel-steered sailboat (left) and tiller one (right).

name on all detachable equipment is an aid in identification and recovery if lost in storm or stolen.

Two anchors with lines.

Ten gallons of water per man, reasonably divided between two or more separate tanks (with separate shutoff valves) or containers.

Stores sufficient for the crew for a period of three weeks.

Two powerful, water-resistant flashlights.

Emergency tiller.

Two life rings, each equipped with a water light, a whistle, and dye marker. (The life rings must be handy to the helmsman. It is recommended that they be of the horseshoe type; orange, red, or yellow in color for greater visibility; and have a drogue attached. White life rings with the boat's name lettered thereon are pretty, but almost impossible to see in breaking water.)

Flag float to put overboard immediately when anyone goes overside. This consists of a six- to eight-foot pole set in a styrofoam or cork float ballasted to stay upright. It should be topped with one or two orange, red, or yellow pennants.

Operable seacocks on all underwater openings except deck scuppers.

Shutters for large deckhouse windows.

All hatches and skylights secured by suitable hinges or lanyards to prevent their being lost overboard.

Small storm trysail and storm jib designed for the boat.

At least two Coast Guard–approved portable fire extinguishers accessibly located in different parts of the vessel.

Coast Guard–approved life jacket for each member of the crew, carried where readily accessible.

Long before it's time to cast off, obtain the United States Coast

Figure 1-8: The bow portion of a racer-cruiser.

and Geodetic Survey and United States Army Corps of Engineers catalog sheets (see page 136). Circle chart numbers for all waters where you're likely to be sailing during the season, and order the charts. Make some type of arrangement so that these charts can be cut to workable size and stored in a combination chart board-holder. One can be made with waterproof plywood covers with bronze bolts as fasteners. The board provides a fine surface for laying out courses with a course protractor or parallel rulers. Also, if your boat doesn't have a bulkhead rack for rulers, dividers, protractor, and tide and current tables, install one. In addition, you might place an old "railroad" type pocket watch next to the chart table or bulkhead rack as an inexpensive and practical substitute for a chronometer. Since most men no longer carry them, the pawnshops are full of excellent watches which can be purchased inexpensively. The daily error on such watches is fairly constant so that an accurate rating card can be made. The watch can be employed for piloting, and for timing runs between landmarks or aids to navigation. For ocean runs, it might even be used for keeping track of Greenwich time for celestial navigation.

The safety of your craft and all aboard can depend upon the accuracy of your compass, so the best you can obtain is none too good. Don't attempt to adapt compasses intended for other services, such as aeronautical or automotive; such instruments seldom meet all of the requirements for marine use. For complete details on marine compasses, see page 136.

There are other items you should have aboard to help you navigate safely. For example, when you sail in deep water it makes little difference how deep the water under the keel is. But when you get into shallower water it is helpful to know that the depths are sufficient for the draft of the boat. Several methods are in common use, particularly in the inland waterway regions where shoaling frequently changes certain depths almost overnight. The time-tested and well-known sounding lead is one of the generally used methods, while a still simpler method is to use a sounding pole. The lead line is nothing more than a heavy weight secured to a line. This is dropped overboard and the depth of the water read off the graduated line. Special marking devices are used so that the depths can be quickly and accurately read. The sounding pole is nothing more than a long stick with the draft of the boat prominently marked. The user stands on the bow of the boat and sounds as the boat moves along. Touching bottom, he can warn the helmsman away from danger spots.

Larger sailing vessels with ample electrical power supply may be fitted with an electronic depth finder or echo device, which transmits an impulse to the bottom, picks it up again on the return, and then translates the minute time element into fathoms. The type of depth finder most often seen on sailing craft is the "indicator" type, which reports depth by means of a moving red light that flashes on a calibrated dial. The more expensive "recorder" variety works with stylus and graph paper and actually draws a continuous profile of the bottom. Actually, a depth finder is one of the most useful pieces of electronic equipment that you can have aboard your sailboat. In addition to indicating depths, which is most valuable to a skipper, it can tell you whether the bottom is hard or soft, and whether a hard bottom is smooth or rocky. Large single fish such as tuna, and schools of smaller fish, can be detected; the depth finder can also be used as a navigational aid. In the latter application, you take several readings around your estimated position and compare them with those on your chart. When a "line of soundings" is found on the navigational chart which agrees, or nearly agrees, with your own soundings, your position may be determined.

Another very useful navigational instrument is the radio directional finder, which is regarded by experienced sailors as an invaluable piece of emergency equipment. With it, you can take bearings on radio stations or Coast Guard or aircraft radio beacons. Plot these bearings on your navigational charts and you've fixed your position exactly, regardless of weather or poor visibility.

While not a navigational device, the radio-telephone is nevertheless very useful in bad weather, but it's essentially a safety instrument. A phone puts you in immediate contact with the Coast Guard or other boats in case of emergency. Further benefits include the convenience of being able to talk with your home, or office, and with other boatsmen. The ship-to-shore radio's use is controlled by the Federal Communications Commission. The radio must have a station license and a call sign; only a licensed operator (usually the skipper) may operate it, and he is required to log all his calls. The FCC demands that its own radio channel be monitored. For further details on the use of the radio-telephone as a safety device, see Chapter 7.

Three more items, less sophisticated than the electronic gear just mentioned, that fall into the near-necessity category are: barometer, portable radio, and binoculars. A barometer and radio help to keep you informed of the weather. Binoculars are most useful in spotting

MARINE
RADIOTELEPHONE PROCEDURE
RULES TO REMEMBER

YOUR RADIO CAN MEAN YOUR SAFE ARRIVAL — USE IT WITH RESPECT

Important points of proper usage recommended by the Radio Technical Commission for Marine Services, Washington, D. C.

PRIORITY CALLS

BE SURE TO GIVE NAME AND POSITION OF VESSEL

EMERGENCY SITUATIONS	CODE WORDS
DISTRESS	MAYDAY MAYDAY MAYDAY
URGENT MESSAGE CONCERNING SAFETY OF VESSEL OR CREW	PAN PAN PAN
SAFETY OR WEATHER INFORMATION	SECURITY SECURITY SECURITY

1. Maintain your watch	Listen to 2182 kc when not in communication with another station. Rule 8.223)
2. Listen before you talk	Avoid interference with calls in progress. (Rule 8.181
3. Identify your vessel	Give your call sign and vessel's name at beginning and end of each communication. (Rule 8.364)
4. Make calls correctly	Call other vessels on 2182 kc then switch to intership channel. (Rule 8.366)
	Call Commercial Shore stations on an appropriate working channel. (Rule 8.366)
5. Use channels properly	2182 kc for emergencies and brief calls and replies. (Rule 8.353)
	Intership for safety, navigation or operational and business needs of vessels. (Rule 8.358)
6. Watch your language	Use of profane or obscene language is a criminal offense.
7. Be brief all the time	Limit calls to 30 seconds; conversations to 5 minutes. (Rule 8.366)
8. Keep an accurate log	Enter all transmissions made and distress calls heard. (Rule 8.368)
9. Have documents handy	Ship Station license, Operator license or permit; Part 8 of the F.C.C. Rules, Log Book. Rule 8.367)
10. Have equipment checked	Periodic checks insure safety and good operation.

Figure 1-9:

buoys, landmarks, and other navigational aids, and in addition they will add a great deal to your awareness and enjoyment of life afloat. There are other pieces of gear in this near-necessity class; they will be covered later in this book. Also, to complete the commissioning of your sailboat, you'll need such items as personal gear, galley equipment, boatkeeping gear, etc. These items will also be discussed in later chapters.

A Home for Your Boat

During the sailing season, you can keep your craft at your dock if you live on the waterfront; at an offshore mooring; or at a boat-yard, marina, or yacht club. The latter three must be paid for.

The Yacht Club. If you plan to race, membership in a class association is a must. Since many of the classes are affiliated locally with yacht clubs and because many yacht clubs hold regattas, it is usually desirable to become a member of a club.

Yacht clubs vary in size, services, activities, and costs. Some are informal groups that pool their resources to buy a patched-up dock and an old shed in which to store gear. They seek new members to reduce individual costs or to get equipment that all can use. Then there are the huge, nonprofit organizations with million-dollar properties that include swimming pools, tennis courts, and a Hollywoodian clubhouse. Somewhere in between is the typical American yacht club. It offers group lessons in sailing, swimming, safety, and seamanship to old and young; winter programs on sailing education; dances and dinners; and a summer calendar of races, cruises, and social functions. You can judge for yourself how vital to your sailing pleasure such clubs are. But, remember that the facilities of a yacht club are for the exclusive use of its members and their guests. Usually, members of other recognized yacht clubs may use the facilities of clubs of which they are not members only if they are visiting the harbor in a yacht, never if they approach by land—in a car, for instance. (It isn't, however, true that membership in a recognized yacht club automatically gives you the right to use facilities of any other club when you're cruising. Some clubs have exchange-visiting privileges, and very few clubs would deny you a vacant mooring in bad weather.) It is *not* proper for members of one club to use the facilities of another club in the same harbor if they are not also members of the second club. Club courtesies to visiting yachtsmen usually include the services of the launch, the use of bathroom facilities in the club, and dining-room privileges. However, it is only polite for the boatowner to go ashore first in his own dinghy, and ascertain which privileges are available by speaking to the steward or manager of the club. The guest book should be signed at this time.

If you join a yacht club, participate in all its activities. It's true that most club work is done by a dedicated minority. Joining it will present you with some of the most rewarding contacts of your life. From club service it's a logical step to interclub or association duties. Here, on the "inside" of boating, you'll meet the vast complex that makes up your marine fraternity, a complex truly international in scope and embracing with equal vigor commercial and pleasure boating. You may learn, to your surprise, that personalities and groups you once believed hostile to boating interests often are dedicated to increasing its safety, preserving its intent, and expanding its facilities.

Many yacht clubs have long waiting lists of people who want to join. The number of new clubs has not kept up with the increased number of boats in use, which accounts for the long prospective-membership lists. The greatly increasing interest in sailing, plus the lack of yacht-club facilities, has led many sailors to form their own organizations, where sailing is the prime activity. In many areas local communities have organized sailing programs and clubs. If you like

Figure 1-10: A fine example of a family-style day-sailer.

to head up committees you might gather a group of friends and neighbors and start your own sailing club.

The Marina. The fastest growing development in the age of the sail is marinas, both municipally and privately owned. The concept of a modern marina offers a wide latitude, but the owner of a recreational craft has come to expect more than the basics in service and facilities from the establishment he chooses as home port. The size, shape, and functions of a marina today are highly flexible, and along with equipment and construction details vary according to the needs and desires of boatowners in the immediate area. Yachtsmen, however, have come to expect certain features and services at a marina, no matter what the size. These include berthing space; dockside electricity; fresh water and telephone outlets; available fuel, groceries, and other supplies; laundry service and garbage disposal; parking space; showers and rest rooms and access to marine stores; and boat hauling and repair and storage service. (But select a marina —either public or private—carefully; some are excellent, while others are little more than busy, noisy service stations.)

The Boatyard. Most boatyards rent lockers and dock space or mooring to customers who use the yard for winter storage as well as to those who use it only for the summer. The facilities in a boatyard are usually limited and very informal but generally quite satisfactory. There is a lavatory, there may be showers, and there are usually a couple of rowboats handy for getting to and from your mooring. Boatyards generally offer dockage or moorage at the lowest possible cost. If you don't keep your boat home during the winter and have to pay for winter storage, year-round cost at a boatyard is generally less than anywhere else. Another advantage is that you have repair and maintenance service close at hand if you should ever need it. But, one word of caution: your boatyard isn't likely to permit you to do unlimited work on your boat, nor to bring in outside labor. Have things understood before you store your boat there.

The Offshore Mooring. When choosing an offshore mooring site, be sure it's protected from the wind as much as possible; out of the direct surge of waves from large areas of open water; not in the main channel of a stream or tidal flow, or beneath the mouth of a feeder stream, dry wash, or gulley where flash floods may suddenly form. Also make sure your mooring isn't in a channel or fairway; if possible, it should be an authorized anchorage or mooring area. You should make arrangements for launching and perhaps storing a dinghy at a point on shore near where the boat is moored so that you can easily get to and back from it. For this reason it's usually a good idea to moor the boat near a friend's waterfront cottage, near a yacht club, marina, boatyard, or public park. In many places mooring spots can be rented for fees ranging from $10 to $100 per season.

Marine Insurance

When you shove off in your boat for a long day or weekend of fun, your daily responsibilities are left behind. Unfortunately a new crop appears. The hazards of boating are similar to those of driving a car. You are liable for property damage you may cause, or injuries sustained from the operation of your boat. Also, many things can happen to your boat. To protect your investment and cover yourself against liability, marine insurance is the only answer.

To keep the cost down, get only what coverage you really need. This is determined by where you use your boat, how much of the year it is in the water, how much protection and indemnity (liability) coverage you want, and, of course, the value of your boat. Yachts insured for $10,000 and over may be covered for any twelve fifteen-day periods, not necessarily consecutive. Yacht policies may be written for any period of navigation up to twelve months by applying the proper rate adjustment. Policies written for a specific period of navigation are subject to "lay-up" credit for any fifteen consecutive days the boat is not used during this time, but these only apply to yachts with a hull value of $10,000 and over.

Property damage liability to another vessel is part of the basic hull policy, but only for an amount equal to the amount of hull insurance. If Protection & Indemnity is included, let's say with $25,000/$50,000/$25,000 limits, the third limit is for property damage, thereby providing a substantial increase in protection for the owner of a $5,000 hull. But remember that insurance rates are promulgated on loss experience and that only you, the assured, can help to keep the rates down by doing your best to safeguard your property. For the same reason that one would consult a doctor of medicine when requiring medical attention, one should consult a marine insurance broker when arranging for marine insurance; the specialist is the best person to answer your needs.

Before You Get Under Way

As with everything in our modern day, there is, to a degree, government regulation of our new age of the sail. For instance, as of April 1, 1963, all boats powered by motors of more than 10 horsepower plying the navigable waters of the United States must be registered and numbered according to the Federal Boating Act of 1958; documented boats are excepted. The Federal Boating Act of 1958 (also known as the Bonner Bill) simply updates this law to permit the states to institute their own registration systems, providing they conform, substantially, to Federal regulations. It also rearranges the numbers so that the letters of the registering state are identified first, instead of the Coast Guard District, as under the old law. The boat must be registered in the state where it operates most. (This includes the time it is berthed.) The numbering fee may be charged either by the state or the Coast Guard. The law provides for reciprocity between states in recognizing the validity of a number awarded by another state or by the Coast Guard. Although Federal laws are to be enforced by Federal enforcement agents and state laws by the law-enforcement officers of that state or its political subdivisions, this act specifically provides that "nothing herein shall preclude enforcement of both State or Federal laws pursuant to agreements or other arrangements" between the Coast Guard and any state designed to "insure that there shall be the fullest cooperation in the enforcement of both State and Federal statutes, rules, and regulations relating to recreation boating." The intent of the law is the promotion of boating safety, to provide coordination and cooperation between the states and with the Federal government in the interest of uniformity of boating laws, and to encourage the highest degree of reciprocity and comity among the several jurisdictions. Nothing in this act interferes with, abrogates, or limits the jurisdiction of any state, and any state system for numbering which is not incompatible with the Federal numbering system will be approved as provided for in the act. The certificate of registration must be on board whenever the boat is in use.

As for the identification numbers themselves, the following regulations must be remembered:

1. Paint or otherwise permanently attach your numbers to the bow so that they will be clearly visible and legible.

2. They should be of the *plain block design* not less than three inches high.

3. The numbers must be of a *solid color* that contrasts with the background.

4. The hyphens or spaces separating the numerals from the letters must be equal to the width of a letter except I, or any numeral except one.

About the only thing left to do before getting under way in this new age of sail is a name for your sailboat. This is a personal matter and I have no real suggestions. But, once you, your wife (the first mate), or your family decide, it should be applied to the stern along with your home port. The name of your yacht, as previously suggested, should also be painted on all safety equipment such as life rings, life jackets, dinghy, etc.

2

Reviewing
the Art
of Sailing

W e all know that it is the wind that makes a sailboat go. Any object floating on the water will have a tendency to drift along before the wind. But, if you're going to learn all of the intricacies of the art of sailing, you have to be ushered through enough theory so you'll be better able to understand why you must handle sails and rudder in certain ways to obtain the desired results. If we were to simply accept the analogy of the object floating on the water, we would be pretty well up against it to account for the fact that a boat can sail in a great many directions other than in the one toward which the wind is blowing. Because of the importance of the art of sailing, it's a good idea for all of us to review the principles of aerodynamics.

Aerodynamics of Sailing

Of all the laws that I had to learn in my college physics course, the one of Sir Isaac Newton—the man who was hit on the head by an apple—that states that for each action there must be an equal reaction, is about the only one I remember, since it explains the theory of sailing. Being as mercifully brief as possible, let's look at the dia-

33

gram here and see how Newton's law of reaction moves your boat. As shown, lines A–C and D–B represent the course we wish our sailboat to go to windward. Lines A–D and C–B represent the sideslip or lee-

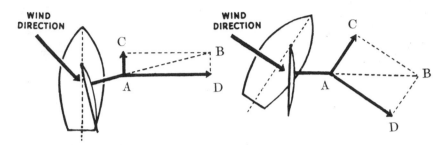

Figure 2-1: The force AB shown at the left is comprised of two component forces AC and AD, one operating sidewise, while the other operates forward. At the right, as the angle with the wind increases and your forward force AC increases, there is a decrease proportionately in the lateral force AD.

way (the opposite side from which the wind strikes) caused by the pressure of the wind on the sail. The diagonal line A–B is the component of the two forces—in other words, the theoretical path of the boat. The sides of the rectangle should be directly proportionate to the forces. (As shown at the right, increase your angle with the wind, and you increase the forward force A–C, and decrease proportionately the later force A–D.) In a heavy breeze, the proportions of the rectangle of forces would vary. As the sides change in length, the diagonal A–B will also change. Line A–B is what we're after, as it represents both forward and sideways motion. By designing boats to exert the least resistance to motion ahead, and the greatest resistance to movement sideways, we change the proportions of the parallelogram so that A–B becomes longer and at less of an angle to the keel. In theory, we are attempting to shorten A–D and C–B and lengthen A–C and D–B so that our pet A–B line is going where we wish—which is ahead and not sideways. Naturally, as the boat turns more off the wind and the sails are farther out, the line of force A–B at right angles to the sail acts in a more forward direction; consequently the force driving the boat ahead is increased, while the force that makes for leeway is reduced.

Going back to my college textbook for a moment, it's a known physical law that wherever your stress is greatest, there you'll require the greatest resistance to that stress. There is one point on the surface of your sail or sails where the force of the wind is centered. (This point is known as the "center of effort" of the sail plan.) Or, it may be stated to be the point where the force of the wind aft of the center of effort is equal to the force of the wind forward of that point. There is likewise a "center of lateral resistance" on keel or centerboard, and the position of these two points in relation to one another is most important in the design of a boat. (If this underwater extension is fixed, it is called a "keel"; if adjustable, so that it can be lowered or raised, it is known as a "centerboard.") For instance, if the center of lateral resistance were near the middle of the boat, and the center of effort of the sail plan were toward the bow, the latter's tendency would be to rotate the bow *away* from the wind, the center of lateral resistance simply acting as an axis. (Such a boat is said to have a "lee helm.") On the other hand, if the center of effort is behind the center of lateral resistance, the stern will go to leeward (away from the wind), and simultaneously bring the bow into the wind. (Such a boat is said to have a "weather helm.") While theoretically any rotary motion could be prevented by having the two centers directly beneath or above one another, actually most boats are designed with a *slight* weather helm. Thus, if you let the helm go for any reason, the boat sails gently and quietly up into the wind for safety.

The rudder is a flat perpendicular plane which is essentially a continuation of the keel. When it is directly in line with the keel it contributes to the resistance to leeway and allows the craft to progress on her course. (The pressure on both sides of the rudder, caused by water flowing past the keel or hull, is equal.) When it is swung to one side or another by either the tiller or wheel, one side of the rudder is more exposed to the force of the flowing water than the other, and an unequal or unbalanced effect is produced which pushes the stern around, thus causing the boat to swing from her original course and turn on its center of rotation. It is important to remember that there is a difference in steering with a tiller and with a wheel. A tiller is always pushed opposite to the direction the boat is to head. If you want to go to the port (left), you push to starboard (right) side; and vice versa. A wheel, used on larger craft, is turned in the direction you want to go. Turn it to the left and the boat steers to the port. Turn to the right, the craft steers to the starboard, like an automobile.

While the fundamental task of the keel or centerboard is to reduce the boat's chance of moving to leeward, and keep her moving forward, it has the additional important function of helping maintain the boat in an upright position when the wind, striking sidewise on the sail, might overturn it. Any sailboat, when "pointing" into the wind, has a natural tendency to "heel" or lean to leeward. Since the lateral force of the wind is resisted below the waterline, it takes it out on the sails above the waterline, where some yielding to this force may be essential as a safety valve. But, too much heel to leeward is dangerous and inefficient. By this I mean that the greater the angle of heel, the less sail area exposed to the wind. This is a safety factor because as a boat heels, the more she tends to spill the wind over the top of the sails—just as water would spill over a dam, if you tilted the dam. Usually before a boat heels far enough to overturn it will be spilling enough of the wind to keep from capsizing. However, too much heel cuts down on the effective drive of the sails. Hiking—crew leaning out on windward side of the boat—to the high side of the craft when it heels in strong winds not only keeps her more upright but keeps more sail in the wind for driving purposes. Actually, the angle of heel between 0 and 10 degrees is not important, but an angle over 50 degrees is most critical. Only about 2 percent of the sail is lost when a craft is heeled 10 degrees to leeward, but at 50 degrees less than 65 percent of the sail area is exposed.

While the hull shape, the rudder, and the keel all contribute to the necessary forward drive, the action of the wind on the sail or sails is the major factor. When properly drawing in the wind a sail has a gently varying curve over its whole area. (This curve is called the "airfoil.") The side away from the wind will take a concave form; the side facing the wind is convex, which permits the flowing wind to pass over the sail quicker than it can on the windward side. As the wind strikes the sail, it divides and is caused to change direction. Thus, on the windward side we have an increased pressure and on the leeward side a decreased pressure. This difference in pressures on opposite sides of the sail create forces that move the boat upwind; the force on the windward side pushing against a lesser or negative force contributes as much as 75 percent of the pulling driving force when sailing as close to the wind as possible. In other words, only approximately 25 percent of the actual force of the wind is utilized in driving the craft forward, and of this, only a very small proportion is actual forward-driving force. Careful experiments in wind tunnels have shown that 75 percent of the pulling force driving a boat is derived from the suction or negative pressure on the leeward side of the sails. The combination of these two is what gets the boat to windward. No craft will sail directly against the wind; the nearness with which it will sail against the wind is determined by a number of factors of hull and sail design. Most boats will sail about 4 points off the wind or at roughly a 45-degree angle to the wind's direction. It will be seen therefore that to sail a course against the wind, you must sail at a 45-degree angle from it, first in one direction and then in the other—a sort of zig-zagging progress.

As stated in Chapter 1, the sloop, with her jib sail, is the most popular type of sailboat afloat today. Besides furnishing some additional drive in itself, the principal function of the jib when sailing close to the wind is to guide the wind around the leeward side of the mainsail. If the wind were not so guided it would not flow evenly around the mainsail, and eddies or "turbulence" would form on the leeward side. It is interesting to note that the slots on the wing of certain types of aircraft perform much the same function as the jib of a boat. This turbulence on the leeward after side of a sail is indicated by the flapping of the sail. It may be caused by a badly setting sail—one that has perhaps stretched out of shape—or by a badly trimmed jib. Thus the jib performs the function of a slot and, in addition, by blanketing the mast (which always causes back eddies of wind), it improves very greatly the efficiency of the sail; this is because the thin forward edge (luff) of the jib makes a good "entry" into the wind, causing little or no back eddies. This guidance of the wind is called the "slot effect," and greatly improves the performance of the boat by directing the wind into the area behind the mainsail, thus increasing the suction or pulling effect.

If my former physics professor at Brown University should read my dissertation on the aerodynamics of sailing, I am sorry, after all his good teaching, for my clumsy attempt to express a scientific explanation of this rather complicated phenomenon. But, for most of us sailors, it should serve as a fairly good basis for the art of sailing.

Figure 2-2: A fine example of the slot effect in action.

Know Your Sails

Most large sailboats carry several special sails for particular purposes. These may include spinnakers, genoa jibs, and a variety of other light sails that are hoisted when more speed is desired than can be obtained from the normal working sails. Let me hasten to say that some small boats also have light and special sails. Many of the little one-designs can carry spinnakers. Most of them are also rigged with genoa jibs.

Mainsail and Jib. Before discussing special sails, it might be a good idea to take a look at the working mainsail and jib. Although we have described the aerodynamics of a sail, let's first give all the relative parts of sails their names, whether the sail is a mainsail, a jib, or a spinnaker:

The leading edge is the luff.

The trailing edge is the leech.

The lower edge is the foot.

The top corner is the head.

The lower leading corner is the tack.

The trailing after corner is the clew.

There are three types of mainsails: the jib-headed (also called the Marconi and Bermudian), the gaff-headed, and loose-footed. The jib-headed mainsail is by far the most commonly employed in the United States. It is long, narrow, and triangular in shape. Its popularity is due to ease of handling and its excellent "on the wind" ability. The gaff-head mainsail is a four-sided (quadrilateral-shaped) sail whose upper edge is fastened to a spar called a gaff, hence its name. The loose-footed type is similar to the jib-headed, but its foot or lower edge isn't fastened; it hangs loose. It's controlled by a single line fastened to the clew and pulled out by a line attached to the end of the boom.

Originally, the sail that we call a jib was named a staysail. Old-timers who still call it by that name are technically correct. Jibs were set from the bowsprit of the old-time sailing vessel. The staysail was inboard and nearest the mast. Today, practically everyone calls the single sail forward of the mast of a small sloop, a working jib. It fits in the area between the mast, jibstay, and deck. Its tack is fastened close to the deck at the jibstay to which the snaphooks on the jib luff are attached.

Most jibs are loose-footed and their curvature is controlled by jib sheets, and the placement of the jib-sheet leads is used to keep the foot straight. The leech, more often than not, has battens to keep it straight and prevent the sail from curling. This is very important; if the leech is allowed to curl it will force the wind flowing off the jib to strike the leeward side of the mainsail. This will defeat the purpose of the jib to a degree.

Genoa Jib. The genoa jib is larger than the working jib, but it is cut with somewhat more of a belly than is a regular jib; and its base, or foot, extends abaft the mast. Practically all cruising craft

Figure 2-3: The three common types of headsails: working jib (left), genoa jib (right), and spinnaker (below).

have this sail in their locker and set it when the wind direction and strength are right. Those craft that go in for cruising-racing often have a lightweight genoa and a heavy genoa made for use in these respective light and heavy winds. The lightweight genoa generally is a larger sail than the heavyweight. The newer ocean-racing yachts are so rigged (the jibstay is run to the masthead) that the sail can extend to the masthead, and when the wind is high it furnishes tremendous drive.

The main difference between it and the ordinary working jib is that usually, although not always, it is sheeted so that it leads outside the main shrouds. An ordinary jib is inevitably sheeted inside the shrouds. Except on rare occasions, the genoa must be sheeted outside the shrouds because, being longer on its base, it could not be flattened properly without chafing against the wire rigging. The genoa furnishes more drive than the working jib and is used for going to windward and close reaching in all winds but the strongest. Some cruiser-racer style boats don't have any other headsail except the genoa. But these boats are designed to contend with the extra-strong forces exerted and created by this sail. They also have enough crew and proper equipment to handle it. It takes a lot of strength to handle the sheets in a strong wind, even though their pull is controlled by a winch.

Spinnaker. The spinnaker is an egg- or bell-shaped nylon cloud that billows out at the top and curves in at the sides so as to drive the boat before the wind. Broadly speaking, it is set across the boat rather than fore and aft. To accomplish that, there must be a spinnaker boom. This is a light spar having a fork, crotch, or special metal fitting at its inboard end to fit the mast. The outer end of the boom has a snap hook to which the tack or outer lower corner of the spinnaker is made fast. The opposite corner, or clew, is attached to the spinnaker sheet, which is passed around the forestay and carried aft outside the shrouds on the side opposite to that on which the spinnaker boom is to be run out. A guy from the end of the boom is carried aft outside the shrouds on the side where the boom is to be rigged.

Weight of Sail Material. A predetermined and exact scale is used to determine the gradations of canvas or synthetic materials when they are used for sailmaking. The gradations are in weight, measured in ounces per yard in length of material that comes 28½ inches wide.

The weight ranges from 1.2 ounces to 15 ounces. Although dacron is much stronger than cotton, other factors in addition to strength must be considered when determining the weight of the cloth to be employed. This is particularly true for mainsails; not only the size of the boat but her primary use must be taken into account. Thus for a 35-foot waterline boat that is to be raced, most experts would recommend a 12-ounce dacron mainsail. However, for a cruising boat of the same size they would advise a 9-ounce dacron mainsail. On a boat carrying a genoa jib, there would be so much back wind coming through the slot that beefing up the weight of the cloth is desirable. The airfoil is ruined when a sail is made of cloth too light in weight.

Spinnakers are the exceptions. For these sails the more strength and the less body the better. Although boats which carry several spinnakers should have one or two of heavier weight for heavy winds; generally speaking, the lighter the spinnaker, the more effective it will be. This has not proven true with working sails. Experimentation with mainsails on some of the smaller classes (sails as nearly identical as they could be made except for weight) have demonstrated conclusively that the heavier sails outperform the lighter ones, particularly in light airs. The following table gives the recommended weight of cloth for various sail areas.

AVERAGE RECOMMENDED WEIGHTS (IN OUNCES)

Working Sail Area (sq. feet)	Working Sail Weights	Genoa Weights*	Nylon Spinnaker Weights
up to 150	4	3	1.2
150–360	5	4	1.2
360–420	6	4	1.2
420–550	8	4–7	1.2
550–1000	10	4–7	1.2–1.5
1000–1500	12	6–7	1.2–1.5
1500–2000	13½	6–12	1.2–1.5

* As stated earlier, in the more highly competitive racing classes, boats will usually carry genoa jibs of different weights and sizes (generally four) as indicated in the table above for all sail areas between 420 and 2000 square feet. (Table courtesy of Ratsey & Lapthorn, Inc.)

Cut of Sail Material. Most mainsails today are crosscut. That is, the length of the sail material is laid at right angles to the leech, which is the same as the direction of pull of the main sheet. On the other hand, practically all jibs, both working and genoa, are "miter cut." The seams of material are laid at right angles to the leech and to the foot of the sail. They meet a line that bisects the angle of the clew. It is made this way to withstand the single line pull

Figure 2-4: The photograph above shows a good example of how sails are cut and fastened together.

coming at the clew. When the jib is very large, as on large cruising craft, it sometimes is cut with three miters and looks much like a large spider web.

As you can see in the various illustrations in this book, there are several ways used to cut the material to make a spinnaker. Often, alternating cloths are used—principally for distinctive decorative purposes, often for ready identification.

Know Your Rigging

To carry all of the sail considered necessary, masts are fitted into the hull; and since the load or thrust of the sails is transmitted to the hull through the masts, they must be strong and well supported. (While wooden masts and spars have been traditional for centuries, special aluminum alloys that are light and aren't corroded by salt water are used in place of wood in the new age of the sail.) In addition to a very substantial mast, stays of wire are employed to help in supporting and distributing the stresses to the hull proper. All rigging of whatever kind used to support and stay the masts is called "standing rigging," as opposed to the various lines which are used to raise or lower the sails and to control their position, which is termed the "running rigging."

The Standing Rigging. The headstay, the backstay, and the shrouds, which all support the mast, are standing rigging. They "stand" permanently, as long as the mast is up. (In larger craft the standing rigging, once set up, is rarely adjusted during the season. Small dinghy owners may have to strip down and set up the rigging for each trip.)

The headstay runs from the bow of the hull to a point high up on the mast, or, on some boats, to her very peak. The backstay runs from the top of the mast to the stern. The stays running from the side of the boat to the mast are called shrouds. All stays attach to the boat's hull by means of turnbuckles, adjustable threaded links with eyes that are rotated to tighten or slacken the stays. The turnbuckles secure the shrouds to metal chain plates built into the hull. Spreaders are small metal struts extending from both sides of the mast aloft. The shrouds lead over the ends of these struts and then to the mast at an angle, providing a stronger rig.

The larger the sailboat, the more support her mast must have. The standing rigging then multiplies. A second headstay, most often called a jibstay, is added; it secures farther down the mast. A second set of shrouds ends at the base of the spreaders. For additional support, a second or even third set of spreaders may be added. Strength at the top of the mast may be provided by a jumper strut, facing forward, with its accompanying jumper stays.

The Running Rigging. As the name implies, running rigging is constantly being adjusted. It doesn't remain fixed like standing rigging. Running rigging is the term given to the lines (ropes) by which the sails are hoisted, set, and trimmed. To trim is to adjust the sails when the wind changes or the boat alters course. To hoist and to trim are two different operations. They require two main types of running rigging for each function: 1) halyards for hoisting sail; and 2) sheets for trimming sail.

The halyards hoist aloft the head of the sail and therefore need to be connected with the top of the mast. This is done in one of two ways: 1) they are rove through a block attached to the mast by a strop or shackled to a mast band. Rove is the past tense of the verb "to reave"—to pass a rope through a hole or block. 2) They are passed over a sheave and down through a hollow mast to deck level. A mainsail is hoisted with a main halyard. This halyard passes over a sheave let into the top of the mast and then either inside or outside the mast down to deck level. Halyards that are led inside a hollow mast are known as internal halyards. The main is usually to the port side of the mast, while the jib halyard, which is used to hoist the jib or genoa, is to the port. If a boat has a spinnaker then a spinnaker halyard is used. Flag halyards, signal halyards or lines are required to hoist the burgee and all flags.

Racing boats that are rigged for the several varieties of sails often have a special halyard for each of the sails so that in shifting from one sail to another, no sail need be taken in until the other is drawing. The multiple halyards and sheets present a problem that only a trained crew can solve. All sorts of stunts to identify the running gear have been tried. Lettered tags work fairly well in daylight. Racing cruisers sailing in total darkness usually have the halyards identified by small metal tags of different shapes. Of course, the positions of the different lengths of running rigging and the cleats to which they are belayed follow a standard pattern. Even the crew of the smallest sailing craft should know the location of every line and cleat.

Sheets are the lines used to trim the sails when under way. They take their names from the sails which they control; thus the mainsail is controlled by the mainsheet. Even on large boats, the mainsheet is always a single line running into the cockpit, but the common arrangement on the jib finds double sheets, one each for port and starboard sides. The mainsheet controls the in-and-out movement of the boom and, therefore, the sail itself. On small boats your mainsheet may be simply a line passing directly from the boom to a cleat close to your helm, or to pegs or cleats next to the tiller. On larger boats the sheets will pass through one or more blocks, and frequently one of these blocks moves on a slide or traveler running crosswise on the deck abaft the helm. The jib sheet may also be a single line sliding on a traveler, but more likely it will comprise two separate lines, each running from the clew down through a fair-lead or a small pulley fastened to the deck and back to the helm where it's made fast near the tiller or wheel. While some manila is still used by old-timers, cotton and dacron rope is the most popular today because it's easier on the hands. Since the running rigging is the lifeblood of any sailing vessel, it must be kept in impeccable condition and be constantly checked for wear.

Other parts of your boat's running rigging include the topping lifts, downhauls, and guys. There are two types of topping lifts, one for the main boom (only on larger boats), the other for the spinnaker pole. The former merely takes the weight off the boom when the mainsail isn't set, while the lift on the spinnaker pole runs from the middle of this pole to a block on the mast; then to the deck. As for the downhauls, the main one, at the inboard end of the boom, pulls down on the tack of the mainsail, thereby making sure that the desired tight fit along the luff of the sail is obtained. The spinnaker downhaul runs from the midsection of the pole through a block on the deck and then to the cockpit. This lowers the pole and gives a crew member in the cockpit control over its outboard end. A guy is employed also to help control the spinnaker.

The Rigging Fittings. The many items of hardware aboard a sailboat are called *fittings.* Starting at the bow of a small sailboat, you'll find the headstay fitting and its turnbuckle which secures the headstay. On the foredeck lies a cleat for either or both the mooring line and the docking line, and the bow chock through which these lines pass. Near the mast, the jib sheets attach to the clew by means of a shackle which snaps shut. Around the mast at deck level a group of fittings can be found. Halyard cleats are located here, either on deck or below it, in which case the halyard runs through the deck.

Then there are cleats for the main downhaul, the spinnaker guy and topping lift. Also here is the gooseneck fitting that secures the boom to the mast. Another item, principally for racing craft, is the boom vang, a detachable fitting that runs from the underside of the boom to the deck. Its purpose is to hold the boom and mainsail down against actions of wind and wave when sailing before the wind.

On larger boats, you'll find it necessary to have means for providing additional power for the control of the halyards and sheets. Power can always be gained by adding blocks to the tackles, but such multiplication of power involves an equal reduction in the speed of hoisting and sheeting. Most sails are hoisted on wire halyards rather than on the older cordage lines rove through two or more sheaves to provide power. Wire running rigging can't be belayed around a cleat. Sometimes such rigging has a rope tail spliced to the wire, the line portion being used for hauling and belaying. It is hopeless to believe that a man can haul in wire running rigging by hand. The diameter is too small to grasp. Rope large enough to be grasped comfortably is often out of proportion to its job. For these reasons, the use of hand winches is becoming more and more popular even though they add to the cost of rigging gear and increase the number of toe-breakers on deck. The larger boats sometimes have electrically driven winches for halyards and sheets.

The Points of Sailing

It may sound too simple to mention, but the key to controlling a boat under sail is to know which way the wind is blowing. It really is as simple as that. And it is a fact that confusion over wind direction is the single biggest source of trouble for sailing novices. Actually, once you know the wind direction, figuring out the proper trim of the sail is a matter of common sense. An important thing to remember about the wind is that it seldom stays constant in direction and strength. It comes in puffs and gusts that vary in power and swing back and forth through a couple of points on the compass. These variations in the wind can cause a beginner trouble and it is important to know how to be on guard for them. First of all, basic wind direction should be ascertained. On larger sailboats a wind indicator is often employed for this purpose. A wind pennant or yacht club burgee at the top of the mast is helpful, and it is also a good practice, on smaller boats, to tie light ribbons or a piece of nylon stocking to the shrouds. (The latter is ideal since nylon sheds rain and doesn't get waterlogged.) These ribbons are called "tell-tales"; watching them can be a big help in determining wind shifts. (More on determining wind direction can be found in Chapter 4.)

As shown on the opposite page, a boat is capable of sailing close-hauled into the wind, with the wind, and at right angles to it. These actions are called "beating," "running," and "reaching," respectively. As you have already read, a sailboat can't be made to go directly to windward. The closest to the wind that a sail can be trimmed effectively to make the craft move forward is approximately 45 degrees from the wind, on either side of it. A point directly upwind can be reached by sailing for a while at 45 degrees to one side of the wind direction and then coming about to sail at 45 degrees to the other side of the wind direction. When the wind is coming over the starboard or right side on any of these points of sailing, the boat is said to be on the "starboard tack." It is on the "port tack" when the wind is coming over the port or left side. The windward objective of this tacking operation is eventually achieved by a series of 90-degree zigzags across the direction of the wind.

It's easier to visualize sailing on the other points. When sailing before the wind, off the wind, with the wind aft, downwind, downhill, sailing free, scudding, running—all these terms have the same meaning—the boat moves with, in the same direction as, the wind. In other words, the wind blows your boat along like a leaf in a country lane. If the sails were lowered the wind would still blow the craft along, but she would move more slowly.

When a boat is not as close-hauled as possible, but sailing closer to wind than at right angles to it, she is said to be on a "close reach." When the wind is coming from slightly abaft the beam to a point close to that of a run, the craft is then on a "broad reach." When wind comes from a point directly abeam—at an angle of about 90 degrees to the wind—the boat is on a "beam reach." This latter position is the simplest of all points of sailing—and the fastest. Actually, when on a beam reach, the driving force is at its greatest and sailboats attain their best speeds.

In all explanations up to now I have left out the apparent wind and dealt only with the true wind. By apparent wind I mean the direction from which the wind appears to come once the ship has started to move ahead. As the ship moves ahead faster and faster, the

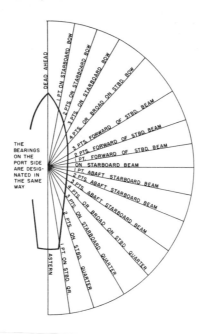

Figure 2-5: Relative bearings used in reporting direction of wind (above) and the points of sailing (below).

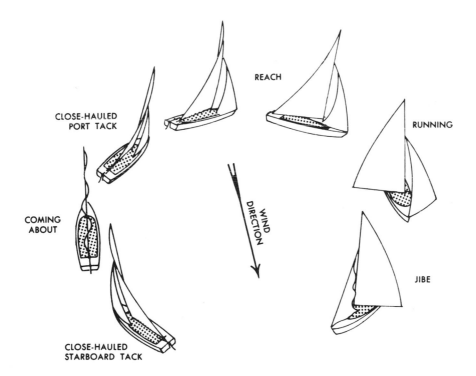

wind will appear to draw more and more ahead, and it will be under the influence of this "apparent wind" that any forward movement will continue. The apparent wind, whose direction is most important to the sailor when handling his boat, will continue to draw ahead until the water resistance set up by the hull form of the boat to any forward movement exactly balances the forward-acting force. When this point is reached the only way in which an increase of speed can be obtained is by increasing the amount of sail carried (assuming that the wind remains constant) and so pushing back the point of balance between the drive of the wind and the resistance of the water. Your wind pennant or telltales show the true wind when your craft is stationary. But, when she is moving, the pennant then indicates the combined direction of the true wind and the apparent wind.

The man at the tiller or wheel must not only keep an eye on the wind but must also watch the water. Very rarely do the wind and the waves come from *exactly* the same direction. Generally steering is easier, and the helmsman will have far greater control, when the waves are running toward the boat and she takes them on the bow.

In addition to the waves, you must consider the effect of tide and current. Rivers flow in only one direction, but in salt water, tide and current flow in one way for a certain number of hours and in the next period they flow in the opposite direction. You should know which way the tide and current are going so that you can use them to your advantage. For instance, when starting a short sail it's generally wise to sail against the tide so that when you're heading back you'll be moving with the tide and will get a lift from it. Tides and currents will be covered more thoroughly in Chapter 5.

Bending and Hoisting Sail

When bending on the mainsail, the slides are fitted on the mast and boom tracks. Make certain that the pins in the tack and clew fittings are so placed that they hold the foot of the sail in a straight line on the boom. The sail was built to be set in this way and is bound to be less than perfect if it angles up or down at the tack or clew. Before hoisting, take up on the topping lift so that it will bear the weight of the boom; in a small boat that is not equipped with a topping lift, have someone hold up the boom. Failure to do this results in an unnecessary strain on the sail.

When a sailmaker goes aboard to check the fit of sails, according to Ernest Ratsey—one of America's foremost sailmakers—the first check he usually makes is to squint up the mast track to make sure the spar is straight. If it is not, the sail can't set correctly. Most sailors check their masts from time to time but comparatively few pay equal attention to the boom. Yet the boom is of equal importance to the

Figure 2-6: Raising the mainsail (left) and the jib (right).

set of the sail. While someone is sailing your boat to windward, go forward and sight along the top of the boom, using the gooseneck much as you would a rifle sight. A curve in the boom may be eliminated merely by a change in the lead of the mainsail sheet but sometimes it may be necessary to replace the boom with a heavier or less rubbery one. Unless you feel qualified to cope with the problem, get an expert's advice.

The correct lead of the jib sheet is frequently a bothersome matter which usually can be solved only through trial and error. However, there are some general principles that may be applied. For working jibs, a projection of a line which cuts the luff about 60 percent below the head of the sail and bisects the clew will, when extended to the deck, indicate the proper fore and aft location for the sheet block. The athwartship position will vary but generally will be about 10 degrees from the centerline of the boat. For a genoa jib the lead of the sheet should be much nearer the horizontal. Generally, the faster the boat, the smaller the angle should be. Since genoa sheets are led through snatch blocks, shackled into a fitting on a track, the lead can be changed readily in a fore or aft direction. Genoa sheets, as previously stated, are always led outside the shrouds.

Battens are a nuisance at best, but they do help, as stated earlier in this chapter, to make a well-fitting sail; and they permit the sailmaker to put roach into the leech, which gives a sail a little greater area than it otherwise would have. Before the advent of crosscut sails, when the seams ran parallel to the leech, battens were used only in exceptional cases. Even today a nonbattened sail has its points for cruising, but such sails are not often seen. Many substitutes for the good old ash batten have been tried, including aluminum, pressed wood, plastic, and fiberglass, to name a few, but a close-grained ash batten still is my choice. The others seem to tear the pockets or to cut the stitching, and if they fly out they almost invariably sink, whereas wooden battens may, with luck, be retrieved. If you don't sail back for a batten some other sailor may pick it up to his profit.

Battens should be an inch or more short of the full length of the pocket and should be an easy, not a tight, fit. They should taper fore and aft; the thinner, more flexible part is the leading end. Well-made battens should have all edges and corners carefully rounded and sanded smooth and should be either varnished or treated with linseed oil. The oil treatment must be applied months before the batten is to be used, for oil dries slowly and undried oil may stain the sails. I have seen two thin battens taped together in an attempt to minimize breaking. If properly done this may have its points; but it makes the batten heavier, which isn't good. It is good practice to remove battens before sails are put into bags; if left in the pockets the battens may break or warp. When batten pockets are provided with small lanyards, these should be passed through the hole in the end of the batten, through the grommet in the opposite side of the pocket, and securely tied into a multiple square knot (not a bow). Tie it four, five, or six times to minimize the possibility that the lanyard will work loose when you bring the boat about or when she lies head to the wind. Dot fasteners have been tried as substitutes for batten ties or lanyards, but they are not in general use. Many modern sails are made with pockets which need no tying, hold the batten in place, yet are so constructed that battens can easily be slipped in or out. This sounds paradoxical but it works well. The pocket at the leech end is curved upward and left open for a short distance so the batten can be inserted or removed by flexing the sail and sliding the batten in or out over the top of the stitched part. This is a really improved pocket and takes a lot of the curse out of the use of battens.

Hoisting the mainsail consists merely in hoisting the halyard until the headboard is as high as it will go. In boisterous weather, care should be taken to hoist it slowly and to look aloft throughout the entire process. When partly hoisted, sometimes the mainsail may flap around so that it wraps itself about the ends of the spreaders. To continue to hoist a sail when it has wrapped itself around a spreader is sure to result in a torn sail. A sail can usually be freed in such cases by a gentle pull on the leech; or it will probably free itself in a couple of minutes with a slight change in the position of the boat. But there should be no pull on the luff or the halyard while the mainsail and the spreaders are playing games. The jib is hoisted in the same manner as the mainsail. But, in either case, keep the following two principles of sail adjustment in mind: 1) sail edge tension; 2) sheet tension and direction.

As previously stated, the jib should aid and not destroy the forces creating drive. A jib that sets well always helps the performance of a mainsail. It increases the wind speed and smooths out the wind flow on the leeward side of the larger mainsail, thereby increasing the speed of the boat. When the jib is raised the halyard must be snugged up tight so no wrinkles or loops form in the luff. This leading edge, the first to strike the wind when under way, must always be kept taut. Should the luff hang loose the shape of the sail is destroyed. It will lose much of its driving power, especially when sailing into the wind. It is most important that the jib be set up correctly, not only for the greater efficiency derived but because most skippers sail by the actions of a taut luff. From its actions, whether shivering, violently shaking, or quietly full, they can tell whether they are sailing correctly.

It is a good idea to mark, as a frame of reference, all the sheets and other adjustable rigging and hardware at appropriate spots so that you will have a continuing frame of reference every time you set or trim a sail. If your boat moved well with the sails set to certain marks, you can easily duplicate the settings on a similar day.

Sailing to Windward

Sailing to windward is usually the wettest, the most challenging, and the most enjoyable part of sailing. A boat can't be sailed directly into the wind, since the sails won't fill and exert the proper pressures. Thus, the whole object in windward sailing is to "point" as high or to sail as close to the wind as possible without stopping the boat's way. Therefore, when sailing close-hauled or "on the wind," the sheets should be hauled in hard so that the sails are trimmed as flat as practicable and the boom is as close to the centerline of the boat as advisable. Care must be taken to get the boom in a proper position so that the craft will sail at its maximum speed and not stall. If a boat points too high into the wind, she will slow down and come to a stop because the airfoil of the sail has been broken. This is called "pinching"; if the boom is too close to the center of the boat it may be heeling at a considerable angle but have little forward movement. Just how far the sails should be sheeted, however, depends on how full or how flat the sail is cut, and how much breeze and sea there is. As a matter of fact, trimming the sails to go to windward depends a great deal on the individual craft. Some sailboats take well to being sheeted in hard; others, generally of a less "racy" type, won't stand such hard sheeting. To begin with, trim the mainsheet so that the end of the boom is just over the lee quarter, that is, the lee corner of the stern, and the jib sheet not quite as hard in as you can get it. The harder it's blowing the harder you can trim in the sheets. To trim them in hard in light airs will "kill the boat's way."

Some sailboats can't sail any closer than 45 degrees to the true wind direction, while others can sail closer to the wind than 45 degrees. The best way to determine if you are sailing as close into the wind as possible is to turn the boat gradually up into the wind until the outer edge of the sail begins to shiver and shake. The jib is generally the first to show signs of pinching; it will flutter at the luff. Then the mainsail will begin to shake at the luff. This indicates that you have sailed too far into the wind, so that the wind is now blowing on both sides of the sails. When this occurs, move the tiller away from the sails so that the boat will head farther from the wind. Since the wind is almost continually changing in strength and slightly in direction, it's a good idea to test frequently by pushing the tiller toward the sails and pointing up to make sure you are sailing as close to the wind as possible. When you see that the telltales or burgee are making a broader angle with the boat than the sail, this is your warning that you're not pointing high enough. You must then put the helm "down" (away from the wind) and bring the bow up into the wind until the luff starts to shake, then bear away just enough to put the luff to sleep again. By experimenting several times, you'll soon know how far you can point up before the sails begin to flutter or luff.

On boats with fixed keels, nothing further in the form of adjustments is required to sail into the wind. In boats having a centerboard, the board as well as the sheets must be adjusted for the different points of sails. When going to windward, the centerboard should be lowered all the way to prevent the boat from sliding leeward.

When sailing close-hauled, there is certain to be some leeway being made, and you should, if possible, take advantage of every little strong puff of the wind to get back a little to windward. As soon as the puff comes and the boat heels to it, ease the helm down very gently and let the craft sail closer to the wind; as the puff dies down, the luff of the mainsail and the back of the jib will begin to quiver and lift and you'll have to bear away again. By following such a procedure, you'll cancel or help to cancel out your leeway and will save a surprising amount of ground.

How the crew is seated can have an effect on your leeway since it helps to control the heel of the craft. Human weight on the high-side rail will counteract excessive heel. Every boat, of course, has her best position with regard to heel and weight distribution. This can be learned only by experimentation and feel. But always remember that a boat always heels more sharply when sailing to windward. It has one great advantage: you can always point the boat's bow up into the wind (luff up) by a quick movement of the tiller downwind. This lets the wind blow on both sides of the sail at the same time; the sails flutter out, doing no work, and the boat can't be knocked down. When running and reaching, the sheets are your safety valve. You can let them fly if a squall should make it necessary. When close-hauled, the best safety valve is to luff up. In very squally weather, the puffs of wind may strike you so suddenly that the boat won't respond quickly enough to be safe; in this event your best safety valve would be the main sheet. Starting the sheet, as it is called, is of course a much quicker safety valve than luffing up. Its effect is immediate; whereas when luffing, the boat takes a second or two to respond to the helm. It is better to luff than to start the sheet, as by luffing up and bearing away again you can keep the boat moving. You should always keep way on a boat. A boat that is moving is under control. When she is stopped she is at the mercy of the elements. Every time you luff you kill the craft's headway, and you must be careful to sail away from the wind again, before headway is lost. In the same way, starting the sheet immediately kills the boat's headway and you must trim the sheet in again quickly before you lose steerage way. Thus, when sailing into the wind you must do a great deal of experimentation to find out just how your boat will handle.

As was stated previously, a boat can arrive at a point directly upwind only by making a series of diagonal slants, or tacks, first one way, then the other. This operation can be compared to a skier climbing a slope on skis. As we know, a skier does this by using the so-called "herringbone" technique—alternately placing one ski before the other at an angle of about 45 degrees to the direction in which he wishes to go. If we consider the wind as being represented as the slope, and flowing downhill, the boat follows the same technique as does the skier to go upwind.

Changing a sailboat's course so that the bow swings past the eye of the wind and pays off on the other tack is called "coming about." If we assume you are sailing on a port tack, swing the tiller sharply to starboard (leeward side) or toward the sail, thus causing the bow to turn to port. At the same time, release the jib sheet (the starboard or leeward sheet) so that the jib won't present any resistance to the wind as the bow swings into the eye of the wind. Be careful to ease the mainsail sheet loose so that you don't heel too suddenly. For an instant the boat will be pointed directly into the wind, with the sails shaking violently. As the boat continues to swing around, the wind will strike the sail more fully and the jib must be trimmed. It will fill and push the bow of the boat around to the starboard tack. Midship the rudder as you approach the new heading (a starboard tack), and when straightaway set the sails again. The reverse procedure is followed when swinging from a starboard tack to a port tack.

Figure 2-7: These boats are sailing to windward.

Be careful when coming about. The boom swings from one side of the boat to the other. If you aren't watching, it can strike you or one of your crew members on the head or even knock someone right out of the boat. To prevent this, the command "Coming about" should be given as a warning to cast off (uncleat) the jib sheet and to prepare a change from one side of the boat to the other. The command "Ready about" or "Hard alee" is given as the tiller is pushed to the lee side of the boat and the bow goes through the eye of the wind, and anyone in the way of the boom ducks. Don't come about too fast or too slowly. Carried out correctly, this will be one smooth, continuous operation and the boat will immediately gather way on the new tack. If coming about is accomplished too fast, you may overshoot the new heading. Also avoid coming about in the middle of a strong puff of wind, since the results may be the same. If done too slowly or in light winds, your boat may get "caught in stays" and get "in irons"; that is, she'll lie up in the wind, all her sails shaking, and refuse to fill on either tack. She has now lost all headway, and commences to go astern. In order to get way on again, haul the head sheets to windward, which we will suppose is the port side. Put the tiller to starboard. As the vessel is going astern, the rudder will now produce the reverse effect of what it would were the boat going ahead; so putting the tiller to starboard turns the craft's head to starboard. To assist her still further in paying off, slack out main and jib sheets; these sails have a tendency to keep her up into the wind. When she has paid off sufficiently, trim the sheets, and she'll soon gather way on the port tack.

When coming about, in a boat with a genoa jib, the clew of this big sail must move itself forward, past the shrouds, and around the mast. For this to occur smoothly, the genoa's sheet must be released in sufficient time for the sail to swing in its path, and the craft must be brought about more slowly than when using a working jib. Sometimes the sheet or the big sail itself will catch on a projection, such as a winch or cleat on the mast, as it flaps its way from one side of the craft to the other. To prevent this, a crew member often takes the genoa's clew forward, and leads it around the shrouds and mast to the other side. While carrying out this operation, don't permit the boat to go into "irons."

When tacking to windward, the duration of a tack may not be the same. Obstructions, channels, sand bars and the like make each of the tacks of different length. (In sailor parlance, a short tack is called a "short board" or "short hitch" and a long tack a "long board" or "long hitch.") All the words in the world couldn't describe the correct length of each tack, for every different condition of the water, the wind, and the ability of the boat to sail close to the eye of the wind will enter into the problem. On long trips in open water, the tacks might be several hours in length. A small boat sailed in restricted waters may have to come about on another tack at intervals of a few minutes. The only rule is to keep a tack as long as possible, for each time you come about reduces the speed of the boat, demands adjusting of sails, and, in small boats, causes the crew to shift from side to side.

Sailing Before the Wind

Sailing or running in the same direction as the wind is blowing—or in nearly the same direction—is rather tricky. Contrary to what you might think, it calls for better seamanship than close-hauling or tacking against the wind. It's probably the least exciting point of sailing, since the boat's speed is usually reduced and the apparent wind is much lighter. Also, the sense of control and response which the helmsman feels when the craft is close-hauled is diminished to a great degree. That is, the boat moves less easily, responds less surely to the helm.

In order to obtain maximum power from the wind, the mainsail is set by letting out its sheet until it is approximately 90 degrees (at right angles) to the centerline of the boat. (Note that I said the *mainsail* should be at 90 degrees, not the boom.) This is done to obtain full pressure of the wind against the greatest possible sail area. If you're sailing dead before the wind, the mainsail may be paid out either to starboard or port; if the wind should be coming from one quarter or the other, the mainsail should be out on the opposite side. After setting the mainsail, the jib sheet should be trimmed so that the jib will be nearly at right angles to the fore-and-aft line of the boat. However, you'll probably find, when running before the wind, that the jib will be completely blanketed by the mainsail and will just flap idly. After you have gained some experience and have become fairly adept at running, you can spread the jib out on the opposite side of the craft to the mainsail (this is commonly called "sailing wing and wing") by using a whisker pole, or in some cases a boat hook. A whisker pole is a light spar with jaws on one end like a gaff and a spike on the other end. The spike is pushed through the clew of the jib, and the jaws rest against the mast. The whisker pole holds the jib out at more-or-less a right angle to the boat. The jib is most effective used this way. To make the whisker pole stay in place, it is necessary to trim the jib sheet to put a strain up the spar, and thus hold it against the mast. As explained later in this chapter, you may wish to substitute a spinnaker for the jib.

In the case of centerboard craft, the centerboard should be raised. Most boats will sail at their fastest (when running) with the centerboard raised entirely, but if she shows a tendency to yaw or swing off her course in either direction, it's wise to lower the board a quarter of its full depth.

When running before the wind, there are two things you must guard against: an accidental jibe and broaching to. For instance, if the person at the helm isn't alert at all times and should allow the boat to alter her course enough to permit the wind to blow behind the sail, there is the very definite danger of the sail being hurled from one side of the craft to the other. An action of this type is called a "jibe," and in a case such as this, an "accidental jibe." The velocity reached by the boom during this swing is sufficient to cause a serious bodily injury to anyone unfortunate enough to be caught in its path. It also can cause a great deal of damage to the craft, such as broken rigging or a broken mast. Thus, an accidental jibe should be avoided at all costs—so that even when your sail is almost at right angles to the boat, you'll do well to keep the wind a little on the opposite side instead of directly astern. If you see your main starting to fill on the leeward side, hold your tiller sharply down to leeward. If the jibe seems inevitable, keep your tiller or wheel to leeward and trim your sheets as fast as possible, so that when the boom swings over it will have a minimum of play.

"Broaching to" is a tendency your boat may have to nose into the wind, in spite of your efforts to keep her on her course. Once allowed to start, the impulse may be difficult to stop, since as the boat is being heeled over, the boom may dip into the water. This can be dangerous, because as soon as the boom is in the water, the rudder becomes useless. The only safeguard against broaching to is alertness. As in the case of accidental jibe, there is no need to worry if you watch your steering. It is easier than it sounds, and the dangers of broaching to or an accidental jibe, while they have to be considered, need never be experienced if you handle your sailboat with the attention she deserves.

The "controlled jibe" is a much-used maneuver and it's essential to sailing. (Only the unintentional jibe can cause trouble.) It is generally employed when sailing before the wind and when you have to round a buoy or breakwater where there is limited space; when the wind has shifted and you wish to avoid sailing by the lee; or when you wish to change your course without coming about. Actually, you could say that jibing (sometimes called "wearing") is the opposite of coming about. In both maneuvers the sail shifts, catching the wind on its other side. The difference is that you come about when you are sailing into the wind, and you jibe when you are sailing with the wind.

Suppose you're sailing with the wind on the port quarter and you want to alter your course. As the wind is behind you and pounding squarely on the sails, you must take care to insure that the mainsail is under complete control at all times during this maneuver. In the case of a centerboard craft, drop the board while jibing—this makes the boat more stable. Commence the jibe by trimming in the sheets as rapidly as possible and keep hauling on the mainsheet until it's almost as tight as when you're tacking. This will reduce the size of the arc through which the boom eventually banks, and will keep the boom from lifting. Release the jib sheet so that the jib swings freely. When the boom gets well inboard, ease the tiller over so that the boat starts turning in the direction you want to go. (The stern will swing into the wind—not the bow, as in coming about.) As soon as the wind is dead astern, ease the mainsheet slightly and push the boom over so that it won't swing suddenly. Should you wish to return from a running position to a windward direction, it's an easy task to swing the boat, just as you do in tacking, by pushing the tiller toward the mainsail. As the craft swings closer to the wind, haul the mainsail sheet in gradually so that the boat doesn't lose its forward motion. It's then only necessary to continue the swing and trim the sails.

Reaching

As we said earlier, when a sailboat is under way and is neither sailing to windward nor before the wind, it is said to be *reaching*. In other words, the craft sails more or less across the wind. When sailing in this manner, your boat is able to sail from one point to another and return with no complicated maneuvering. To trim the sails correctly for a reach, as soon as the vessel is on her correct course, ease out the mainsheet and head sheets until the luffs of the sails are beginning to shake. Then haul in on the sheets until they cease to shake, and then haul in a little more to get the best trim.

Now make fast the sheets. You'll be able to tell if the wind draws ahead or aft by watching the wind pennant, the sails, the direction of the waves, and by the feel of your boat when you have had more experience. To get the best out of your craft you should always study the wind's direction and trim your sheets accordingly. For example, if the wind draws ahead, the luffs of the sails will start to shake, and in order to trim the sheets correctly for the course you are sailing, you should haul them in until the luffs cease to shake. If, on the other hand, the wind draws further aft, the boat will be heeled over, but you will lose speed; the burgee or telltale will point further ahead and the feel of the wind on your face will be less. To trim the sheets correctly, ease them until the sail is making roughly the same angle with the craft's centerline as the wind pennant. The pennant is always a good guide to the trim of the sails when reaching or sailing close-hauled.

To change from sailing close-hauled to close-reaching, move the tiller up (toward the wind). Then, as the boat's head falls off to leeward, set the sails until both the jib and mainsail start to flutter along the luff. Both sheets are then hauled in until the fluttering stops. The sails should be trimmed in a nearly parallel position to the centerline of the craft. The boat will move faster and have less heel than when sailing to windward close-hauled.

When on a broad reach, the same procedure is followed after the craft has been put on her desired course. The sheets are hauled in just enough to stop fluttering of the sails. The boom is usually kept at an angle halfway between the centerline of the craft and the direction the burgee or telltale is pointing. Broad-reaching is possibly the easiest maneuver in sailing, since the boat then has its best balance, though some care should be taken to keep the sails at their full drawing angle to the wind. When sailing on a beam reach, you handle the sails in the same way as when sailing on a broad or a close reach. In the case of centerboard craft on a beam reach, the board should be about halfway down; on a close-reach it should be about three-quarters down; and for broad-reaching about one-quarter down.

When you're on a reach course, it generally is a good idea to choose some landmark, or if none is in sight, to sail by compass bearing, so that you keep the craft going in the desired direction. You'll find that it is rather difficult to keep any small sailing vessel on an *exact* course, especially if there is a heavy sea running.

The only concern, when reaching, is from a beam sea, since it may cause the craft to roll slightly and may slop over the windward

Figure 2-8: This boat is on a reach.

side. But serious rolling seldom occurs except when the seas are very high, because in this sailing position the sails have an excellent steadying influence. If yours is a centerboard craft, it's advisable to carry about three-fourths of your board. It need not be down quite so far as when you are going to windward.

Handling the Spinnaker

The spinnaker can be effectively employed when sailing before the wind and when broad-reaching. It is effective in very light airs, where it does more to keep a boat moving than the mainsail. In strong winds it "pulls like a mule" and care must be taken in its handling.

In setting, clear the spinnaker of any twists. Then, with the boat sailing along, one crew member should go forward and secure the head of the spinnaker to the spinnaker halyard. The spinnaker halyard is generally kept cleated to the mast ready for use. It should have a swivel shackle and a snap hook that can be snapped into the becket (or loop) at the head of the spinnaker. The spinnaker boom is placed on the deck with the outboard end headed forward. The tack of the spinnaker is secured to the outboard end of the boom. The sheet, which is fast to the clew, is held by one member of the crew aft. The crew member forward should now pass the boom guy, which is secured to the boom's outer end, around outside the shrouds back to the cockpit. Now the helmsman ties the line to a cleat and the hand forward begins to hoist on the halyard, and at the same time pushes the boom out over the bows and secures its inboard end to the mast either by a conical socket device or a small gooseneck, or, if the boom has jaws, by resting them against the mast. The spinnaker goes up. When it is high enough, the man hoisting makes fast to any convenient cleat, while the hand controlling the guy hauls the boom aft until it is at right angles to the boat. If there is much wind there will be a hard strain on the guy when the boom is pulled aft. When the boom is at right angles to the boat, the sail will be drawing and the line can be tied to a cleat. The sail is now kept drawing by the sheet hand, who keeps his eyes glued to the sail, particularly the luff. As soon as this begins to shake and the sail shows signs of collapsing, he hauls in the sheet smartly until

Figure 2-9: Setting of the spinnaker.

the sail is drawing again, while the guy hand eases away on the guy. As soon as the sail is drawing again the sheet is eased and the boom pulled aft once again.

When setting the spinnaker, remember to keep the foot of the sail absolutely parallel to the water. Also, the spinnaker pole should always ride perpendicular to the mast. And it should stand at the same level as the tack, to which its outer end is secured. The pole should *not* tilt skyward nor droop to the water, because this will bend the spinnaker out of shape. The sail should have a belly and lift to it, accomplished by careful trimming of sheet and guy. On calm days, lightweight sheets will help the sail to lift itself. As for the jib, it is a point of controversy. Some skippers believe that it should be brought down fast, so that it doesn't interfere when the spinnaker is broken out. Others say that the jib can be left hoisted, and you should try to trim your sails so that the spent wind of one sail is spilt into another. The mainsail should spill into the spinnaker and the spinnaker into the jib. While I must admit that I am one who believes in the former procedure, the best advice I can give you is to try both ways and see what is best for your boat.

One way of setting a spinnaker (this method is often used on larger sailboats) is to set it in stops. To do this, first lay out the spinnaker on the deck with the luff and the leech alongside each other. Roll up the center portion of the sail tightly. You should now have a long, thin sausage with the luff and leech together on the outside, and the clew and tack together at the bottom. Now take some light cotton cord—don't use anything heavier—and tie the sail with a single turn of the thread at intervals of two feet or so. The sail, thus stopped, is then sent up the mast by the halyard and the foot made fast until the spinnaker is wanted. To break it out, make the sheet

Figure 2-10: Sailing with a jib and spinnaker (left) and just the spinnaker (right).

fast to a cleat and the tack fast to the outboard end of the boom. When the boom is secured to the mast and guyed aft, the rest of the stops will go. The advantage of setting a spinnaker in stops is that you can break it out more easily and quickly than if you had to bend it on and hoist it. In racing, this time-saving factor is very important. When cruising, apart from the fun of watching the stops go as the sail fills, it has no very great advantage except on certain occasions when it may be useful to have the spinnaker ready waiting for an expected alteration of course on which it will be needed.

In the larger racer-cruiser boats, the setting of a spinnaker may be much simplified by reeving an outhaul through a sheave on the outboard end of the spinnaker boom. The boom, having been secured at its inboard end to the mast in the usual way, is kept at right angles to the craft's fore and aft by being guyed aft with the guy. The spinnaker is then bent and hoisted, the tack being bent not to the end of the boom, but to the outhaul. The spinnaker is now up and down the mast, lying in the lee of the mainsail. Now haul away on the outhaul and the sail is set and may be trimmed with sheet and guy as usual. Here are some additional hints that may prove helpful in handling the modern spinnaker:

First, on a dead run the spinnaker pole should be worked back to windward as far as practicable so that as much of the spinnaker as possible is exposed on the windward side of the boat, clear of the mainsail's wind shadow.

Second, above 6 or 7 knots the halyard can be eased some 6 inches to 1 foot away from the mast on small boats and from 1 to 3 feet on larger boats, in order to get the spinnaker away from the mast and out into clearer air. This should be a gradual process so that the halyard is kept in close to the mast in very light air, eased slightly at winds of 7 and 8 knots, and gradually let out to the maximum in 15- and 20-knot winds.

Third, on a beam reach in anything except light air, the pole should be raised so that it is at least square with the mast and sometimes a little above square. This will release downward tensions on the leading edge of the spinnaker, allowing it to curve to leeward in a higher angle of attack for reaching. It requires some experimentation to get the best setting of the height of the pole on a reach with any given boat; but it will be noticed that as the pole is raised, the leeches will spread wider, which is very advantageous.

The spinnaker setting in extremely light air is probably the most difficult, particularly when there is really not enough wind to fill out the spinnaker. In this case, the best solution simply is to expose a flat, stable surface of cloth to pick up any slight breeze that may occur. To do this, the spinnaker pole should be on the lowest setting on the mast, and dropped below the perpendicular so that there is a very slight tension on the luff. The head of the spinnaker should also be raised as close to the halyard block as it will go. If any fresh air comes in that fills out the spinnaker, the pole should immediately be raised and the halyard eased off in accordance with the wind velocity.

The leech of a spinnaker, while reaching, should be treated in the same way as the leech of a jib. There is air flowing off the leech, and if the leech is too close to the main, it will back-wind the main severely, sometimes even rendering it useless. In some cases, if the spinnaker is brought around to a point where the clew is trimmed almost as close inboard as the tack, the major thrust of the spinnaker will be directly to leeward, laying the boat over but not driving her forward as fast as with the jib or genoa.

The point at which the spinnaker should be taken down is a hard one to judge. But if with the acting perpendicular forces in mind, it is observed that there is no appreciable angle away from the boat's centerline along the foot, the chances are that no practical benefit is being derived from the sail. To take in the spinnaker, just reverse the process of setting it. That is, slack off the guy, allowing the boom to go forward, spilling the wind out of the sail. The forward hand unships the inboard end of the boom and brings the boom carefully inboard. As soon as it is inboard, the clew and the tack are cast off and the sheet hand gathers in the foot of the sail in the lee of the mainsail. When doing this, he should let go the halyard. As the sail comes down he makes the two ends of the halyard fast to their appropriate cleat and coils down the guy. The sail is folded and returned to the sail locker or bag.

3

Reviewing Sailing Seamanship

Seamanship pertains to all the skills used in operating a sailboat. It's the sum total of every sailor's knowledge, and how well he puts it to use determines how good a yachtsman he is. However, seamanship is far too big a subject to be covered adequately in the limited space at my command, and I must therefore confine myself to practical hints. Actually, a book as big as a jet airliner would not be able to tell you what to do under every possible contingency. Much of the correct seamanship of a sailboat depends largely on the skill of the helmsman, but the art of properly handling the tiller, watching the set of the sails, and getting the most out of the boat can't be learned quickly. In other words, you simply can't read a few chapters in a how-to-do-it book and expect to become a proficient sailor overnight. Most of the really expert sailors started at it in boyhood and have been sailing and practicing the art for many years. When I was about eight years old, I started my sailing on the Kickamuit River in a square punt with leeboards. I just took the sailboat out on the river and learned by myself how to get the craft to move about. From the punt, I advanced to the White Cap Class, the Town Class, and finally to the Herreshoff "S" Class. I still actively race in the S-Class. In addition, I have taken part in ocean racing events such as the Newport-Bermuda Race and the Annapolis-Newport Race, as well as taking many cruises with my family. But, I must honestly admit that I never really stop learning sailing seamanship, and maybe that is a good thing, because there are few sports where learning can be so much fun.

Leaving the Mooring

To get to your boat on a mooring or at anchor, of course, you can use a tender or dinghy. Generally it is rowed, or powered by a small outboard motor. Upon leaving the dock, aim your tender to pass other boats just astern rather than to cut close across their bows. Look out for mooring lines, which may hold you up. To make a direct crossing of an anchorage with a strong tide running, it may be necessary to point the boat obliquely up tide, that is, into the tide, for the crossing.

Unless there is an adverse stronger tide to contend with, the sailboat will always be facing into the wind while at her mooring. Thus, if you approach the moored craft from aft you'll also be pointing into the wind (or tide), which will act as a brake. Come alongside the moored boat on the lee side, which is most sheltered from the wind. Ship one oar and make your dinghy's painter (a short line attached to the tender's stem) fast to a cleat on the deck. Be sure to make fast as soon as possible and put out fenders from your dinghy. The dinghy may be towed or may be secured to the sailboat's mooring; it will probably be used to get back ashore.

On arriving at your moored boat, check to see that the tiller is firmly in place, the centerboard (if you have one) lowered to its desired sailing position, and all sheets coiled so that they will run freely through the blocks. If there is a topping lift, take up on it until the boom has lifted from its crotch (if it has one). Remove the crotch and stow it where you won't fall over it while out on the water. Also be sure to stow it where none of the running rigging can get tangled about it. Then bend on the mainsail or remove the sail covers.

When you're leaving your mooring, it is well to plan in advance in which direction you intend to sail. Let's say that there are several boats close to your port side, so you decide to go off to starboard—in other words, on a port tack. (A boat is sailing on a port tack when the wind is coming over her port side.) With both sails hoisted, haul in the starboard jib sheet, taking up all the slack. Push the clew of the jib to port; the wind will fill the sail and force the bow of the boat to starboard. Untie your mooring line; but before casting off, walk back with it along the port deck. This will throw the boat's bow to starboard and bring the wind over the port side. As soon as the boat begins to swing around, let go of the mooring line and take up on the starboard jib sheet. Swing the tiller to port; this will help push the nose of the boat to starboard. Then trim the mainsail by taking in the mainsheet until the sail is fairly flat. As the jib pushes the boat around, the mainsail will fill and the boat will move forward. As your boat begins to make headway, bring the tiller back to starboard, so that the craft doesn't fall off too much. When the boat is on the desired course, bring the tiller amidships (to the center).

In casting off the mooring line make certain that everything is clear. In the above example, let's assume you go out to your mooring in a dinghy. Your mooring line should be over the starboard bow and your dinghy's painter taken aft and brought around forward on the port side outside all shrouds and stays. Then pass it around the bow to the starboard side and secure it to the mooring line. By following this procedure you won't have any fouling of lines when casting off. To help in all this sort of close-quarters work, the rudder may or may not be of much use. Bear in mind that a rudder is of little value unless the boat is either moving through the water at an appreciable speed or (and this is a point too often ignored) fast to her mooring with a current flowing by her.

If the wind is light, the current sometimes may have more effect on a boat lying to a mooring than the wind, and, instead of finding the boat lying head to wind when you board her, you may find her heading into the current with her stern to the wind, or tailing to the wind, or "tide rode," as it is called. In other words, the current and wind are in opposite directions from each other. In such a situation, it is best to leave the mooring under the jib alone. But you should get the gaskets or stops off the mainsail to be ready to hoist it promptly, then set the jib, sheet it on the side opposite to which you intend to sail out, cast off the mooring, and, under jib alone, sail before the wind or with the wind on the quarter until you have gotten into clear water. Then, when there are no boats or other ob-

Figure 3-1: Getting ready for a sail. Note that there are no suitcases. All clothing is stored in sea bags.

structions to interfere with the maneuver, set the mainsail as quickly as possible, first putting the boat's head as much into the wind as it will go by shoving the tiller down and letting go the jib sheet. When this sail is set, the jib being already set, both sails can be sheeted in and the boat will gather headway immediately. Remember, however, that the boat will drift some, and the tide may turn you, so allow sea room. Put the jib aback so that the bow falls off. Now, with all the sail up, sail on a reach to again pick up momentum. A yawl is perfect in this respect. With everything furled but the mizzen, such a boat will head up and, if moored, lie more or less quietly awaiting your next move. If she is adrift, she will still lie up into the wind and drift astern. If there are exceptions to this rule, they will occur when the wind is light and the current strong.

If the wind is across the tide you can adopt either of two previously mentioned methods. You'll usually be able to hoist the main-sail, but you will have to let the sheet well out, to prevent the sail's filling before you're ready to move. All you have to do to get under way is to cast off the mooring and at the same time haul in your sheets.

Getting away from a mooring at a crowded anchorage can some-times become a ticklish undertaking. Before attaining proper sea room and speed, the question frequently arises whether to attempt to pass ahead or astern of other craft at anchor or moored. It's always safer to pass astern under crowded conditions, as wind and current leeway could readily set you back to foul mooring buoys and lines, or even the boat itself, if you attempt to pass ahead of other boats with insufficient clearance. When maneuvering in a crowded anchorage remember that you must be on constant alert. Winds may quickly go flat and fail, leaving the boat to drift. While the speed of drift will be low, the boat may collide with others, and the crew can do little to prevent contact. The simplest scheme is to hold the boats apart by hands and feet, boat hook, and fenders as they pass and secure a bow line to the moored craft as you go by. This will serve to check the drifting and hold you safely astern of the other boat until the wind freshens and you can again make headway and get clear. If there should be no moored vessel in reach there is of course no danger of contact; then it might be practical to grab a mooring and hold on until again able to proceed.

None of the remarks about the difficulty of getting under way in a crowded anchorage or from a wind-stoppered bottleneck apply if you have auxiliary power on board. You then start the engine, motor out to a less crowded area, and get up your sails in a leisurely manner.

Getting Under Way from a Dock

Casting off from a dock is usually considered more difficult than clearing from a mooring only because there are generally more boats closer at hand. Actually, leaving a dock is easy if the craft is to lee-ward or should she head to the wind. First, unfasten the bow and stern lines and then pull on the jib sheet. As the bow swings away from the side of the pier, trim the mainsail until it's at the proper angle and the boat moves ahead. Adjust the course to steer by the tiller, and keep the sheets well in hand. Set your sails close-hauled to get clear.

When leaving from a downwind dock, the mainsail should not be set and the boat should be maneuvered clear of the dock under the jib alone, using a boat hook to fend off. Once your boat is sufficiently clear, raise the mainsail.

These two situations present no difficulties. It is a bit harder when the wind is blowing onto the dock. In this instance run the light anchor out in a dinghy to a point as far away as possible and at right angles to the dock face. When the anchor has been laid, cast off docking lines from the dock and haul out to the anchor. The boat will then be lying to anchor and you can proceed as described earlier in this chapter, bearing in mind the fact that dock is still comparatively close. In all cases, once you get under way, take in and stow all fenders, lines, and other docking gear.

Getting under way from a dock can be simpler if you have auxiliary power. When the wind is blowing off the dock, just cast off and you'll drift away. Then start your engine to get clear of other boats. When the breeze is blowing against the dock, let go the stern line and tighten up on the bow line until the bow is snug against the dock (fenders out, of course). When the stern is far enough out, cast off the bow line, reverse the engine, and go astern until you're sufficiently in the clear to swing the bow out and go ahead. When the wind is blowing parallel to the dock, push the bow and stern away, and when clear, use your auxiliary power.

Helmsmanship and Trim

There is one good rule in helmsmanship: let the boat do the sailing. A well-balanced and well-designed boat can quite often sail herself better than you can sail her. As stated earlier, a boat that tries to turn up into the wind is said to carry a "weather" helm; while a boat with the opposite characteristic is said to carry a "lee" helm. In most cases, a properly designed sailboat will usually have a *slight* weather helm. This means that the tiller must be held toward the windward side. If the tiller is unattended, the boat will turn into the wind and luff. This can be a very important safety factor. Such a balance means that if you get into any trouble, you can let go of the tiller and slack off both main- and jib sheets. The boat will swing around and lie more or less quietly, looking up at the wind. If your boat has a *heavy* weather helm, it is an indication that something is wrong. The first thing to do is to examine the trim of your sails.

In trimming the sails, the forces acting on a sail, mentioned in Chapter 2, must always be kept in mind. As was previously stated, sails are cut to provide the greatest amount of forward drive force and the least amount of heeling action and drag. The manner in which they are trimmed, however, appreciably affects their ability to do their best job. Actually, all boats differ somewhat in actual performance. Thus for any given boat, proper athwartship adjustments and the best settings for different airs can be determined only through experimentation.

The ballast of your boat can have an effect on the helm. In our keelboats the ballast is usually sealed inside the shell of the hull, and, unless the boat is being raced, the live ballast (your crew) and gear on board are usually of little concern. But, in the smaller day-sailer and sailing dinghy, you must make sure that her fore-and-aft trim is correct. A modern day-sailer is designed so that the crew members may be in their normal sailing positions and maintain the trim, but there has to be some adjustment of the conditions and for the relative weight of helmsman and crew. A properly trimmed craft should have a clean wake, her transom just dipping below the surface of the water, and the wake streaming away smoothly without eddies or bubbling.

Right-of-Way Rules

A good skipper anticipates the movements of those ships or boats which may affect his vessel's course and speed. This comes with knowledge gained through experience, observation, and full understanding of the Rules of the Road. These rules are the regulations governing water traffic, and they're the basis upon which maritime law is maintained. They cover all crossings, convergings, and meetings, and they establish which vessel is responsible for keeping clear of another.

According to the Rules of the Road, sailboats always have the right-of-way over powerboats, except in the not-very-likely possibility of a boat under sail overtaking one under power. In this case, the motorboat would have the right-of-way. As a matter of fact, *every* vessel overtaking any other vessel must keep out of the way of the overtaken one. Also, remember that *all* vessels must keep out of the way of any vessels fishing with nets or lines or trawls. However, even

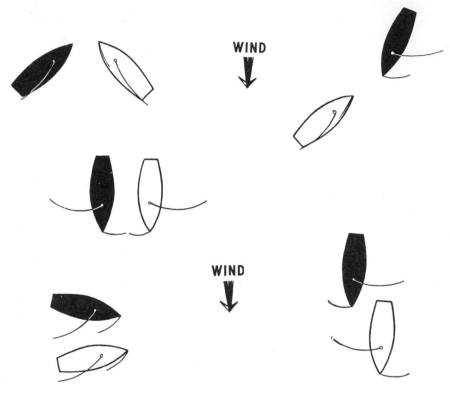

Figure 3-2: Rules of the Road. The white boat has the right-of-way in each case. (Courtesy of United States Coast Guard)

if you have the right-of-way, don't press your advantage. It can be dangerous! Don't expect all motorboaters to understand your intentions, such as when jibing or coming about in tight areas. In such cases, keep in mind that the only purpose of the Rules of the Road is to prevent collisions, and to do this, they must be mixed with common sense and courtesy.

The rules of right-of-way for sailing craft are determined by direction of the wind and sailing directions of the boats at their time of meeting. The following are the most common situations you will encounter during normal sailing:

1. When both sailboats are running free, with the wind on the same side, the one which is to the windward must keep out of the way of the craft which is to the leeward. In other words, when both sailboats are running free before the wind, the one upwind, which receives the wind first, must give away to the other.

2. When both sailboats are running free, with the wind on different sides, the one which has the wind on the port side must keep out of the way of the craft with the wind on the starboard.

3. A sailboat running free before the wind must keep clear of one that is close-hauled tacking into the wind.

4. A sailboat close-hauled on a port tack, with the wind coming over the port side, must give way to a craft close-hauled on a starboard tack.

5. A sailboat which has the wind aft must keep out of the way of the other craft.

When your sailboat is under auxiliary power, remember that according to law you're operating a motorboat and not a sailboat, and therefore you must follow the motorboat's Rules of the Road, which are as follows:

1. Two motorboats approaching each other should pass port side to port side (give way to the right). In some channels with a current, on the Great Lakes and specified rivers, the vessel riding with the current has the right of way over the one going against the current.

2. A motorboat having another boat in her danger zone (from dead ahead to two points abaft the starboard beam) must give way, and shall, if necessary, slow down, alter her course, stop, or reverse direction.

3. Boats coming out of slips into the open, or leaving berths at piers and docks, have no rights until they are entirely clear.

When a powerboat alters course to give way to another vessel, she indicates her movements by signaling with her whistle or horn in the following manner:

One short blast—I am directing my course to starboard.

Two short blasts—I am directing my course to port.

Three short blasts—I am proceeding astern (in reverse).

Four or more blasts—Danger! (Can imply an emergency or indicate inability to understand or comply with signal received.)

If you haven't an auxiliary engine yourself, it is still important for you to know the regulations for motorboats and other mechanically propelled craft, for even if you keep clear of traffic-infested waters, you're sure to meet many cruisers and auxiliary yachts in the course of your travels. It is sometimes difficult to determine whether a craft under sail has her engine running also, and if you have any doubts about the matter, it will be safer to assume that she is under sail alone, and give way, if the steering rules for sailing craft demand it.

There is another rule to which I would call your attention. This states that a vessel which does not have to give way to another shall keep her course and speed, but it must not be taken too literally, as it is only intended to apply when the other vessel fulfills her obligations. There is an overriding rule that states that "nothing in these rules shall exonerate any vessel, or the owner, or the master, or crew thereof, from the consequences of any neglect . . . of any precaution which may be required by the ordinary practice of seamen, or by the special circumstances of the case." If the other vessel fails to give way when she should, you must do all you can to avert a collision; if you don't you may be held to be guilty of contributory negligence.

Anchoring and Leaving an Anchorage

There are many considerations in anchoring safely. Not the least of these is selecting the best spot. The factors to consider are shelter, swinging room, holding ground, and anticipated weather. If a choice of ports offers, plan to anchor in óne which provides protection from sea or ground swell. If configuration of the land can provide a lee from prevailing or anticipated winds, so much the better. If the United States Coast and Geodetic Survey chart shows more than one variety of bottom, choose the best holding ground for the type of anchor used. Symbols shown on the chart will tell the nature of the bottom—sand, gravel, mud, coral, rocky, etc. Abbreviations for the different types of bottom will be found in the masthead of these U.S.C. & G.S. charts. To anchor safely it is imperative to know the kind of bottom in order to estimate the amount of scope needed for that particular bottom considering the type of anchor used. Trial and error is the only substitute for experience.

In most harbors and inshore anchorages it is best, of course, to anchor where there's enough water under the keel, but avoid locations where it is too deep because the burden of weighing anchor increases with the depth of water. Always keep in mind that deeper parts of a harbor are usually rougher, which, of course, is opposite to conditions when in open water. Also, in coastal waters, you must not only know how much water you have under your boat at the time you anchor, but how much you'll have at low tide. This latter vital information can be learned from the tide tables (see Chapter 4).

After verifying the depth of water and stage of tide, figure the scope needed to hold the boat when the tide is high. As stated in Chapter 1, this is perhaps the most important facet of anchoring. While the advent of nylon line has supposedly made all the old anchoring formulas obsolete, it is still my firm belief that a scope of six times the distance from the deck to the bottom at maximum tide is the absolute *minimum* for anchoring under ideal conditions. Actually, no rule can be formulated except that it's better to use too much scope than too little. But, all too frequently, it is not possible to let out as much scope as you would like because of crowded anchorages. Let out too much scope under these circumstances, and you will be the scourge of the harbor, running into everyone around you as they swing to short scope and you swing long.

In such cases, the use of chain instead of line tends to keep the pull on the anchor horizontal with somewhat less scope than with line. If an entire anchor cable of chain is out of the question, some advantage may be gained by using a length of chain at the anchor end of the anchor rode. The remainder may be of manila or nylon, with the latter fiber line having the added advantage of being shock absorbent because of its greater elasticity. The extra weight of the chain will help to keep the anchor's shank down and thus will keep chafing of the fiber portion of the line down to a minimum. Another way of keeping the anchor pull at the best angle is to hang some type of weight—a length of chain or another anchor. This will also reduce any strain as the boat surges. Often, in crowded anchorages, it may be advisable to employ a stern anchor to prevent the boat from swinging into any of her neighboring vessels. But this should be done only when there is very little possibility of strong cross currents or winds, because a strong push from the side would exert a great pull on the two anchors, which could cause either or both of them to drag.

It is always wise to mark an anchor rode so that the scope can be ascertained at once. It isn't good seamanship just to estimate the length of rode payed out; since one fathom of rode looks like another, it is all too easy to miscalculate. While I have used the plastic anchor rode markers that are available at most marine stores for a number of years, I supplement them by a marking system based on the traditional seaman's way of marking sounding lead lines, and I would recommend it unreservedly. This traditional system consists of having two strips of leather at the 2-fathom mark, three strips of leather at 3 fathoms, a white cotton rag at 5, a red flannel rag at 7, a piece of leather with a hole in it at 10, and repeating the marks for 3, 5, and 7 fathoms at 13, 15, and 17 fathoms. At 20 fathoms two knots were tied in a piece of marline; at 25, one knot; at 30, three knots; and one knot again at 35 fathoms. Actually the system is simple and logical. Since the plastic marker system depends on being able to see the markers in order to read them, the plastic markers are useless at night unless a light is available; and it is just when the night is most angry that lights and people to hold them are not available. The traditional seamen's method, which depends on touch—even the cloths have different textures—rather than on sight, does not have this considerable shortcoming during a furious night at sea.

How do I get to my desired anchorage spot? Here are the three situations that usually occur:

1. *When close-hauled, and wind and tide are in the same direction:* Luff or swing upwind; lower jib; wait until the boat gathers sternway; and then let go the anchor. This technique is also used where there is no tide or where it is negligible.

2. *When running, and the wind is against the tide:* Lower mainsail and approach under jib only; just before reaching desired anchorage spot lower jib; wait until boat gathers sternway; and then let go the anchor.

3. *When running, and wind and tide are in the same direction:* Lower mainsail and approach under jib only; lower jib a little way from the chosen location; let go the anchor; and then snub (stop the running out of) the anchor line and allow the boat to swing to the tide.

Except in the latter case, it's usually wise not to let go of the anchor until the boat has stopped forereaching and has begun to gather sternway. Make sure that the anchor rode is laid out along the deck or coiled down carefully so that it will run free. Don't stand in the coils, and make sure that they can't take a turn around your legs or around any other object on board. Then lower the anchor until you feel it strike bottom, and as your boat gathers sternway, pay out the amount of rode necessary for the desired ratio of scope to depth. (If you have an engine, it's not a bad idea to start it and back away from the anchor.) When the anchor is set and scope adjusted, make your anchor rode or cable fast.

After anchoring, in most places it is good practice to set an anchor light before dark. Usually this is located on, or suspended from, the forestay. Also before darkness sets in, take cross bearings on your anchorage; or better still, note ranges by two prominent objects in line on shore. These ranges should preferably be at right angles to one another, and they should be of such a nature that you can recognize them in the dark. You can easily determine whether or not you're dragging by subsequently noting these ranges.   .

If you're anchoring in company with other craft, watch the radius and direction of their swing and place yourself accordingly. Be careful of fouling someone else's line and allow for a sudden wind shift that might cause a collision or beaching. One hint, when anchoring in a fleet, that might help you avoid midnight fending parties, is to anchor, if possible, with a group of boats that are similar in size and type to yours. When doing this, locate your boat at least three or four boat lengths away from the nearest boat, whether that boat is ahead, astern, or on either beam. If you anchor among larger boats, allowances must be made for their greater swinging radius.

When you're ready to weigh anchor, follow much the same procedure as when leaving a mooring, except that the anchor and anchor line must be contended with. Recovering the anchor, itself, is best accomplished by moving up to a position over the anchor under power (or if necessary, under sail in short tacks), taking in slack until the shank of the anchor lifts from the bottom. This action should loosen the buried fluke sufficiently to permit the anchor to be broken out easily under power or sail unless caught on some unknown obstruction or hooked in a rock crevice. If it won't budge, take a few turns around the cleat and back your engine slowly for a few seconds to pull it loose. If you don't have an engine, take a turn around the cleat, lead the line over the gunwale amidships, and rock the boat. Also, it is sometimes possible to break an anchor free by "sailing it out." This is done by raising all sail, then sailing in a complete circle, yet constantly maintaining full strain on the anchor by keeping the anchor line taut. The pulling, turning effect created can twist the anchor loose.

The best way to prevent a caught anchor is to use a trip line. While a trip line is a small nuisance, it will pay big dividends if it is needed. A light, but strong, buoyed line—just long enough to reach the surface—attached to the crown of the anchor, will enable you to back the anchor out should it become wedged under an old log or cable. The buoy will also let you know at a glance where your anchor is located in relation to the boat. This can be useful intelligence when wind and tide are at cross-purposes, and boats are hanging in haphazard disarray in a crowded anchorage. At all times, when hauling in the anchor, wash the mud and sand off when it's at the surface of the water. Then coil the anchor rode and stow the anchor in its proper position.

Laying To

While sailing, there are often times you wish to "lay to"—to stop the boat and maintain its approximate position without the use of an anchor. As was already explained, a boat can be stopped from going ahead by pointing it into the wind. But, as you will remember, in this position the boat will begin to drift backward until it falls off the wind and fills away, at which point it will start sailing again. If you wish the boat not to fall away, you can arrange the tiller to the leeward side of the boat and trim the sheets to the point where the craft won't sail. The exact position of tiller and the trim of sheets varies from boat to boat, and only by practice can you determine the proper positions for laying to. But, as the size of the boat increases, the harder it is to make her lay to.

Approaching and Picking up the Mooring

The easiest way to pick up a buoy is to pass to its lee and then "shoot" up into the wind with sufficient way to carry the boat up to the buoy. The object is to come dead in the water as the bow is laid alongside the buoy. To accomplish this, as you approach the spot where the buoy is located, the momentum of the boat should be checked by letting go the jib halyard and taking in the jib. This should slow the boat up, if sailing close-hauled or on a reach, and will leave the forward part of the boat clear for you to handle the mooring line. If the boat is still going too fast, the main sheet can be slacked a bit until the sail shivers along its luff. When directly to leeward of the buoy, shove the tiller hard down (to leeward) and the boat will spin around head to wind while the momentum will make her forereach, with the mainsail fluttering, as she glides up to the mooring buoy under control of the rudder. If the main boom has been well off, the sheet can be trimmed in a little as the tiller is shoved down, and this will accelerate the turn. Care must be taken to make sure that the sail doesn't fill from one side or the other as the boat shoots for the mooring. Filling will add to the boat's headway and may make her overshoot the buoy, so the sheet should be left with plenty of slack after the boat has come head to the wind. The boat will coast toward the mooring. Your crewman should be ready at the bow to pick up the buoy and make the mooring line fast to the cleat in the bow. A boat hook will help in the picking-up operation.

If you have estimated the "shooting" distance of your craft correctly, you will have little or no difficulty in picking up the mooring, but if the boat is still moving ahead when she reaches the buoy, it may even then be possible to pick up the mooring line, get it over the cleat, and check her on that. However, if the boat has too much headway for this, there is nothing to do but to trim in the sheet, put the tiller over (the side to put it depending on which way you want to pay off), gather headway, and try it again, allowing a little greater distance this time for the boat to shoot. It may or may not be necessary to set your jib again to do this. If you have plenty of headway you can probably maneuver under the mainsail alone.

As stated previously, the easiest way to approach a mooring is close-hauled, or on a reach, for it is then easy to slack the mainsheet and check your headway as you approach the point where you swing up into the wind, and the turn is more quickly made through an arc of from 50 to 90 degrees. However, there may be times, owing to the direction of the wind, the position of the mooring buoy, or the presence of other boats, when it is necessary to approach from windward, while sailing before the wind, with the main boom well off. But there is no need to get panicky just because these conditions prevail. In this case, as you are sailing dead before the wind, you can get your jib off in plenty of time, without hurrying, as it isn t drawing much anyhow and the boat will steer as well without it as with it. As you approach the place where your buoy is located, you should check the headway of the boat by taking in on the mainsheet. Before the wind, a boat sails fastest with her boom and sail at right angles to the wind. As you take them in and decrease this angle, the boat's speed slackens. When you have spotted your buoy, sail by it on the side opposite to that on which you're carrying your boom, giving it a good berth of perhaps fifty feet or more. When you have reached a point that will permit room to swing, put the tiller hard down (to leeward), letting the mainsheet run as you do so, and the boat will swing around head to wind and point for the buoy. This swinging suddenly through an arc of 180 degrees, with the tiller hard over, will usually kill a boat's headway entirely, and, if you've estimated your distance and the direction of the wind properly, the boat's momentum will be checked almost on top of the buoy and the mooring can be reached easily with a boat hook.

How far a boat will shoot into the wind, or carry her headway, when picking up a mooring, and what her turning radius is, can be determined only by practice. They vary with different boats and depend on the weight, shape, and size of the boat. They also depend on the strength of the wind and the speed at which the craft is moving. Generally, the craft should first be steered to a point several boat lengths to leeward of the mooring. The number of lengths usually depends on whether the craft has either a keel or centerboard. In the case of a centerboard boat, because of the lack of forward movement (way) when beating, a distance of one to two boat lengths is sufficient in light air, and three to four in heavy air. Because of more forward movement when coming into the wind, keelboats require more distance from the luffing point to the buoy. This distance is generally about half again as much as that allowed for a centerboard boat. But remember that every boat is different and the only way to determine the distance for your boat is to experiment. Also, winds and tides will change the amount of distance needed for this operation. In any case, the maneuvering up wind must be thoroughly planned if one is to pick up the mooring in a seamanlike manner. It is not uncommon to see skippers miss several times before making the mooring.

When picking up a mooring under power—the easiest way, but

the least yachtsmanlike manner—come up to it with the cruiser heading into the wind or current, whichever is the stronger. To be sure about this, simply note the direction in which other anchored boats are pointing and approach your mooring in the same direction. Now slip the clutch into neutral when you estimate that you have just way enough to carry you up to the buoy. Be sure to station a crew member on the bow to pick up the mooring when it comes within

Figure 3-3: Steps in picking up a mooring.

reach. Should you fall short, give a few extra kicks ahead with the engine; if you overshoot your mark, reverse enough to check the headway as the bow comes up to the buoy.

Rafting

A popular form of mooring several boats at a club rendezvous or similar social gathering, is to tie up or raft alongside a friendly earlier arrival. This is sociable, for it is possible for people to visit back and forth between the boats. Generally, such tie-ups are of short duration and the visitor doesn't drop his own anchor. He merely ties up to the first boat using bow and stern lines with fenders between to protect both craft. Often a spring line is required to prevent movement fore and aft. If there is dragging of the one anchor, or should the group wish to raft overnight, other anchors should be properly lowered (see page 79). When rafting, follow the same general sailing procedure you would follow in picking up a mooring.

When you want to leave a rafting situation, walk your boat astern by the use of light lines. This will permit her to be under complete control at all times, and with a couple of fenders between the hulls

Figure 3-4: A fore and aft view of how boats can be rafted together.

no harm can result. The boat should be carried far enough along so that she can hang to the stern of the anchored craft by a bow line while the sails are being hoisted. When all is ready the bow line is cast off exactly as when leaving a mooring and your boat can then proceed on your chosen tack. The chosen tack should be one which will allow the greatest freedom of movement, as well being the most expeditious from the standpoint of getting way on and retaining full control of the craft. Generally winds would be light, for boats shouldn't tie up alongside in heavy weather, so ease the sheets and get moving as quickly as possible so that the boat will respond to her rudder and be under control.

Docking Procedure

In coming alongside a dock or another boat, under sail, follow the same general procedure as when picking up a mooring. Approaching a dock from leeward or windward is simple. If it's leeward, head-reach up to the dock with the sheets loose and attach the mooring lines to the dock. A member of the crew should be up forward to see that the bow of the boat doesn't ram the dock. Landing on the windward side, sail downwind until you are beam-on to the dock. Put out the fenders, break out docking lines, and make ready the boat hook. Push the tiller hard over so that the boat swings around into the wind. The hard-over rudder acts as a brake and the vessel will be almost dead in the water about a boat length away from the dock. The craft will drift broadside against the dock. Tie up, and the job is done.

If you're coming in too fast to a dock, you can hold or fend a small sailboat off with a boat hook, or one of your crew members can do it with his feet. But when a crewman fends off a boat with his feet, be sure he sits down on the bow and holds both his feet straight out, balancing himself with his hands on the jibstay. In this way his legs will better take the shock of fending off the boat and yet he won't be pushed overboard. If you don't have quite enough speed to make a dock, a light line can be heaved to someone on the dock. But be sure that one end of the line is made fast to your boat. If your heaving line misses the dock and you start drifting backward, you can follow the same procedure as when caught in stays or in irons. However, the action of the tiller is reversed. Usually you can get enough momentum to get to the dock; if not, you will have to catch the wind and make a fresh attempt to dock your boat.

Should you run into a situation where there is simply not enough room to come about and approach a dock into the wind, it might be expedient to drop an anchor out from the dock and then allow the boat to drift back under check from the anchor until close enough to reach the dock from the stern of the boat. It's generally the best practice to lower all sails when at a dock so that the boat will lie quietly without the possibility of stray gusts of wind surging it ahead or sideways into possible trouble with neighboring craft. Fenders, where used, should be employed with intelligence. If they are secured to the boat, as is the normal practice, there is always the chance that the vessel will move along the dock and the fender slip into a void, leaving her unprotected. If the fenders are made fast to the dock the protection is better, but there is again the possibility of sailing away leaving the fenders behind.

Three lines are vital for tying up a larger boat—bow, stern, and spring. The spring line is fastened to the stern cleat and is brought amidships and fastened to a dock cleat. This third line keeps the boat parallel to the dock and prevents the boat from swinging and

Figure 3-5: Steps in docking under auxiliary power. The bottom photograph shows the crew getting everything ready to go ashore.

banging against the dock. It also provides enough slack on bow and stern lines to allow for the rise and fall of the tide.

Of course, if you have an engine aboard, the docking procedure is much easier. When docking under power, always approach a dock on the downwind side to prevent crashing into it. Slow down and maintain just enough headway to maintain maneuverability, and to observe the forces of wind and current. Approach the dock at an angle from 30 to 45 degrees. Nearing the dock, put the engine in neutral, letting the boat glide under her own momentum. If docking on the port side, throw the wheel over to the right. This forces the stern to come left and the boat to approach a more parallel position to the landing. When the bow is a few feet from the dock, reverse the engine enough to check headway. If necessary, throw the wheel hard left to swing the bow in closer. Reverse the process when anchoring on the starboard side. Put fenders over the side when close to the dock.

Leaving Her Shipshape

When you have secured to a mooring or tied up at a dock, you should then "stow ship." While every skipper has his own ideas about how to leave his boat after a sail, there are certain things that *must* be done. If you have a boom crutch, for example, ease down the boom on the topping lift until it rests in its crutch. Haul in the mainsheet to keep the boom and crutch in a secure position. We now come to the subject of stowing and furling the sails. Methods vary for the small-boat owner and the cruiser-racer skipper.

When small-boat sails arrive from the sailmaker they will probably come in a small box. This is done from a combination of habit and the need to conserve space and minimize shipping charges. Leave the spinnaker as is for the present, but unpack the main and jib and fold them in a flaking manner along the foot. The theory is that the sailmaker has gone to a lot of trouble to develop a fabric with an extra smooth finish—and it should be kept that way. The fewer creases the better, and those that are necessary should run fore and aft. Some sailmakers also have recommended rolling sails entirely. They should be kept in sail bags. But, a few skippers I know (bachelors of course) hang their sails between races in the living room.

As mentioned before, the cruising and distance-racing enthusiasts have gained most from the development of nylon and dacron. Where sails must be furled on spars or stowed below, synthetics have reduced to a fraction the time needed for drying and airing compared to cotton. However, certain precautions should be taken. Sail covers are a must. A light dacron cover that will stow away easily is adequate, as its prime function is to keep out the sun and dirt. There have been cases where gases from factories have done serious damage to synthetic sails; and soot itself, while possibly not harmful, seems to adhere to dacron and is difficult to wash off.

There are two ways to start a furl of the mainsail. One is to roll the bunt up on the boom in a neat roll. The other is to "flake" or "fake" the sail down in folds on the boom as it is lowered. It is easier to "fake down" a large sail than to roll it up (see illustration 3-6). Before lowering away it is good practice to rig the stops (strips of material or lines) between the boom and the foot rope ready for instant use when the sail is down. The battens should be removed before the sail is faked down; once the sail is faked, install the sail cover.

The next thing to do is to put the jib or jibs into their respective sail bags after the battens have been removed. Put the head of the sail in the bag first—the foot last. But the cruising-boat owner should be sure his sail lockers are ventilated and that sail bags don't rest against the skin of the vessel. Last year we had a half-dozen sail bags brought in that showed a lot of mildew. The owner explained he had left his boat closed up for three weeks. Naturally there had been some sweating in the lockers. Nylon spinnakers should be given special care as the fabric will weaken and colors may bleed if wet or salty (attracting more moisture when put away). It is still a good idea to dry sails whenever possible, and synthetics dry faster than natural fibers. I do not recommend hoisting them at the mooring in a breeze! Dacron and nylon are tough, but the fibers will break down, and enough slatting occurs while racing without adding to it.

One last point on furling. Some do not feel it is necessary to ease outhauls after sailing, primarily because dacron does not shrink. But for no other reason than to retain the spring in the bolt rope, I ease mine. The tension you apply the next time you sail will depend on the wind velocity, so there is no point in keeping outhauls taut.

Having finished with the sails, belay all halyards around their proper cleats and coil down the ends. Then, to prevent their beating a tattoo on the mast when it blows, either secure them to the main shrouds with thin line, or twist one of them, say the main halyard, around the mast and then belay it to its cleat. Coil and make fast all other cordage. Collect all the life preservers and other gear; either

Figure 3-6: A boat must always be left shipshape after a sail.

stow them in compartments on the boat or take them ashore. Make fast all loose gear.

In centerboard craft, be sure to raise the board and leave it secured with the pin provided for that purpose. The board should always be left in the full up position; for if left down, it may work back and forth causing serious wear of the bearings or strain on the centerboard well. On some small boats, it's good practice also to unship the rudder and stow it. If the rudder is left shipped, the tiller should be lashed to prevent excessive movement of the rudder as the boat rides at her moorings.

Check your boat very carefully and make note of anything and everything that should be done before your next outing. It's far better to do any repairs now while they're fresh in your mind than to wait until a later time. Maintenance and repair work are fully discussed in Chapter 11.

It is well too to break out a sponge and swab, and tidy up the sides and deck. Scum or dirt is far easier to remove while it is still wet than later, when it has dried and hardened. Also make sure that the cabin area is clean and straightened up. Check your plumbing closing and engine (if used) closing schedule as recommended in the boat's instruction manual. This usually includes closing certain sea cocks, opening the main battery switch, and shutting off the gasoline supply line. Turn ventilators against the chance of rain, close and lock all hatches. Some sailboats have cockpit covers. These are canvas coverings that fit over the cockpit, enclosing it completely. If you have one, unroll the cockpit cover and lash it in place securely.

Finally, check the mooring line very carefully. Be sure that it runs from the mooring cleat through the bow chock and then to the mooring. If you're tying up at a dock, be sure your boat fenders are down to prevent any damage to the hull. When all these tasks have been accomplished, you're ready to go ashore.

Marlinspike Seamanship

It's nearly impossible to take an active part in any form of pleasure sailing without being required to know your ropes, how and where to use them and how to take care of them. Someone once said, "Give a man enough rope and he'll hang himself." He obviously wasn't thinking of a sailing yachtsman. Though there have been hangings at sea, mutiny on pleasure craft is a rarity and capital punishment for a mutinous crew of family and friends is frowned upon. Give a seaman enough rope of the right kind and if it's used properly it will add to pleasure and safety of crew and craft. A competent yachtsman is quickly distinguished from a landlubber by a knowledge of marlinspike seamanship, which entails a knowledge of ropes and skill in working with them.

Knots and How to Tie Them. While some 1,500 knots, hitches, and splices have been invented, there are only about six to nine that the pleasure sailor is likely to use. But, in order to learn to tie these knots properly, an understanding of rope and knot definitions and their application is necessary. The most basic of terms are those applied to the three parts into which a rope divides when it is being knotted, bent, or hitched. These are the *standing part,* which is the long unused or belayed section; the *bight,* which is a loop or half loop made when rope is turned back on itself; and the *end,* which is the short, remaining end of the rope. (With an anchor cable, the inboard end is usually secured to a bitt, hence the term "bitter end.") And when a rope comes aboard your boat for nautical purposes, it becomes a "line."

Whenever two sections of rope cross, one section must go *over* and the other *under.* The over and under arrangement for each knot must be followed exactly; if an overhand loop is called for, an underhand loop won't work. The wrong knot for the job—or no knot at all—will result.

The *bowline* is a knot that can neither slip nor jam. It is used for lowering a man over the side to do some particular work, for forming an eye in the end of a hawser to be thrown over a bollard when handling a vessel alongside a dock, and for a great variety of similar purposes. A bowline is made by forming a bight in the line with the end part on top; bringing the end part up through the bight; then passing it under the standing part above the bight, and back through the bight. The length of bight depends upon the purpose for which a knot is required.

The *sheepshank* is used for shortening ropes that will require lengthening again. Take up the amount necessary to shorten the rope and then lay out the rope in three parts. Then each part is half hitched around the bight of the other two parts.

The *figure eight knot* resembles the figure eight, and is used to prevent the end of the rope from unreeving when rove through blocks. The end of the rope is passed around the bight over its own part and through the loop. The figure eight knot is used primarily as a "sheet stopper" to prevent the sheet from running through blocks when it isn't desirable.

The *square* or *reef knot* is used as a binding knot for joining two pieces of twine or small rope. It is a simple knot to tie but it should *never* be used as a bend (to tie two ropes together). A sheet bend is recommended for this purpose. The square knot is formed by making an overhand knot (made by passing the end of a rope over the standing part and through the bight), then crossing the ends and bringing one end up through the bight.

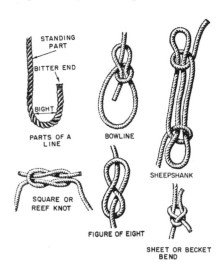

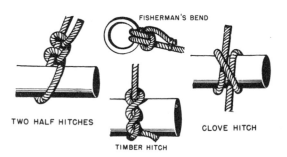

Figure 3-7: Common sailing knots. (Courtesy of Columbian Rope Company)

The *sheet bend* or *weaver's knot* is probably the best knot to use to join two ropes, even when they are unequal in size. It is made by forming a bight in one of the ropes, bringing up the other rope end through the bight, twisting it over and under the bight, and then bringing it under itself.

The *anchor knot* or *fisherman's bend* is formed by passing the end twice around the ring and under the turns, and seizing the end back. This bend is used for securing a rope to a buoy, or a hawser to the ring or harp of an anchor.

Two half hitches are formed by leading the end over and under and up through the standing part and repeating the process. This is one of the most popular methods of bending a rope's end to a spar, stanchion, bollard, or ring.

The *clove hitch* is another common hitch for attaching a rope to a spar and for fastening ratlines to shrouds or to the standing part of a rope. To form this knot, the end is passed around the spar, crossing the standing part, then around the spar again, bringing the end through between the end part and standing part under its own part.

The *timber hitch* is formed by passing the end around the spar and its own standing part; then passing several turns around its own part.

How to Make Fast. (Shown on page 101) The following is an easy but effective method of making fast: Loop the running part of the rope around the cleat's far side, away from the direction of the strain. Then take a turn around the stem with the running part and up and over the center (additional turns would jam the line). Add several more figure eights or slip a half hitch over a horn of the cleat immediately if there is little strain. Your line is now made fast, yet ready for prompt castoff with no part under tension binding loops.

This method makes it easy to cast off without having to take up the slack in the standing part and ensures against accidents that occur when lines can't be freed quickly.

Splicing Rope. Remember that every time you tie a knot in a rope, you substantially lessen the strength of the rope. The fewer the knots, the better. Never knot a rope at a break; cut away the broken ends and splice it together. There are three kinds of splices you should know: the short splice, eye or side splice, and the long splice.

Where it isn't necessary for a rope to pass through a small pulley or where only a small amount of rope can be spared for making a splice, the *short splice* is very satisfactory. To make it, the ends of the lines to be joined are unlaid for about a foot or more, according to the size of line, and the strands are interlaced. Beginning with any one strand, tuck it from right to left; the lay of the line can be easily opened by using a wooden fid. The other two strands are similarly tucked from right to left. Threads are then cut away from the ends of each tucked strand until they are two-thirds their

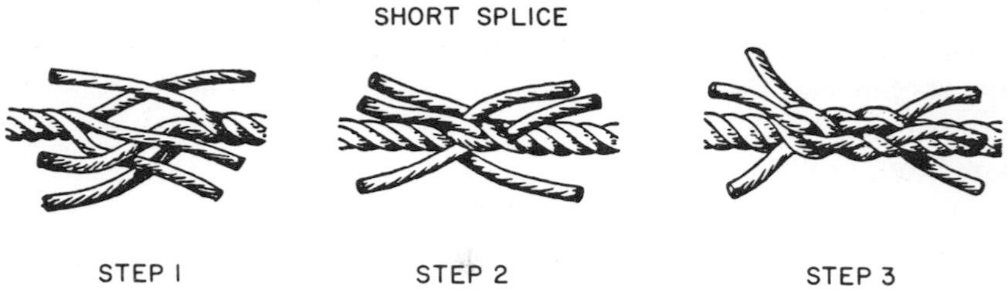

SHORT SPLICE

STEP 1   STEP 2   STEP 3

Figure 3-8: Steps in making a short splice. (Courtesy of Columbian Rope Company)

original size; then they are again tucked. After this they are similarly cut away until one-third their original size; then a third and last tuck is taken. Cut all the ends off and roll the splice beneath your foot, or between two boards, to give a smooth appearance. This produces a neatly tapered splice. The same procedure is used for a four-strand line, except the first strand is tucked under two parts of the first tucking only.

The *long splice* is used for pulley work since it permits the ropes that have been spliced to be run through sheave blocks without jamming or chafing. Unlike a short-spliced rope, the diameter of the long-spliced rope is increased *very* slightly. To make the long splice, the ends of the lines to be joined are unlaid for a greater length than in the short splice, but similarly interlaced. At this point the procedure differs from that of the short splice. A strand of one piece is unlaid for a considerable distance, and the corresponding strand of the other piece is laid in the opening thus left. The length of this lay should be from 1½ to 2 feet. The two remaining strands are twisted together for convenience, the line turned end for end, and then the operation repeated on the other piece of line. The remaining strands of each part are left at the original position. This leaves pairs of strands at three positions along the line. Each of the strands is halved, two of these halves at each position are tied together with an overhand knot, the remaining two halves are tucked over one and under one of the full remaining strands of the line. After all strands have been tucked, the loose ends are trimmed until smooth. Pound down each part of the splice and roll it on the floor, underfoot.

The *side splice* is often called the *eye splice* because it is used for forming an eye or loop in the end of a rope by splicing the end into the side. This splice is made in the same way as a short splice, except that the line is first brought back upon itself enough to give the desired size of the eye, and the strands tucked into the body of the line. The splice may be finished by dividing each strand as in the short splice and rolling the finished splice underfoot.

Splicing Wire Rope. This type of work usually requires special tools, equipment, and a degree of skill that can only be learned through expert instruction and plenty of practice. In addition, making a single-eye-splice wire rope as just described for fiber ones can take several hours of work, not to mention wear and tear on your fingers. Because of this, several types of fittings have been designed to

LONG SPLICE

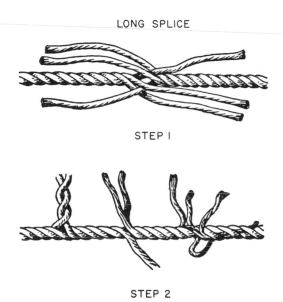

STEP I

STEP 2

Figure 3-9: Steps in making a long splice. (Courtesy of Columbian Rope Company)

simplify the job of getting an eye on the end of a cable. This affords a convenient means of connecting two ropes or otherwise securing a rope. A number of these appliances and their use are shown in the accompanying illustration. While the neatest and strongest wire rope splices are generally those turned out by professional riggers, these do-it-yourself fittings will serve very well if your requirements are not

EYE SPLICE

STEP 1   STEP 2   STEP 3

Figure 3-10: Steps in making an eye splice. (Courtesy of Columbian Rope Company)

too exacting, and are a great deal less expense.

Whipping. A whipping is a binding on the end of a line to prevent unraveling. When employing fiber ropes, the common or plain whipping is used; it's tied by laying a loop along the rope and then making a series of turns over it. The working end is finally stuck through this loop and the end hauled back out of sight. Both ends are then trimmed short. A whipping should be, in width, about equal to the diameter of the rope on which it is put.

With nylon, dacron, or polyethylene ropes, the best rope end is obtained after whipping by cutting with a hot knife. However, great care must be taken that the hot knife doesn't come in contact with the rope at any place but at the point of cut. The knife should be very sharp and hot so that, when it is drawn quickly through the rope, the filaments will be fused together at the point of cut. If a cold knife must be used, a somewhat ragged end results. It may be evened by heating the fiber ends in a match flame sufficiently to fuse them together. Again, this must be done carefully, and the match flame kept away from the whipping itself.

Coiling a Line. When not in use on the boat, any line should be coiled neatly and compactly. This makes for easy stowage and handling, and prevents knotting, twisting, and kinking. Should a new line have a twist in it, tow it astern for about twenty minutes (be sure you're clear of other boats); then haul it in. The twist should be gone. If it isn't toss the line astern again and tow a while longer.

When coiling a line begin with the standing part and coil to the free end. In other words, coil the free end last. Coil it clockwise—from east to west by way of south—and it will pay out smoothly. If the coil is to be hung on a cleat, reach through the coil, lay hold of the part between the coil and cleat, bring the bight of it out through the coil, twist it once or twice to prevent it from coming undone, and hang this small bight on the cleat. If you are putting the coil on

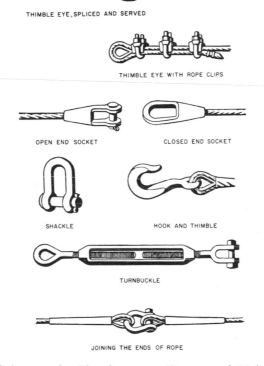

THIMBLE EYE, SPLICED AND SERVED

THIMBLE EYE WITH ROPE CLIPS

OPEN END SOCKET   CLOSED END SOCKET

SHACKLE   HOOK AND THIMBLE

TURNBUCKLE

JOINING THE ENDS OF ROPE

Figure 3-11: Fittings used with wire rope. (Courtesy of United States Coast Guard)

deck rather than on a cleat, turn it upside down so as to bring the standing part on top, thus permitting the line to run off the top. It will foul if it has to run off the bottom.

To throw a line, make it up into two coils—about two-thirds of the rope held in the left hand, about one-third in the right hand for throwing, and the whole ready to run out easily. The end of the

Figure 3-12: How to hand coil a line. (Courtesy of Columbian Rope Company)

left-hand coil should be made fast. The right-hand coil is thrown by swinging the arm and body.

Use and Care of Line. An important part in the ways of marlinspike seamanship is to know the proper care of your lines, especially those of fiber construction. To do this, observe the following suggestions:

1. Make sure all kinks are out of the line before using it.

2. Keep your line clean.

3. Store the line in a dry place away from excessive heat and moisture.

4. Protect it from chafing and abrasion. Chafing gear can be wrapped around lines where they pass over the sheer rail or through chocks.

5. Protect the line from chemicals such as acid from batteries, paint, drying oils, as well as metallic rust. Also don't lubricate the rope itself.

6. Never use a line that has been frozen without allowing it to thaw out and dry.

7. To make sure the line is serviceable during a season's usage, it should be inspected inside and out. On the outside, you should look for signs of abrasion and broken fibers. The fibers should also

have a certain luster to them without any signs of brittleness or limpness.

8. Inside, the line may be inspected by twisting the strands against the lay. If the inside is bright, clear, and free from spots of

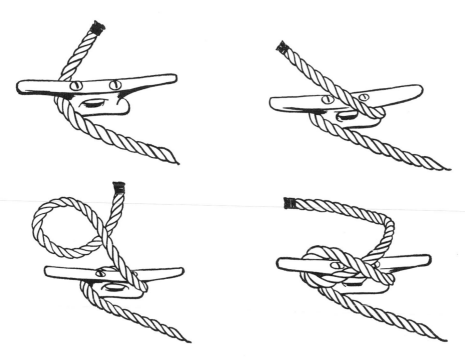

Figure 3-13: How to make fast. (Courtesy of Columbian Rope Company)

discoloration, chances are that the line is in good workable condition. Never overload a line.

The line, be it the anchor "rode," the "painter," the mooring "line," or the bell "rope," is a vital part of sailing and as much a part of your yacht's equipment as the compass and running lights. It's truly a seasoned yachtsman who knows how to tie, care for, and inspect lines, for the safety of the craft depends upon it.

4

Weather Wisdom and Sailing

Agood yachtsman is always weather-conscious. The weather conditions that you encounter are important to a sailor. But you don't have to be a meteorologist, since there are many aids to help you foretell the weather with a high degree of accuracy. Also, your radio gives up-to-the-minute reports on local conditions. You should learn how to read the daily weather map that is published in leading newspapers across the country, and interpret the symbols and systems shown. Also learn to read nature's signs and to use the various weather instruments at your disposal. While in your office, you're not generally appreciably concerned, but once out on the water the weather becomes of major importance, and rightfully so, as your entire well-being is dependent on it.

Radio Weather Reports

A radio set is invaluable for keeping up with local weather forecasts. Even an inexpensive portable radio that will pick up weather reports from regular commercial broadcasting stations is a big help, and one equipped to receive the mariners' weather reports regularly transmitted by the Coast Guard and other government stations is very worthwhile. The Coast Guard broadcasts, in addition, include notices to mariners and hydrographic information; special broadcasts include storm warnings, advisories, and urgent marine information. These are broadcast upon receipt and thereafter on either the odd or the even hour for a period of six hours unless cancelled or superseded. *Coastal Warning Facilities Charts* list telephone numbers of Weather Bureau and Coast Guard offices plus time, station, and wavelength of these broadcasts. These charts are available through the Superintendent of Documents, Washington 25, D.C., for ten cents each.

Yacht owners having radio receivers or direction finders covering the 200- to 415-kc. band may be able to pick up interesting and valuable up-to-the-minute weather data broadcasts by one or more of the Civil Aeronautics Administration airfield control towers in their vicinity. These broadcasts are now being made 15 and 45 minutes after each hour and include current reports in visibility, barometer readings, wind direction and velocity, ceiling heights, sky conditions, weather, temperature, and, as a rule, dew point. These are not forecasts, but offer valuable information on the progress of changes previously forecasted.

Certain additional coast stations have been authorized on very high frequencies utilizing frequency modulation. For our coast areas the following stations have been established: all stations authorized in the 152- to 161-mc. band may now receive and transmit on the calling and safety frequency of 156.8 mc.

Often, your radio can give you tips on the weather even when you are not tuned in on a weather report. For instance, when there is static, your radio is telling you there is an electrical storm somewhere within the range of 25 miles, and the chances are you can expect it to rain within an hour.

Storm Signals

Storm warnings issued by the United States Weather Bureau are conveyed to vessels during the day by flags and pennants, and at night by lights. These signals are flown at Coast Guard installations and other locations, such as certain yacht clubs. Check to see if provisions have been made to fly these signals somewhere in your vicinity. If so, make it a point to look for them on every possible occasion. The storm signals are as follows:

Small Craft Warning. One red pennant displayed by day and a red light over a white light at night to indicate winds up to 38 mph (33 knots), or sea conditions dangerous to small craft operations, or both, are forecast for the area.

Gale Warning. Two red pennants displayed by day and a white light above a red light at night to indicate winds ranging from 39

DAYTIME SIGNALS

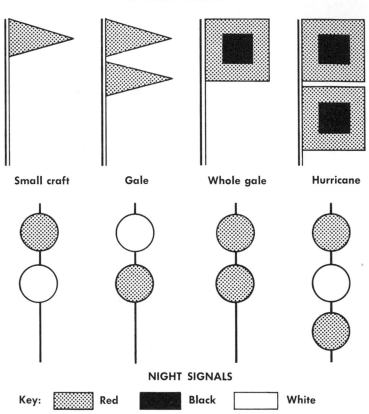

| Small craft | Gale | Whole gale | Hurricane |

NIGHT SIGNALS

Key: ░░░ Red   ███ Black   ☐ White

Figure 4-1: The day and night storm-warning signals.

to 54 mph (34 to 48 knots) are forecast for the area.

Whole Gale Warning. A single square red flag with a black center displayed during daytime and two red lights at night to indicate winds ranging from 55 to 73 mph (48 to 63 knots) are forecast for the area.

Hurricane Warning. Two square red flags with black centers displayed by day and a white light between two red lights at night to indicate that winds of 74 mph (64 knots) and above are forecast for the area.

Weather Maps

Almost all newspapers carry some type of weather report; and a great many, especially in yachting areas, publish daily weather maps which are based on the Daily Surface Weather Map issued by the Weather Bureau. Sometimes you can find one of these maps on the post office bulletin board, at a Coast Guard station, or at the local airport. At first glance, of course, a weather map looks like an overwhelming confusion of figures, symbols, and shadings. These are nothing but the scientist's shorthand, and a complete explanation of all the symbols and funny little marks is printed right on the back of the map. The typical weather map illustrated here shows usual summer conditions and is an excellent portrayal of existing weather and a means of forecasting local conditions for the next one to four days.

Familiarity with the concept of air masses is essential to understanding and interpreting weather maps. Air masses are large oceans of atmosphere with nearly homogeneous properties throughout, both vertically from the earth's surface and horizontally, along it. They are generated over large areas of land, ice, or water which transmit to the stagnant air mass their own characteristics of temperature, wetness, or dryness. The basic and conflicting air masses are the polar and the tropical, and throughout the year these are alternately backing and filling over much of the continental United States.

As you peer at a weather map or hear a detailed weather forecast, the word *front* will usually be mentioned quite often. A front, in the simplest of terms, could be described as a weather factory. It develops when two different masses of air, each striving to retain its individuality, meet. Cold, dry air from the polar regions flowing south over the United States meets warm, moist air moving northward from the tropics; the two kinds of air do not mix well, so the cold air, being heavier, slides under the warm air and lifts it. A sloping boundary, rather sharply defined, is formed between the two air masses, and this separation is called a front.

A *cold front* usually is accompanied by strong, shifting surface winds, squalls, and thunderstorms. Altocumulus clouds, a sign in themselves, may precede a cold front by as much as 300 miles. Cold-front weather is often severe but of short duration. On the other hand, a *warm front* normally brings less violent winds, but the sky will be heavy with great expanses of low clouds. There will be rain, maybe fog and poor visibility. The foul weather accompanying such

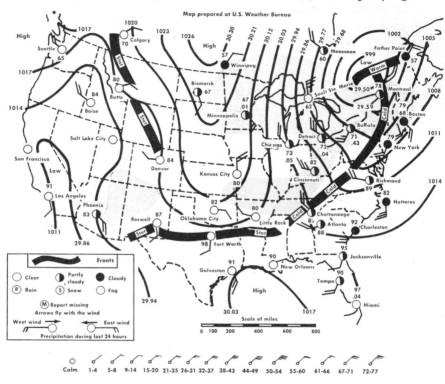

Figure 4-2: Typical summer's day weather map. Note Beaufort Wind Scale symbols at the bottom of the map. Velocity is given in miles per hour. (Courtesy of United States Department of Commerce, Weather Bureau)

a front lasts a long while, as a rule, because the system covers a large area and moves slowly.

An *occluded front* is a line along which warm air has been lifted from the earth's surface by the action of the opposing wedges of cold air. This lifting of the warm air often causes precipitation along the entire front. A *stationary front* is an air mass boundary which shows little or no movement.

Two other terms that are commonly found on weather maps are

high and *low*. They actually mean high-pressure and low-pressure areas. A high-pressure area is a weather system in which the air pressure or atmospheric pressure is high. The air is heavier, colder, and drier. A low, on the other hand, is made up of a mass of low-pressure air that is lighter, warmer, and wetter. In general, lows bring bad weather, because their air contains more moisture. Highs, being made up of colder, drier air, generally bring good weather. Winds are counterclockwise toward the center of low-pressure systems, and clockwise and outward from high-pressure areas.

Our weather, for the most part, flows in a continuous procession from the west to the east. It travels about 700 miles a day in the winter and 500 miles a day in the summer. In other words, as a general rule, tomorrow's weather is always directly to the west of us. As a result, if a town 200 to 300 miles to the west of you is having bad weather tonight it's a pretty safe bet that you shouldn't plan on doing any yachting tomorrow.

The map reproduced here indicates the presence of three air masses over the country. Most prominent is the cool, dry polar air flowing down through the Great Lakes region and covering everything within the boundaries marked by the heavy dark lines indicating the cold and stationary fronts. Second is a maritime tropical air mass, hot and moist, extending inland from the warm summer seas over which it formed, and covering the area from Texas to Maine. Third is the maritime polar air mass from the northern Pacific Ocean which has moved in over the coasts of Washington and Oregon and tapers off into a stagnant area west of the Rockies and out to the California coast.

A prominent feature of this map is the low-pressure area or extratropical cyclone centered in eastern Canada. This formed a day or so earlier, well to the west of its position shown here, as a result of warm tropical air flowing up the Mississippi Valley and overriding the cool polar air mass. This "low," deepening as it moved eastward, developed the well-defined warm and cold fronts extending out from its center. The warm front has brought rain and general cloudiness as it moved through the Great Lakes states and New England. The cool, dry air sweeping in behind the cold front has pushed rapidly south and west through the Mississippi Valley, causing showers and rain, but not halting until it became warmed by the heat of the previous day and the extremely hot land of the lower plains states.

In northern Texas it has become a stationary front and there it will probably lose its identity.

The whole-number figures given at each observation point indicate the temperature. Note that temperatures are uniformly higher south and east of the cold-front line despite greater cloudiness and the proximity of the cooling ocean along the Atlantic Coast.

The thin black lines are isobars, lines connecting points of equal barometric pressures. They are labeled in both inches of mercury and millibars. The closer together the isobars, the greater the wind velocity. Note that at Sault Sainte Marie, Detroit, and Buffalo, where the isobars are closely spaced, wind velocities of 20 to 31 miles per hour—relatively high for summer—are shown by the numbers of feathers on the arrows, which fly with the wind. (These wind symbols are those of the Beaufort scale, discussed later in this chapter.) From Denver westward to Salt Lake City and San Francisco, where the isobars are far apart, winds are less than seven miles per hour, with a calm indicated throughout the western half of this area. Along the Gulf and lower Atlantic Coast the isobars are far apart too, but in the coastal cities there, a considerable sea breeze effect is noticeable (air rising over the hot land draws in cooler air from over the sea).

The forecast from this map indicates that the "low" will continue to move eastward into the North Atlantic, with its cold front trailing off into the ocean all the way down the coast and bringing cool, dry air and clear to partly cloudy skies behind it, with brisk northwesterly winds. In the Great Lakes area and throughout the Middle West and plains states, winds will diminish as the isobars widen out, and temperatures will turn upward again as the polar air is warmed by the summer sun and cloudless skies. Along the Gulf Coast and throughout the South, the stationary front will probably dissipate and maritime tropical air push slowly back northward again. Without a more complete picture of conditions over the Pacific it is difficult to forecast for the area west of the Rockies, but the almost equal barometric pressure there indicates that no sudden or violent changes are to be expected.

Visual Weather Indications

The weather bureaus, with all their data and instruments, occasionally come to wrong conclusions. In addition, most professional weathermen are inclined to look at the weather picture in the terms of general or long-range predictions. But for the yachtsman it's better to become familiar with the conditions in his own region, or in the area where he plans to do his sailing. Local predictions by the skillful amateur are seldom accurate when they're made more than twelve hours in advance of a shift in weather, because local signs are seldom noticeable more than that length of time ahead. But when these predictions are made by a careful observer for a specific place, and on a short-time basis, they are likely to be more reliable than those of the professional prognosticator.

The color of the sky can foretell the weather for the following day. No doubt you have heard of the old saw or rhyme that goes as follows:

> A red sky in the morning
> Is the sailor's warning.
> A red sky at night
> Is the sailor's delight.

> or

> Evening red and morning gray,
> Are certain signs of a fine day.

While these little poems are part of marine folklore, they may have some sound basis in meteorology. Observe for yourself:

Blue skies, bright and clear—fair weather.

A red sky at sunset—fair weather for the following day.

A gray sky in the morning—fair weather for the day.

A purple sky early in the morning or late afternoon—good weather.

A yellow sunset—wind is coming.

A red morning sky—brings wind and rain.

Greenish tints at sunset—rain and wind to follow.

A thin brown haze on the horizon—be ready for fog.

Clouds. One of the most important means of forecasting for seamen, however, is reading messages spelled out in the sky by clouds. Clouds aren't mere collections of water vapor, shapeless blobs offering picturesque background, for their movement and formation are vital weather signs. They are usually classified according to their height: cirrus, cirrostratus, and cirrocumulus are considered high clouds (above 20,000 feet); altostratus and altocumulus are called middle clouds (6,500 to 20,000 feet); and stratus, nimbostratus, and stratocumulus are known as low clouds. One type of cloud, cumulonimbus, the thunderhead, belongs to all three height categories, since the cloud begins at the ground and extends upward to great heights—40,000 feet or more. As described below, each type indicates that certain conditions will be soon at hand.

CIRRUS. Detached clouds, delicate and fibrous-looking, which take various forms such as featherlike plumes, curved lines ending in tufts, lines drawn across a blue sky, isolated tufts, and so forth. They are often arranged in bands which cross the sky like meridian lines and, owing to the effect of perspective, converge to a point on the horizon or to two opposite points. Cirrus cloud formations can indicate rain or foul weather when moving rapidly, especially from the southwest; thickening, especially with a south wind; backed by overcast or gray sky; converging in bands near the horizon; and moving east to west (rain in twenty-four hours). When they build up into an anvil, a thunderstorm is near. Cirrus also can mean fair weather when not increasing; drifting slowly or standing still; and dissolving as the sun rises.

CIRROCUMULUS. Small globular masses or white flakes, having no shadows, or only very slight shadows, arranged in groups and often in lines. Such clouds indicate changeable weather and can be a sign of rain when driven by northeast, east to south winds.

CIRROSTRATUS. A thin, whitish sheet, sometimes completely covering the sky and only giving it a whitish appearance, or at other times presenting, more or less distinctly, a formation like a tangled web. This sheet often produces halos around the sun and moon. They often mean rain when they start to thicken.

ALTOCUMULUS. Rather large globular masses, white or grayish, partially shaded, arranged in groups or lines, and often so closely packed that their edges appear confused. The detached masses are generally larger and more compact at the center of the group; at the margin they form into finer flakes. They often spread themselves out in lines in one or two directions. Should they form into a domed shape, a thunderstorm is possible, but when in small, isolated patches, chances for fair weather are good.

ALTOSTRATUS. A thick sheet of a gray or bluish color, showing a brilliant patch in the neighborhood of the sun or moon. These

Figure 4-3: Various cloud forms (left to right, top to bottom): altocumulus in parallel bands; stratocumulus formed from cumulus; stratus; cumulus of fair weather; squall line clouds; waterspout. (Courtesy of United States Department of Commerce, Weather Bureau)

clouds are like thick cirrostratus but without the halo phenomena. Rain may fall from altostratus clouds when they grow thick enough and become lower in the sky.

STRATOCUMULUS. Large globular masses or rolls of dark cloud, frequently covering the whole sky, and occasionally giving it a wavy appearance. The layer of stratocumulus is not, as a rule, very thick, and patches of blue sky are often visible through the intervening spaces. All sorts of transitions between this form and altocumulus are observable. It may be distinguished from nimbostratus by its globular or rolled appearance and because it does not bring rain. Stratocumulus usually precede or follow a storm.

CUMULUS. These are often called woolpack clouds, thick clouds of which the upper surface is dome-shaped and exhibits protuberances, while the base is horizontal. When these clouds are opposite the sun the surfaces usually presented to the observer have a greater brilliance than the margins of the protuberances. When the light falls aslant, they give deep shadows; when, on the contrary, the clouds are on the same side as the sun, they appear dark, with bright edges. If they turn gray or black, they are getting all the water they can hold, and a thunderstorm could occur. Also, when they are massing to windward, chances of a storm are good. On the other hand, small, isolated patches of cumulus clouds usually indicate fair weather.

NIMBOSTRATUS. Rain clouds; a thick layer of dark clouds, without shape and with ragged edges, from which continued rain generally falls. If the layer of nimbostratus separates into shreds or if small loose clouds are visible floating at a low level underneath a large nimbostratus, they may be described as *fractonimbus,* the "scud" of sailors.

STRATUS. A low uniform cloud layer which gives the water a hazy appearance and resembles fog except that they are not resting off the water. They are usually present during a light, steady rain. When this very low layer is broken up into irregular shreds, it is designated *fractostratus;* and they generally indicate a long rainy spell when driven by northeast, east to south winds.

CUMULONIMBUS. Thunderheads or thunderclouds; heavy masses of clouds rising in the form of mountains, turrents, or anvils; generally they have a sheet or screen of fibrous appearance above, and a mass of clouds similar to nimbostratus underneath. From the base local thundershowers usually fall.

While it is important to be able to identify cloud types, their sequence helps more in making a forecast. The following cloud sequences usually mean the approach of foul yachting weather:

1. Cirrostratus to altocumulus (thunderstorm).
2. Altostratus to altocumulus to nimbostratus or cumulonimbus (thunderstorm).
3. Altocumulus to cumulus (thunderstorm).
4. Cumulus to cumulonimbus (thunderstorm).
5. Cirrus to cirrostratus (thunderstorm).
6. Cirrocumulus to altocumulus to cumulonimbus (thunderstorm).
7. Cirrus to cirrocumulus or cirrostratus (rain).
8. Altostratus to nimbostratus (rain).
9. Stratocumulus to stratus (rain).
10. Cirrus to cirrostratus to altostratus to nimbostratus (rain).

Fog. Fog is a problem that all yachtsmen must face at one time or another, though its occurrence can generally be predicted and, if predicted, the sailor can prepare by planning a course and estimated time for a run to a safe area. Actually, fog is merely a cloud resting on land or water. It results from the cooling of the air that remains at the earth's surface. Air temperature may be cooled in a number of ways, but the most common situation is that of a warm, moisture-laden offshore breeze blowing in over cold coastal water. This type of fog occurs along saltwater coastal areas where cold rivers flow into the ocean. Another situation is that of warm moist air moving from a low to a higher altitude where it may be cooled to such an extent that fog will form over large areas. This type is more common over sea than land. Fog also may form as the spread between air temperature and dewpoint decreases. As the temperature approaches the dewpoint, fog is likely.

Other Signs. There are other signs that can be seen in the sky; for example, halos caused by cloud cover over the moon and sun. A halo around the moon usually means changeable weather, generally bad before good. A halo around the sun also means bad weather coming.

The weather-savvy yachtsman knows about the birds, too. If you don't, here are some clues that will help you to be a better weather prophet, which sometime may save you a rough time afloat. For example, when seabirds and gulls fly out early in the day and go far to seaward, fair weather and moderate wind may be expected. When they hang about the land, or over it, or fly inward screaming, expect a strong wind with stormy weather. Also, most birds perch on wires, tree limbs, or any handy resting spot when bad weather is approaching.

If, on your way to your sailing area, you pass industrial plants or have an opportunity to observe commercial ships, you should learn to make a mental note of the direction of the smoke flow from the stacks. When smoke leaves stacks and drifts downward, this is a sure sign of mean weather. Smoke will rise straight upward in calm, clear air. This is found in high-pressure areas and is a sure indication of fair weather ahead. Canny sailors often check the top of marsh grass. Dew on grass at night or in the early morning is a good indication of fair weather, for it will form only when the atmosphere is clear and the air is dry. Also, remarkable clearness of atmosphere near the horizon; distant objects such as hills unusually visible, or raised (by refraction); and what is called "a good hearing day"—these may be mentioned as signs that moisture, if not wind, is to be expected. Aside from the obvious wind indicators, you have to keep your eye on the water for the way puffs and gusts move across the surface. With a little familiarity, you can detect a change in wind strength and direction by the progress of a gust, indicated by moving dark areas on the surface and increased whitecaps. Keep an eye out to windward—the origin of the expression "weather eye"—for the approach of these dark patches. In a harbor with obstructions around it, they may come from radically different directions. On the open sea, their variations are usually not as extreme.

Weather Instruments

Various kinds of instruments are used for gathering the data necessary to forecast weather. Of all of them, the barometer—some yachtsmen consider it the next most important instrument to the compass—is by far the most valuable. It is an instrument used to measure atmospheric pressure. Atmospheric pressure at sea level is approximately 14.7 pounds per square inch; this means that height is expressed as a barometric reading of 29.53 inches of mercury. Variations of the atmospheric pressure serve to indicate changes in weather.

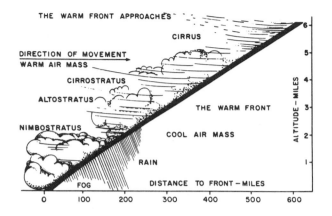

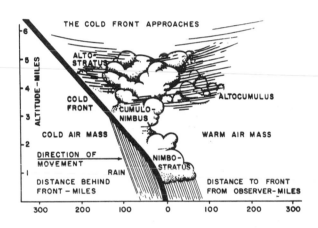

Figure 4-4: Characteristics of warm and cold fronts. (Courtesy of United States Department of Commerce, Weather Bureau)

Use of the Barometer. A record of barometric readings made at regular intervals will indicate the pressure being exerted on the earth's surface at the instant of observation. If several readings have been logged, as on the following page, significance may be attached to them.

In this case, the barometric pressure falling at an increasing rate denotes foul weather. A fall of 0.02 inch an hour is a low rate of fall and not particularly disturbing, whereas a fall of 0.05 inch per hour is a high rate and normally indicates stormy weather.

Time (in hours)	Pressure (in inches)	Change (in inches)
0700	30.04	
0800	30.02	−0.02
0900	29.99	−0.03
1000	29.95	−0.04
1100	29.90	−0.05
1200	29.84	−0.06

With the use of a barometer in conjunction with your compass, you can determine air pressure and wind direction, the two most important elements in weather prognostication. As a loose guide to barometer-wind correlation the United States Weather Bureau offers these three rules:

1. Foul weather is usually forecast by a falling barometer with winds from the east quadrants. Fair and clearing weather is usually forecast by winds shifting to west quadrants with a rising barometer.

2. When the wind sets in from points between south and southeast and the barometer falls steadily, a storm is approaching from the west or northwest. The center of the storm will pass near or north of the observer within twelve to twenty-four hours and the wind will shift to the northwest by way of south and southwest.

3. When the wind sets in from points between east and northeast and the barometer falls steadily, a storm is approaching from the south or southwest. The storm center will pass near or to the south of the observer within twelve to twenty-four hours and the wind will shift to southwest by way of north.

However, there are almost as many exceptions to these rules as there are examples that prove it. From the Mississippi and Missouri valleys to the Atlantic Coast, and on the Pacific Coast, rain generally begins on a falling barometer; whereas in the Rocky Mountain and plateau districts, and on the eastern Rocky Mountain slope, precipitation seldom begins until the barometer begins to rise, after a fall. This is true as regards the eastern half of the country, however, only during the colder months and in the presence of general storms that may occur at other seasons. In the warmer months, summer showers and thunderstorms usually come about the time the barometer turns from falling to rising. It is important to note the fact that during practically the entire year precipitation on the great Western plains and in the mountain regions that lie between the plains and the Pacific Coast districts doesn't begin until the center of the low-barometer area has passed to the eastward or southward and the wind has shifted to the north quadrants, with rising barometer. For this reason, the following more detailed Weather Bureau wind-barometer chart below is well worth keeping handy:

Wind Direction	Barometer Reduced to Sea Level	Character of Weather
SW to NW	30.10 to 30.20 and steady	Fair, with slight temperature changes for one or two days
SW to NW	30.10 to 30.20 and rising rapidly	Fair followed within two days by rain
SW to NW	30.20 and above and stationary	Continued fair with no decided temperature change
SW to NW	30.20 and above and falling slowly	Slowly rising temperature and fair for two days
S to SE	30.10 to 30.20 and falling slowly	Rain within 24 hours
S to SE	30.10 to 30.20 and falling rapidly	Wind increasing in force, with rain within 12 to 24 hours
SE to NE	30.10 to 30.20 and falling slowly	Rain in 12 to 18 hours
SE to NE	30.10 to 30.20 and falling rapidly	Increasing wind and rain within 12 hours
E to NE	30.10 and above and falling slowly	In summer, with light winds, rain may not fall for several days. In winter, rain in 24 hours
E to NE	30.10 and above and falling fast	In summer, rain probably in 12 hours. In winter, rain or snow, with increasing winds, will often set in when the barometer begins to fall and the wind sets in NE

Wind Direction	Barometer Reduced to Sea Level	Character of Weather
SE to NE	30.00 or below and falling slowly	Rain will continue one or two days
SE to NE	30.00 or below and falling rapidly	Rain with high wind, followed within 36 hours by clearing, and, in winter, colder
S to SW	30.00 or below and rising slowly	Clearing in a few hours and fair for several days
S to E	29.80 or below and falling rapidly	Severe storm imminent, followed in 24 hours by clearing and, in winter, colder
E to N	29.80 or below and falling rapidly	Severe NE gale and heavy rain; in winter, heavy snow and cold wave
Going to W	29.80 or below and rising rapidly	Clearing and colder

Use of the Anemometer. The anemometer is an instrument used for measuring wind velocity and, in most cases, wind direction. It is mounted at the masthead with the indicator located near the helm. Some units are designed so that the indicator buzzes and flashes a light the number of times per minute that directly corresponds to the wind velocity in knots; others are direct-reading units. Readings made under way indicate apparent wind speed and direction; they should be corrected for vessel speed and direction to obtain *true* wind readings. When measuring velocity and direction of wind, the high degree of accuracy usually essential in bearings isn't required. It is sufficient if velocity be estimated within one Beaufort number, and direction within 5 percent. (See page 121)

Most yachtsmen are aware of the Beaufort scale as simply a standardized manner of designating the force of winds. It is, however, a great deal more; it's a clear and careful compilation of the manifestations, symptoms, and results of winds of various forces, and the relationship of these factors on land and sea. Even by judicious use of the Beaufort scale plus careful observation of the wind reaction on trees, it's often very possible to predict the water conditions you're likely to encounter long before arriving there. But, remember these are only predictions, because there are times, even after arriving at the dock, when you can't make a positive judgment of the wind's strength. For instance, wind coming from the ocean soon gets broken up by trees, shore banks and hills so that if you are a mile or two inland its effect is greatly reduced; it then seems to be less than you will actually experience when afloat. If the wind is blowing out to sea, its effect on the waves will be masked and the water will appear much smoother to the watcher on the shore than in fact it is. The tide also has a considerable influence on the amount of sea raised by the wind. If the wind is against the tide, the friction between the two raises waves which are steeply undercut, forming short chopping seas. These seas will often moderate or even disappear with a change in the direction of the tidal current.

Reefing

As has been stated several times, sails are designed to give maximum power for ordinary light winds known as a whole-sail breeze. When it's blowing real hard, it is a good idea to reduce the sail area by reefing. While the uninitiated may feel that reefing is, in some way, a show of cowardice, this is not so. Although sailing with decks awash may be thrilling, a boat is designed to sail upright and the sail area for a particular strength of wind should be adjusted to permit this. A reefed boat properly trimmed should make better progress than an overcanvased one, which has to be luffed up or the sheets slackened every time the wind freshens a bit more.

There are two basic ways of reefing the mainsail. Most modern sailboats use a variation of roller reefing. The second and older method, still preferred by some experienced ocean-racing skippers, uses lines and eyes, and doesn't involve turning the boom. By this I mean that the area of a mainsail is reduced by gathering up some of its foot along the boom and then the surplus sail is bunched along the boom by a series of short lines, called reef points. There may be one, two, or three rows of points permanently attached to the sail in line with eyes (called cringles) in the bolt rope. It is important to remember that the points are only intended for securing the slack of the sail and that it is the end fastenings which should take the strain. With a small sail the material may be pulled down by direct hand hold and secured to the boom end with a loose line. With a larger sail there may be a rope called an earing or pendant, which is fastened to the boom, taken through the reef cringle, down to the eye in the corner of the sail to the hand, giving a purchase. Several turns around the boom or through an eye will secure that end of the sail. At the other end the procedure is rather different because of the slope of the edge of the sail. In a small boat a line may be used in a similar way to the other end to pull down the sail and haul out the line of reef points. Some turns around the boom and through the cringle will secure it.

When both ends are secured, the surplus canvas at the foot of the sail is pulled out and rolled up as neatly as possible, then held by bringing the reef points together between the sail and the boom. It is wrong to take them below the boom. The knot used is a reef— this is the job which gave it its name (see the previous chapter). So that the points can be let go easily, the ends should be turned back to make a bow or slip reef.

In principle, roller reefing is simple and straightforward, and is preferred by most yachtsmen in this modern age of the sail. In theory, after the main halyard has been slackened, one man working a mechanism at the mast end of the boom should be able to lower the sail and take in a reef. Usually an assistant is needed to see that the sail rolls properly. A little thought will show that the boom must be at right angles to the mast if more than one turn is to be taken without the material piling up at the end. It is usually sufficiently near a right angle in large boats, but in a smaller craft the boom often has to be raised to clear heads, and roller reefing can't be used to shorten sail very much. If the boom is parallel, although not necessarily round, and the sail cut fairly flat, the sail should roll evenly. If the sail is very full, it would be an advantage to have the boom thicker near the middle. How the boom is turned to reef depends to some extent on the size of the boat and the builder's choice.

Forward of the mast, reefing is almost a thing of the past. An assortment of jibs to be drawn on to suit the weather is more usual for any craft with a claim to speed. Many cruising boats that have only one jib are often equipped with furling gear. This allows the jib to be rolled along its luff, either completely for stowing or partly for reefing.

Sails may be reefed when the boat is ashore or at anchor, when the job is easy and can be tackled leisurely. If a reef has to be taken afloat, it is seamanlike to think out the steps so that the work may be

Beaufort Number*	Descriptive term used by U.S. Weather Bureau	Wind mean velocity† Knots per hour	Miles per hour	Land	Sea	Probable wave height‡ (in feet)
0	Calm	less than 1	less than 1	Calm, smoke rises vertically.	Sea like a mirror.	
1	Light air	1–3	1–3	Direction of wind shown by smoke drift but not by windvanes.	Ripples with the appearance of scales are formed, but without foam crests.	¼ (¼)
2	Light breeze	4–6	4–7	Wind felt on face; leaves rustle; ordinary vanes moved by wind.	Small wavelets, still short but more pronounced; crests have a glassy appearance and do not break.	½ (½)
3	Gentle breeze	7–10	8–12	Leaves and small twigs in constant motion; wind extends light flag.	Large wavelets; crests begin to break; foam of glassy appearance; perhaps scattered whitecaps.	2 (3)
4	Moderate breeze	11–16	13–18	Raises dust and loose paper; small branches are moved.	Moderate waves, becoming longer; fairly frequent whitecaps.	3½ (5)
5	Fresh breeze	17–21	19–24	Small trees in leaf begin to sway; crested wavelets form on inland waters.	Moderate waves, taking a more pronounced long form; many whitecaps are formed (chance of some spray).	6 (8½)

| Beaufort Number* | Descriptive term used by U.S. Weather Bureau | Wind mean velocity† | | Locations | | Probable wave height‡ (in feet) |
		Knots per hour	Miles per hour	Land	Sea	
6	Strong breeze	22–27	25–31	Large branches in motion; whistling heard in telegraph wires; umbrellas used with difficulty.	Large waves begin to form; the white foam crests are more extensive everywhere (probably some spray).	9½ (13)
7	Near gale or moderate gale	28–33	32–38	Whole trees in motion; inconvenience felt when walking against wind.	Sea heaps up and white foam from breaking waves begins to be blown in streaks along the direction of the wind.	13½ (19)
8	Gale	34–40	39–46	Breaks twigs off trees; generally impedes progress.	Moderately high waves of greater length; edges of crests begin to break into the spindrift; the foam is blown in well-marked streaks along the direction of the wind.	18 (25)
9	Strong gale	41–47	47–54	Slight structural damage occurs.	High waves; dense streaks of foam along the direction of the wind; crests of waves begin to topple, tumble, and roll over; spray may affect visibility.	23 (32)

10	Storm or strong gale	48–55	55–63	Seldom experienced inland; trees uprooted; considerable structural damage occurs.	Very high waves with long overhanging crests; the resulting foam, in great patches, is blown in dense streaks along the direction of the wind; on the whole, the surface of the sea takes a white appearance; the tumbling of the sea becomes heavy and shocklike; visibility affected.	29 (41)
11	Violent storm or whole gale	56–63	64–74	Very rarely experienced; accompanied by widespread damage.	Exceptionally high waves; the sea is completely covered with long white patches of foam lying along the direction of the wind; everywhere the edges of the wave crests are blown into froth, visibility affected.	37 (52)
12	Hurricane	above 64	above 74		The air is filled with foam and spray; sea completely white with driving spray; visibility very seriously affected.	45 (–)

* In the era of sailing vessels, Admiral Beaufort introduced a wind scale for judging wind on the sails of a vessel. The Beaufort numbers have since then been correlated into a range of wind velocities, and the scale has continued in universal use for describing wind velocity.

† Velocity equivalent at a standard height of 10 meters above open flat ground.

‡ This portion of the scale is only intended as a guide to show roughly what can be expected in the open sea, remote from land. It should never be used in the reverse way; i.e., for logging or reporting the state of the sea. In enclosed waters, or when near land, with an off-shore wind, wave heights will be smaller and the waves steeper. Figures in the brackets indicate the probable maximum height of waves.

done efficiently and quickly. The boat should be headed into the wind. The helmsman may be able to keep her there while other members of the crew do the reefing. If the crew is shorthanded the boat should heave to. How this is done depends on the boat. Maybe the jib can be pulled in hard and the mainsheet kept short. Take the weight of the boom on the topping lift until creases begin to appear in the clew of the sail. But, reducing the area of the mainsail and keeping full jib may affect the balance of the boat under sail, and you'll probably feel this change of balance on the tiller. However, it's not likely to change to such an extent that you can't handle the boat easily. You will probably find that the pull on the tiller is reduced by reefing. Another point worth remembering is that it is always easier to reef while at anchor or alongside a dock, and it is always easier to shake out a reef than to put one in, so it is seamanlike to leave harbor already reefed if you have any doubts about the strength of the wind, and to let the reef out if you find that you have overestimated it when you get outside.

Tactics in Bad Weather

How much more agreeable a cruise can be when it is favored with sunshine and pleasant winds! Inevitably, however, a day will come when the elements decide to go on a rampage, and then all the skill and ability of a skipper are called upon. He may be winding up an extended weekend, and even though the weather has turned bad, he is under the necessity of carrying on to reach his home port so that he may resume his prosaic activities on the morrow.

If there is sufficient advance warning of the approach of bad weather, the wise skipper will take what steps he can to prepare for it. The first thing to do is to secure and lash all heavier objects—such as anchors, the dinghy, and the like—so that they will remain where they are put. Then go about and pick up any smaller effects—books, glassware, tools, and what have you—and make certain these are stowed so they can't come adrift. The best place to care for miscellaneous gear which normally would not be lashed down would be to wrap it in a blanket and then wedge it securely in a corner of the cabin floor. In this way it can't fall any further and is safe against damage. If time permits, it might also be wise to prepare a few sandwiches and fill a thermos bottle with coffee or perhaps some hot soup. There is no telling in advance how welcome a bit of food may be later on.

You and crew should don foul-weather gear (see page 170). Also, everyone on deck should wear a short line made fast around his middle and secured to a deck fitting. I have seen people argue against this procedure and seen them saved by the line in the same hour. When the going is really rough everyone on deck must wear a life belt. A man working on the foredeck or some other place where he must move around should wear a line with a snap hook on it. He can use both hands getting forward, and when he gets there he can clip his life line to the rigging or a deck fitting. Some newer life belts consist of a harness to be fastened around the person's body and a strong line or a strap attached to the harness at one end, with a strong snap hook at the other. The length of the line or strap can be adjusted, but should be no longer than necessary to reach a convenient, strong place for attaching the snap hook and allowing reasonable room in which to work. The length between the harness and the place of attachment should not be enough to allow the person to be washed overboard, and the harness should be so designed that the wearer's head will be kept above water if he happens to find himself overboard and being towed alongside the boat. It is a good idea to wear life belts or jackets when sailing at night. Also, attach a flashlight (with good batteries), and a whistle, to your life jacket. These two items saved many lives during World War II and they could save yours someday.

Luffing Through a Puff. It will happen very often, even when sailing in good weather, that the breeze will freshen considerably, or a strong puff of wind will strike your boat. This may not be sufficient to make it necessary to reef but will require you to nurse your boat along. If this happens, and the increasing weight of the wind from either of these conditions heels the boat over more than you desire, you can ease the mainsheet until the entire forward part of the sail, the luff, is shaking and only the after two-thirds or so is filled. The jib sheet may also be slacked a little. This will at once ease the pressure, and the boat will recover herself while you sail her along, steering on your course or perhaps more nearly into the wind than you were before. You will, of course, have to watch your boat while in this condition and be ready to put your tiller down still more if the wind continues to increase or if a puff should suddenly fill the sail. In such a case, the boat can be luffed sharply until the puff passes. One can sail a boat a long way with her mainsail only half full; but if there is indication of the wind increasing, or no signs of its slacking off, reefing is usually advisable for all but the real expert.

When luffing, care should be taken to see that the boat is kept moving and that she doesn't lose headway. A well-balanced boat, as I stated earlier, will always respond to the tiller or wheel and will always come up into the wind if the tiller or wheel is let go while the boat is moving. That is why it is always better to slack the sheet when you are sailing close-hauled in a puff or squall and let the wind spill from the luff of the sail rather than to just luff her with the sail trimmed in. But, as long as the boat keeps moving, you can do almost anything with her. If you must come about to change your course, remember that the action of the sea and the height of the waves play an important part in this maneuver. Generally there are three or four steep, high waves, then a series of short rollers, then three or four more steep ones, and so on. The trick is to luff and come about when the seas run low. Don't come around fast, for there is constant handling of straining sheets. Make a big wide loop broad-reaching, then swing to a close reach. Time yourself so that when the seas run low, you quickly come about. When the sails are on the opposite side let the sheets out (see that they don't snarl) to the point of reaching. Then let out more sheet so as to again run before the wind.

Sailing in Very Strong Winds. If strong winds increase in velocity and reefing doesn't help, drop the sails. Actually, if ever in doubt as to the force of wind or whether to carry sail or not, drop the sails for safety; drop the mainsail first as this has the greater sail area. As the sails come down gather them in, lean on them, and hold them down until they are tied up securely. Then run before the wind under bare poles, or, if you have an auxiliary engine aboard, use it to continue on your course. Remember that it's best to cut through the waves at about a 45-degree angle; adjust your course accordingly, therefore.

There are times, of course, when the winds haven't sufficient velocity to require the dropping of *all* sails, but their strength is still enough to create a degree of concern for the safety of your crew and craft. In such cases, it's usually safest and easiest to drop the mainsail and sail on with the jib alone. You'll be surprised how well you can reach, and, often, how high you can point, with just this one sail. But the best sailing point with such a rig is running before the wind.

On some occasions you'll want more exposed sail area so that you can move faster. In such cases, you achieve this with the mainsail alone; however, be prepared to luff if a real strong wind puff comes along. You can luff very quickly with the main alone, because there is a tendency in such an arrangement to make the bow swing into the wind. This, of course, creates a weather helm, so much so that the craft will automatically come up into the wind should you let go of the tiller or wheel.

If close to a lee shore, or a hazard of a kind that could damage the boat, or (the exact reverse) the storm is pushing you out to sea, anchor. Let out as much anchor line as possible so that the boat rides easily and does not drag. If the anchor does drag, or if the water is too deep, trail a sea anchor from the bow to keep your boat heading into the wind. For centuries the technique of "lying to" or "heaving to" has been the ultimate safety resort of mariners caught in weather conditions which prohibit a boat from continuing on her desired course.

A sea anchor is an item that every cruiser-racer should have aboard. It consists of a heavy canvas or dacron cone perhaps four or five feet in length, securely lashed to a stainless steel or galvanized metal circular rod 20 to 24 inches in diameter. The cone is left open at the small end so that the water funnels through it and the device furnishes a most effective drag or brake. It doesn't sink to the bottom but is dragged along just below the surface. Because it is effective as a drag, it can hardly be pulled back aboard when it is no longer needed. For this reason a trip line is attached to the small end, and by this means the sea anchor can be reversed and pulled back aboard when the need for its use no longer exists. Most sailboats, because of their design, will easily ride bow-on to the waves with a sea anchor out. If the boat is a yawl, a small trysail, set on the mizzenmast, will do wonders to keep the bow pointed into the wind. Even sloops will ride better if a riding sail (generally the jib) is set.

If you don't have a sea anchor on board, but need one, you'll have to improvise a drag of some sort from whatever you can find aboard. Such things as a bucket, a couple of oars lashed together with some canvas, a few life preservers reinforced by oars or boat hooks, or even a dinghy, capsized and full of water—anything which

Figure 4-5: Fog coming in from the Pacific Ocean through the Golden Gate, San Francisco, California. (Courtesy of United States Department of Commerce, Weather Bureau)

will serve as a drag—will also serve to slow up the rate of drifting and keep the boat headed into the seas and weather. Remember also that the stresses and strains on all this gear at such times are very great, so use line of ample strength, well-protected by chafing gear.

Sailing in a Fog. While handling a boat under severe storm conditions can sometimes be an ordeal, there are other circumstances, which prevail more frequently, that call for piloting ability. This pertains to operating your sailboat in a fog. While fog appears more frequently than heavy storms, ordinarily it would be present in weather with only a very light wind. While this in itself can be a problem for sailboat skippers, there is the added difficulty of reduced visibility and the resultant danger of colliding with other craft or objects. If you have auxiliary power on board, here's surely the time to use it. You don't have to worry about the disgrace—the boys at the yacht club can't see you because of the fog.

The Rules of the Road definitely call for operating the ship's whistle or a foghorn as a warning signal when under way in a fog. The following sound signals are intended to show, as far as possible, that boats are near to each other, and their approximate position. Be sure to use the proper signal to identify the action of your craft.

Since reduced visibility and the uncertainty of what lies ahead are the big problems in sailing through fog, it is necessary that look-

SOUND SIGNALS IN FOG OR IN CONDITIONS OF NO VISIBILITY

Type of Vessel	Method of Signaling	Frequency
Vessel under sail*		At intervals of
(Both International and Inland Rules)		
Under way, starboard tack	1 blast	1 minute
Under way, port tack	2 blasts in succession	1 minute
Under way, running free	3 blasts in succession	1 minute
Vessel under power†		
Under way (International Rules)	1 long blast	2 minutes
Under way (Inland Rules)	1 long blast	1 minute
Under way but stopped (International Rules)	2 long blasts in succession	2 minutes
Vessel at anchor		
(Both International‡ and Inland Rules)	Ring ship's bell vigorously for 5 seconds	1 minute
Vessel aground‡		
(International Rules)	Basic signal: ring ship's bell vigorously for 5 seconds. In addition, strike three separate and distinct strokes on the bell immediately before and after the basic signal.	1 minute

SOUND SIGNALS IN FOG OR IN CONDITIONS OF NO VISIBILITY (*Continued*)

Type of Vessel	Method of Signaling	Frequency At intervals of
Vessel towing†		
(Both International and Inland Rules)	1 long blast and 2 short blasts in succession	1 minute
Vessel towed		
(International Rules§)	1 long blast and 3 short blasts in succession	1 minute
(Inland Rules¶)	1 long blast and 2 short blasts in succession	1 minute
Fishing vessel (20 tons or upward)		
(International Rules)	1 short blast followed by ringing the ship's bell	1 minute

* Signal given on foghorn.

† Signal given on whistle.

‡ On International waters a vessel longer than 350 feet rings a bell in the forward part of the vessel; and a gong, or other different-sounding signal, in the stern, both for about five seconds at intervals of about one minute. To give additional warning of the possibility of collision by an approaching vessel, a boat may also sound one short, one prolonged, then one short blast of her horn.

§ Signal given on foghorn or whistle immediately following the signal made by the towing vessel.

¶ (Optional) Signal given on foghorn immediately following the signal made by the towing vessel.

outs be posted at bow, stern, and amidships. This assumes, of course, that there are sufficient persons on board to man all the stations. If shorthanded, the bow position is probably the most important. The bow lookout confines his attention particularly to the zone ahead of the boat, and should include the water surface for possible drift, debris, or anything else which might appear. The lookouts on the beam confine their attention to their respective sides while the lookout at the stern watches for overtaking vessels and any other indications of objects over the stern. (Be sure that you or your crew don't wear the ear flaps down on your foul-weather gear.) Should you hear the signals of another craft, you must be alert to determine the direction from which it comes, as sound is the medium which functions most effectively at such times. Even this may be erratic on occasion, and every care should be taken to observe that the signal is properly identified. Bell buoys and navigation aids in lighthouses or on shore can also be located by their sound signals. A careful sounding should be taken at known intervals; then a chain of soundings can be plotted which will help a great deal in keeping track of your position. While the usual small boat's running lights are not very powerful, it will help to turn them on because a thin spot in the fog may reveal your presence to the lookout on an approaching vessel who may not be able to hear your fog signals. Some boats that sail in traffic areas, carry radar reflectors from their masts so that big vessels can spot them on this piece of electronic navigating gear. Be sure to keep track of your position on your chart.

When in doubt as to where you are, use your sounding lead or electronic depth finder. If you still don't know, you may have to anchor. But keep an alert watch in case of traffic, which may be on or off its course.

Tides and Their Effects

Tides are caused by the gravitational forces, or "pull," of the moon and sun. The moon, being much closer to the earth, exerts the greater influence. Twice each 24 hours the tide pours out of the bays and away from the coast, pauses for a short time, and then rushes back. Because the moon rises approximately 50 minutes later each day, the tide is that much later each 24 hours. There are local variances, particularly in bays, which may make a difference of 30 minutes or more. For all practical purposes, however, you can estimate the tide at a given location as being one hour later each day.

The incoming tide at its crest is known as high tide, and the outgoing tide becomes low tide when it has reached its maximum retreat. The tide is said to be "flooding" on the way in, at "half tide" three hours later, and at "high-water slack" after six hours, when it reaches its peak. The tide is said to be "ebbing" on the way out, and reaches "low-water slack" just before the "turn of the tide" starts the flood on its way back. "Dead water" occurs at both high-water and low-water slacks, when the tidal current stops and the water is apparently at a standstill. There are exceptions when tides ebb from bays through narrow inlets. Great amounts of water, almost land-locked, continue to ebb through the inlets long after the turn of the tide. The result, choppy water where both currents meet, is dangerous for small boats and inexperienced boatmen. The tide fall may be one or two feet at one point but seven or eight feet just a few miles away. Oceanographers attribute this to contours of the ocean floor. Near the equator the tide fall is less—often just a few inches less—but it becomes greater toward the poles. In the Aleutians or the Bay of Fundy it is normally 40 to 60 feet, and sometimes more.

The relationship of the moon and sun also influences the tide. For example, *spring tides* (unrelated to the season) occur twice each month at full and new moons when the moon and the sun are in direct line with the earth and together exert their greatest force. These tides are abnormally high and often reach flood stage. *Perigee tides,* which occur when the moon is closest to the earth, are exceptionally high tides. *Neap tides* are abnormally low and occur at the first and last quarter of the moon, when the moon, earth, and sun are at right angles and the gravitational pull is weak. *Apogee tides* occur when the moon is farthest from the earth and also are exceptionally low.

The hours of the tides may be learned by reading the daily tide tables published in leading newspapers along the seaboard, in various local boating publications, and in some almanacs. More detailed information on the subject of tides and currents may be found in two publications of the United States Coast and Geodetic Survey: The *Tide Table* and *Current Tables.*

The *Tide Table* lists the times and heights of high and low tide for every day of the year at many major reference stations along the coast. The second part lists a multitude of intermediate stations, with differences and constants to apply to the tide at the nearest reference station. The *Current Tables* are used to find the time of high and low slack. They also show the times and velocities of the maximum flood and ebb currents (currents induced by the rising or falling tide). In addition, another section of the *Current Tables* gives "Current Differences and Constants," to be applied in a fashion similar to those in the *Tide Table.* Information on obtaining these publications as well as other government publications mentioned in this book can be had by writing to the Government Printing Office, Washington 25, D.C.

You can use the ebb and flow of the tide to your advantage. When planning a trip on the water, keep the following in mind:

1. Try to sail out of a harbor with the ebb and return on the flood.

2. Try to sail up a river going inland on the flood and return to the harbor near the coast on the ebb.

3. Study local conditions to find out where the tide ebbs and flows most strongly, where there are eddy currents and where there is slacker water. If you can't use the strong current to your best advantage, try to avoid such areas. Remember that currents are named exactly opposite to the winds. Thus, an easterly current is a current running *to* the east, not *from* the east. The direction of the current is termed the "set" and its velocity the "drift."

5

Getting Where You Want to Go

W hen you cast off from your mooring, or from a dock, you're under way—going somewhere—and the task of navigating your boat begins. As we know, navigation is the art of getting a vessel from one place to another. And, no matter what kind of boat you have, you must be able to navigate her safely and efficiently, according to her ability, and according to your waters. There are two basic types of navigation: coastwise navigation or piloting, and offshore navigation. The former is the act of navigating a boat by means of sight and hearing, while in offshore navigating you don't use these faculties in the normal manner. In other words, while the pilot can actually see the shore and lighthouses, ranges and buoys, read the depth under him, and listen to various radio aids, foghorns, and bells, the offshore navigator must proceed without these aids.

In this chapter, we will concern ourselves primarily with coastwise navigation for three reasons. First, it is the type of navigation employed by most sailors because inshore sailing is the most popular phase of the sport. Second, the subject of offshore navigation would require more space than this book could possibly allot to it. And, thirdly, electronic navigation is replacing the principal form of offshore navigation—celestial navigation—in all but ocean racing. This new form of offshore navigation requires, in general, little or no skill and mathematics to work out a position. But, if you are interested in the traditional offshore navigational methods, I would suggest reading Benjamin Dutton's *Navigation and Piloting*, edited by John C. Hill and others; or the *Primer of Navigation* by George W. Mixter.

Nautical Charts and Pilot Aids

The nautical charts published by the United States Coast and Geodetic Survey are the yachtsman's road map. With them, the skipper can pilot a course from point to point in safety. These charts, executed in great detail, tell you the depth of water, type of bottom, coast or shoreline, land contours, aids and dangers to navigation, tides and currents, anchorages. They also show the location of radio and Coast Guard stations, towns, cities, high towers, and scores of other things. Here are some tips to follow on the proper use of nautical charts:

1. Keep your chart up to date by applying all *Notices to Mariners* corrections when you receive them. A weekly pamphlet prepared jointly by the U.S. Coast Guard and the U.S. Naval Oceanographic Office is issued free to those who desire copies regularly. (See page 136 for address.) It is issued as a safety aid to keep mariners advised of changes so they may keep their nautical charts and related publications up-to-date.

2. Read carefully all notes printed on your chart; each is vital to your safety afloat.

3. Learn the meaning of each symbol and abbreviation on your chart from United States Coast and Geodetic Survey Chart No. 1, price $0.25.

4. The compass on your chart shows the variation from true north; however, you must also correct your bearing for the deviation of your boat (see page 137).

5. Constantly use your chart from the beginning to end of each trip. Keep in mind the orientation of your boat with respect to the chart.

6. Maintain your position on the chart by relating charted features with those you can identify in your surroundings.

7. Storm-warning display locations and small-craft warning signals have been charted for your safety.

8. Many times it is good practice to make notes directly on the chart so that you will have the information for the next time you come that way. "Bridge does not open between 5:15 and 6:00 P.M.," or "Strong current here when tide is ebbing," for example.

Nautical charts can be purchased from the United States Coast and Geodetic Survey, Washington 25, D.C., or their authorized agents in major boating areas. A free catalog of charts is also available from U.S.C. & G.S.

The Mariner's Compass

The magnetic or mariner's compass is probably the oldest, yet most vital, instrument used by seamen. It's functioning is based on the fact that a magnetic needle, freely suspended, will align itself parallel to the lines of the magnetic force of the earth itself, a stable, continuous, and predictable source of power. Modern compasses generally use two magnets, which are suspended from the compass card and fixed parallel to its north and south markings. A pivot and synthetic sapphire provide virtually frictionless support, thus permitting the card to rotate freely. To dampen the motion of the card, the compass bowl is filled either with an alcohol-and-water mixture; or more commonly today, a fine oil. Expansion and contraction of the liquid is compensated for by an expansion chamber in the bowl. The bowl is enclosed at the top with a flat glass in the older-type compasses, through which the compass heading may be read. Modern compasses have a ground, polished, glass dome which gives the compass much greater freedom of movement as well as magnifying the card, and beyond this the quality of greater steadiness. In the past, this bowl was gimbaled externally against the rolling of the boat, but the modern compasses are internally gimbaled to keep them level regardless of the motion of the craft. A shading cover or hood is useful to reduce reflections and glare, and a built-in light or a provision for external illumination is necessary for night operation.

The compass should never be located in close proximity to masses of iron or steel. Keep it away from instrument panels, steel steering wheels (they may be steel even if coated with a plastic), and in general from all circuits carrying heavy amperage such as ammeters, etc.

The lubber's line must be properly aligned parallel with the fore-and-aft line of the ship. Generally, it should be located at an angle of about 25 degrees below the helmsman's eye level.

Variation and deviation are the two sources of compass error. As stated previously, the magnets of the compass align themselves with the earth's magnetic field. This field is composed of magnetic lines of force—called "magnetic meridians"—which are considered to travel from the south magnetic pole to the north magnetic pole. The compass aligns itself with the magnetic meridians, but the magnetic meridians do not coincide—except in a very few places—with the geographical meridians, because the magnetic and geographical poles aren't coincident. Therefore, the compass will not indicate true north. The difference in direction between the magnetic and geographical meridian at any given point is called the variation at that point. If the direction of the magnetic meridian is to the right of true north, the variation is called easterly and labeled E. If the direction of the magnetic meridian is to the left of true north, the variation is westerly and labeled W. On a nautical chart meridians are useful in this connection because each chart carries a "compass rose." A compass rose is a diagram of the compass points based on true north, superimposed upon a diagram of the compass points based on the magnetic north. This enables you to tell the compass variation in your vicinity.

Deviation, the second source of compass error, is the angle between the magnetic meridian and the north-south axis of the compass card. Deviation is caused by the earth's magnetic field acting on the metal in the ship. It is labeled in the same manner as variation. But, while variation is easily found by looking at the chart, deviation, on the other hand, varies from boat to boat, from latitude to latitude, and with changes in heading. It is caused by magnetic influence of metal in the boat itself, such as the engine, iron ballast, electrical gear, etc. Your compass should be compensated for these factors. It's best to employ a professional to do this for you, and at the same time, have a deviation card made up. This card will show how far off your compass is in degrees, and you then can correct easily for your true course. The auxiliary sailboat should have two deviation cards, one made with the power off and one with it on.

To get the exact bearing you wish to sail, you must correct for the errors of both variation and deviation. To get the correct com-

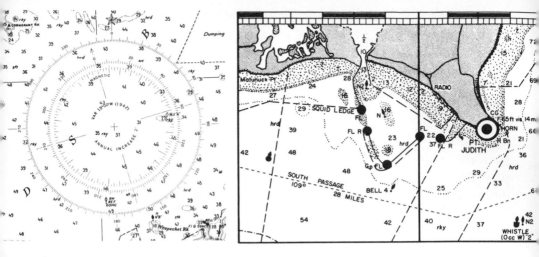

Figure 5-1: Typical compass rose (left), while a section of the U.S.C. & G.S. chart is shown at the right.

pass course to steer also requires correction. When you combine these you get what is called *total compass error*. This error, when correctly applied to the compass course in accordance with the directional symbol of E or W, gives the true course. The mariner's rule is "East, you add; west, you subtract, when correcting." This is the method used to convert a compass course to a true course. The procedure is reversed to convert a true course to a compass course. For example:

Compass Course to True Course

Compass Course	227°	
Dev. W −3		
Var. E +9		
Error +6		+ 6
True Course	233°	

Compass Course	176°	
Dev. W −9		
Var. W −2		
Error −11		− 11
True Course	165°	

True Course to Compass Course

True Course	288°	
Dev. W +3		
Var. E −10		
Error −7		− 7
Compass Course	281°	

True Course	131°	
Dev. W +3		
Var. W +10		
Error +13		+ 13
Compass Course	144°	

With many keel-type sailboats there is sometimes a slightly different compass deviation error when she is heeled over. This so-called *heeling error* is probably most easily determined by running between known objects such as buoys or other aids to navigation on a given course on various tacks and heel angles. While this error is slight in many cases and ignored in others, it can be corrected, if desired. It is a task, however, for a professional compass adjuster. Before leaving the subject of the compass itself, I would like to point out that a compass calibration and correction won't stay accurate forever, since the deviation may change from time to time during the sailing season. For this reason, it is wise to check your compass frequently against known bearing.

Steering by Compass. No matter how good a compass is on board, it won't do you any good unless you know how to use it properly. When using a compass, it is important to remember that the compass card itself never moves. It remains stationary, aligned with the earth's magnetic field.

To practice steering by means of a compass, lay out a compass course (see page 141) between objects in sight of each other; then steer between them, using no aids other than the compass—no peeking either, except to be sure you don't hit something. When you're able to come close to the second object on every attempt, then you have the compass steering technique down pat. But to really become proficient in the compass steering procedure you should practice in all types of sea and wind conditions. Thus, you'll have a full knowledge of steering by compass should the circumstances ever arise when you may be forced to sail under conditions that demand it.

Using a Pelorus. This is a navigating instrument that is seldom used by amateur sailors, but is highly regarded by professionals. I first learned how to use the pelorus while in NROTC, and found it most helpful in taking bearings on my sailboat. Actually, this instrument is only a dummy compass fitted with sight vanes for taking bearings of celestial or terrestrial objects. It is generally made of brass. It has no magnets and is wholly nonmagnetic. The pelorus is suspended in gimbals and is usually mounted on a stand. To keep it in a horizontal position, a weight is attached to the underside of the instrument. The dial, or card, has a compass rose painted or engraved upon it and is divided into 360 degrees. The card and the sight vanes revolve, independently of each other, upon a pivot. Two clamps, one above the other on the top of the pivot, permit the card and the sight vanes to be set in any desired position. One clamp is used to set the card, the other to set the sight vanes. Because of the lack of space on board, some smaller boats use a portable pelorus and find it more practical than the one just described. The portable type can be set up when needed on the cabin top or in the cockpit.

A bearing is taken on an object by first aligning the pelorus card with the compass card and clamping it in position. The lubber's line must be aligned with the boat's keel. The sighting vanes of the pelorus are then aligned on the object of the bearing and are clamped in position. The bearing is read from the pelorus dial. For the bearing to be accurate, the craft must be kept exactly on the course on which the pelorus dial is clamped. Because of currents, wind, and seas, it is sometimes difficult to hold course; therefore, the helmsman must call out "Mark" when the vessel is on course. The crewman who takes the bearing, clamps the sighting vane in position at this instant and an accurate bearing is obtained.

The bearing thus taken from a pelorus is a compass bearing and must be corrected in the same manner as a compass reading. The pelorus is also used to obtain relative bearings. In obtaining a bearing of this kind the pelorus dial is clamped in position with 000 (zero) on the lubber's line. After the lubber's line is aligned with the boat's keel, a bearing can be taken, the sighting vanes clamped in position, and the bearing read. This bearing is relative to the vessel's heading at the time the bearing was taken and must be added to the boat's heading to obtain the compass bearing of the object.

The pelorus has another important use. It can warn you that your craft is on a possible collision course with another vessel on a crossing path ahead. To do this, lock the dial either in the compass heading or at 000 degrees and line up the other vessel in the sighting vane. While observing her, you can determine your course by the following:

1. If the bearing decreases, the other vessel will cross safely ahead.

2. If the bearing increases, the other vessel will cross safely astern.

3. If the bearing remains constant (you do not have to move the vane to keep the other vessel lined up), you are on a collision course and will collide, or pass very close by, if both vessels maintain the same course and speed. Observing a vessel on a crossing course ahead, or a rock or other dangerous obstacle, a constant bearing is a collision bearing.

Plotting a Course

For the greater part of the time you're at sea—if you're an average skipper—you will do most of your piloting "by the seat of your pants"; that is, you'll largely navigate visually. Because you are familiar with the waters in which you operate your boat, you'll lay courses between navigational markers and watch for them to appear over the bow. But as your cruising gets more ambitious, on long overnight trips, for example, or when fog closes in, your navigation must become more precise. This means that you'll have to plot your course on a nautical chart. This is the process of making a scale drawing of the theoretical movements of your craft, covering the ground from where you have been to where you want to go. It involves the measuring and laying out of angles, distances, recording and projection of time, applying corrections for total compass error, and the effect of current. You need three simple instruments to do the job: parallel rulers (to lay out directions on the chart), a pair of dividers (for measuring distances), and a course protractor with a straight edge (to take a bearing from one object to another). These items can be purchased at almost any store carrying marine supplies.

Let's start with the simplest of courses; that is, one between two points such as buoys, docks, or other fixed and recognizable objects. (The object you leave from is the "point of departure," while the point of arrival is known as the "destination.") To determine the course between the two points, place the center line of the protractor or the parallel rulers on your point of departure and align it with the destination. The true course to be steered can be read directly from the protractor or obtained by transferring the line with the parallel rulers to the nearest compass rose. (If your parallel rulers won't reach from the course you want to sail to the compass rose you can "walk" them across the face of the chart by (a) placing one ruler along the course you want to sail, (b) moving the second ruler as far toward the compass rose as it will go, (c) holding the second ruler firmly in position, and moving the first up against it, (d) repeating this process till your second ruler reaches the center of the compass rose.) A correction should, of course, be made for both variation and deviation while steering in this direction. Once you have obtained the total compass error, you can determine the exact compass course to be steered.

It is generally a good idea to lay off a series of short courses, or legs, rather than one long one. Locate several intermediate checkpoints, such as navigational buoys or other similar aids, and use these as points of destinations or points of turning. It's much easier to

Figure 5-2: A marine compass mounted in front of the wheel.

maintain an accurate course with short legs because you can correct your position automatically at each intermediate checkpoint. When a course changes direction, the turning point of the new course is laid out in the same manner as previously described, using the turning place as the new point of departure. The distance of the legs of a course can be determined by drawing the compass course lightly on the chart in pencil. Then set the arms of your pair of dividers on your points of departure and destination, or turning point. These distances can be measured off on the chart's nautical-miles scale.

It is usually possible, by estimating how many knots you're making, to give a fairly reasonable guess as how far you have proceeded along your selected compass course. You can check your speed over the course continuously by timing yourself between buoys or other known objects, measuring the distance between them on your chart with your dividers, and transferring this to your nautical-miles scale. If your course is such that you have to tack to windward, by applying the same procedure you should be able to locate yourself at any time. Naturally, if you can hold to a given tack for the same length of time whenever you tack, your calculation will be simpler. If you can time yourself for a mile, you can estimate your speed by using the table below:

Time for 1 Mile in Minutes	Boat's Speed in Knots	Time for 1 Mile in Minutes	Boat's Speed in Knots
60	1	5½	11
30	2	5	12
20	3	4½	13
15	4	4¼	14
12	5	4	15
10	6	3¾	16
8½	7	3½	17
7½	8	3¼	18
6½	9	3⅛	19
6	10	3	20

On a well-equipped cruising sailboat, guesswork will be reduced by trailing a taffrail log, which will give you the distance traveled through the water. Timing this, of course, allows you to compute your speed.

There are two other factors that must be taken into consideration when plotting a course. One is the allowance for leeway and the other is the direction of the current or tidal current. An easy way to determine your leeway is to sail the compass course for a short distance and then look back at your wake. Estimate the angle that the wake makes with the craft's course, and this will show you how much you should allow for leeway. If your leeway shows you are being set half a point down to leeward, you will have to steer half a point to windward to compensate for it. Actually, the amount of leeway your own boat makes can only be judged accurately by experience. But the average well-built cruising craft only makes appreciable leeway when close-hauled, and in good weather doesn't make very much then. If there is much sea running, you'll find it very difficult to judge the angle of the wake owing to the broken water. Making an accurate leeway allowance is, in point of fact, dependent on knowing your own particular craft.

Correcting courses for tidal current is fairly easy for a "stinkpotter" (powerboat man), but fairly difficult for the sailor. When you find it necessary to compensate for the current, use the current tables for times of slacks and times and velocities of strengths. Tidal current charts will show you hourly velocities and directions. The direction is equally important because this will greatly affect the course you make. Technically speaking, current velocities are directly added to or subtracted from a boat's speed when the boat's course is directly in line with the current. It should be understood that if the current is "fair," that is, running in the same direction as you wish to sail, it will merely increase your speed. If it is "foul," that is, when it's against you, it will have the opposite effect. It is when the current is setting across your course, pushing you to one side or the other of your destination, that you will have to allow for it by steering an equal amount in the opposite direction to which it is setting. For instance, suppose you're leaving point X bound for point Y and with the wind that is blowing you're making an average speed of seven knots. Let's assume your compass course is 97 degrees (this is the corrected compass course) for a distance of about 25 miles, and that you have a current running approximately 159 degrees at the rate of 2 knots. To lay out the corrected course, run a line at 159 degrees from point X and mark off 2 miles, marked at point Z. Now take your dividers, set them for seven miles, and holding one leg at point Z, swing the other around until it cuts your sailing course line. Mark this point T; a line drawn between Z and T will give you the course to steer. Frequently the scale of the chart on which you're working is too small to make a satisfactory diagram to chart scale. However, you may use any scale you desire. Line XY is two units, line ZT is seven units; as long as the units are the same, the line ZT will give you the course in order to make good your sailing direction. After you have run seven miles, make a guess as to your average speed (use the chart on page 143 as a guide) during the next hour and look at your current tables to ascertain whether the set and drift of the current has changed, and refigure the course for the succeeding hour. Because the speed of a sailing vessel is rarely constant, these calculations must be made at hourly intervals, but a powerboat man who can depend on constant speed may calculate an average for set and drift of tidal current over the entire course and shape a course which will allow for it.

Aids to Navigation

It would be difficult to drive cross-country without road signs to point the way. It would be even more difficult on the waterways if it were not for the various aids to navigation.

Buoyage System of the United States. The primary function of buoys is to warn the mariner of some danger, obstruction, or contour in the sea bottom. The system of buoyage in the United States, as all good yachtsmen know, employs a simple arrangement of colors, shapes, numbers, and light characteristics to show on which side of a buoy a vessel should pass when proceeding in a given direction. For instance, the expression "red right returning" has long been used by the seafaring man to remind him that red buoys are passed on his starboard (right) side when proceeding from the open sea into harbor (upstream). Black buoys are kept to port (left) side. Red starboard buoys may be "nun" buoys, shaped like an inverted cone with the top sliced off, or "spar" buoys, which look like a long tapered pole. Black port markers may be either spar or cylindrical "can" types. When entering a channel from seaward or a harbor from the main channel, buoys marking the starboard side of the fairway are even-numbered consecutively: 2, 4, 6, and so on; buoys marking the port side of the channel are odd-numbered: 3, 5, 7, and so on. Thus, you should stay between the two strings of buoys, keeping red to your right and black to your left, and you should keep to the right side, just as ashore. Conversely, when proceeding toward the sea or leaving a harbor, red and even-numbered buoys are left, to port, and black and odd-numbered buoys to starboard.

Since all channels don't lead from seaward, arbitrary assumptions must at times be made in order that the buoyage system may be consistently applied. Proceeding from seaward is considered in a southerly direction along the Atlantic Coast, in a westerly and northerly direction along the Gulf Coast, and in a northerly direction on the Pacific Coast. On the Great Lakes, proceeding in a westerly and northerly direction is proceeding from seaward; and on the Intracoastal Waterway, proceeding generally southerly along the Atlantic Coast and in a generally westerly direction along the Gulf

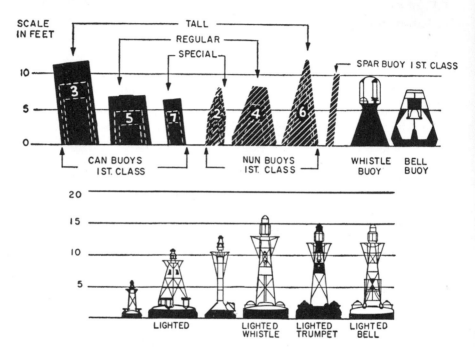

Figure 5-3: The United States buoyage system. (Courtesy of United States Coast Guard)

Coast is considered proceeding from seaward. The characteristics of aids to navigation on the Mississippi and Ohio rivers and their tributaries follow the basic assumption that proceeding from the sea toward the head of navigation will find red on starboard (the right side).

Afloat, we don't have a white line down the middle of the street, but we do have mid-channel buoys. These are black-and-white, vertically striped, and may be of any shape. They'll tell you if you're wandering over into the "oncoming traffic lane."

Buoys are also used to mark obstructions, channel junctions, sunken wrecks, and other areas of special danger. Junction and obstruction markers are red-and-black, horizontally striped, with the top band indicating the best channel. Thus, from seaward, a red top band means the channel is to the left of the buoy—in other words, keep the buoy off your starboard. A black top band, then, means that the best channel is to the right of the buoy. Some buoys have a white top to enable searchlights to pick them up easily; however, the white color has no significance. Some other types occasionally met by yachtsmen are white anchorage buoys, yellow quarantine buoys, and white buoys with a green top, which mark dredging areas.

Bell buoys are generally used to mark channel entrances and obstructions such as hidden rocks, wrecks, and shoal water. These are a metal framework in which bells are mounted. As waves cause such a buoy to rock, the tongue swings back and forth, striking the bell. Some buoys of this type are equipped with whistles or groaners in place of bells.

Red lights (marked R on charts) are used only on red buoys and red-and-black horizontally banded buoys with the topmost band red. Green lights (marked G on the charts) are used only on the black buoys or red-and-black horizontally banded buoys with the topmost band black. White lights are used on buoys of any color and are frequently employed at points where lights of considerable brilliance are required. The purpose of the buoy with a white light is indicated by its color, number, or light phase characteristics.

Lights on red buoys or black buoys, if not fixed (lights that don't flash), will always be regularly flashing or occulting. An occulting light is a steady light that is suddenly and totally eclipsed at regular intervals: the duration of light is always longer than or equal to that of darkness. On flashing lights, the frequency of flashes won't exceed 30 per minute (slow flashing). Where distinct cautionary significance is required, as at sharp turns and obstructions, the frequency of flashes will never be less than 60 per minute (quick flashing). Red-and-black-banded buoys show quick flashes for about 4 seconds followed by a dark period of about 4 seconds—a cycle occurring about 8 times per minute; this is known as an interrupted-quick-flashing buoy. Lights on vertically striped buoys always show a white short-long flash.

Reflectors are placed on certain unlighted buoys to assist the

Figure 5-4: A sailboat approaching a bell buoy.

yachtsman in locating them. The colors of the reflectors have the same significance as the colors of the lights.

The yachtsman must not place *complete* reliance upon buoys as aids to navigation; he should also use bearings from fixed aids on shore. Buoys are liable to be carried away, shifted, capsized, or sunk. Lighted buoys may be extinguished; sound buoys may not function.

Day Beacons. These are unlighted fixed aids to navigation used as a guide for mariners. It is either a landmark, erected on an eminence near the shore, or a mark moored or driven into the bottom in shoal water. In many instances beacons are tall masonry structures built on headlands for recognition purposes. All day beacons have some distinguishing mark; those on land are generally painted a distinctive color, whereas those on sandbanks are surmounted by a top mark (globe, diamond, triangle). Sandbank beacons are very often steel masts sunk in the sand.

Range Lights. These are usually small or skeleton-type structures which when in line (i.e., one over the other) indicate to the yachtsman that he is on a safe course. Generally they are visible in one direction, and by steering a course which keeps these lights in line (range-up) you will remain within the confines of the channel. Remember that quite a few range lights are on shore; that's where you'll be if you don't consult your chart as to where to change course. The range lights may be white, red, or green in color, and may also be fixed or flashing.

Lighthouses. These are found upon the coasts of the United States and along some of the interior waterways. They are placed where they will be of most use; on prominent headlands, at entrances, on isolated dangers, or at other points where it is necessary to warn or guide the navigator. These structures are painted solid colors, bands of colors, and various other patterns to make them readily distinguishable from the background and to distinguish one structure from another. The lights are given distinctive characteristics (different light colors, different-type flashes, and so on) so that one lighthouse may be distinguished from another. There are manned or automatically operated lights. In addition to their visual characteristics, they are usually equipped with fog and radio-beacon signals.

Lightships. These serve the same purpose as lighthouses, being equipped with lights, fog signals, and radio beacons. They mark the entrances to important harbors or estuaries, as well as dangerous shoals lying in much-frequented waters. The masthead lights, fog signals, and radio-beacon signals of these lightships all have definite characteristics, so that each ship may be distinguished from others and also from nearby lighthouses. Lights are displayed from one hour before sunset until one hour after sunrise and at all times when the sound signal is operating.

All lightships in United States waters, except Lake Huron Lightship, are painted red with the name of the station in white on both sides. (The Lake Huron Lightship is painted black with the name of the station painted in white on both sides.) Relief lightships are painted the same color as the regular station ships, with the word RELIEF in white letters on the sides. When practicable, these vessels will exhibit lights and radio signals having the same characteristics of the regular station.

The visibility of the lights given on nautical charts is at 15 feet above sea level—the assumed height of the observer's eye. This visibility must be modified proportionately for any other height. For example, when the observer is 10 feet above sea level and the observed light is known to be 50 feet above sea level (given on the chart), the distance from the light, using the table given here, is:

	Height in Feet	*Visibility in Nautical Miles*
Observer	10	
Observer's Range of Vision		3.6
Light	50	
Arc of Illumination (Light)		8.1
Distance of observer from light		11.7

Distance by Visibility

Height in Feet	*Distance in Nautical Miles*	*Height in Feet*	*Distance in Nautical Miles*
1	1.1	30	6.3
2	1.6	40	7.2
3	2.0	50	8.1
4	2.3	60	8.9
5	2.6	70	9.6
6	2.8	80	10.3
7	3.0	90	10.9
8	3.1	100	11.5
9	3.5	150	14.6
10	3.6	200	16.2
12	4.0	250	18.2
14	4.3	300	19.9
16	4.6	400	22.9
18	4.9	500	25.6
20	5.1	1000	36.2

Light Lists covering the lights of the United States are published by the Treasury Department, United States Coast Guard, in six volumes (CG 158). CG 158 contains the *North Atlantic List, South Atlantic List, Pacific List, Great Lakes List, Intracoastal Waterway List,* and *Mississippi River List.* These lists describe the lighthouses, lightships, radio beacons, and buoys maintained by the Coast Guard in all navigable waters of the United States. The data include the official name of the aid, the characteristics of its light, sound, and radio signals, structural appearance, position, and dimensions for taking angles.

Reduced-Visibility Audio Aids. Fog signals warn of danger when visibility is limited by fog, rain, smoke, or thick weather. They also provide a means of determining position when such conditions exist. There are several devices for this purpose, generally termed "reduced-visibility audio aids." There are reed horns. There are diaphones with low-pitched and high-pitched notes. There are sirens with characteristic rising notes. There are diaphragms, which tremble. As with lights, you should, in a fog, acquaint yourself with the characteristics of the various sound signals which you are likely to pick up, and when one is heard its periods should be timed and compared with those in the *Light Lists* to insure its proper identity.

Finding Your Position

Being able to pinpoint your position at any given time is the purpose of navigation. It is a real science which I spent two years of courses at college learning the many details of. Thankfully, you don't need a great deal of complicated mathematics to do the calculations required for average inshore piloting. (I'm also glad that I don't have to explain it either, because I am afraid that I may have forgotten a great deal of the theory involved.) If you know the basic principles of some of the more common methods, you'll be able to select the systems that are best for your needs.

Cross Bearings. This is the most widely used method of obtaining a fix. (A fix is an accurately known position.) It affords a high degree of accuracy, especially when three bearings can be used for lines of position. The most accurate fixes are those obtained from lines of position that are at a 60- to 90-degree angle from each other and are made from established navigational marks. It is well to remember that whenever possible the navigational mark should be a landmark or a lightship. Buoys may shift position and are relatively hard to locate and identify from small craft. It is most important to be sure that the mark being used for a bearing has been identified properly.

After the bearing is taken on each object quickly, draw the lines on the chart, and find the position of your vessel at their intersection. If three or more cross bearings are taken, it's usually a certainty that all three bearings won't intersect in a point, but rather in a small triangle. The size of the triangle is proportionate to the accuracy of your bearings. The more accurate your plotting, the smaller the triangle formed. In drawing a bearing line on your chart, remember to use the inner (magnetic) compass rose and to correct for deviation.

The Bow-and-Beam Method. In coastwise navigation it isn't always possible to see more than one established navigational mark. One method under this circumstance is the bow-and-beam method illustrated below. The bearings used in this method of obtaining a fix are "relative bearings." The term means that the bearing is in relation to the centerline or keel of the ship. The bow of the vessel, therefore, is considered as being 000 (zero) degrees, whereas the stern is considered as being 180 degrees. Two relative bearings are used in

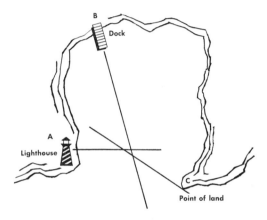

Figure 5-5: The cross-bearing method of finding your position.

this method, 45 degrees and 90 degrees. It makes no difference whether these bearings are taken to the left or right of the bow. The vessel in the illustration has noted the exact time the light bore 45 degrees to port. The time is again noted when the light bears exactly abeam, or at 90 degrees, as at B. The run between points A and B is estimated (see next page), and this distance run is equal to the distance the vessel is off the light when the vessel reaches point B. This holds true only if the vessel maintains the same course throughout the run. A fix can be plotted on the chart with this method by noting that the ship's heading during the run was 064 degrees true. At B, the angle of the bearing was 090 degrees. The line of position then, from B to the light, must be 064 degrees less 090 degrees. In this case, 090 degrees cannot be subtracted from 064 degrees, therefore, add 360 degrees to 064 degrees and then subtract, giving a *true* bearing from the ship to the light of 334 degrees *true*. This line of position is drawn on the chart, then, with a pair of dividers, the distance run along this line is measured from the light to the ship, and a fix is obtained.

The Seven-Tenths Rule. This method makes use of two angles, 22½ and 45 degrees. Here, the time is first noted when the navigational mark bears 22½ degrees off the bow. The time is again noted when the mark bears 45 degrees off the bow. Again, the distance off is equal to the run between bearings. If the vessel maintains course until the mark is directly abeam, the distance off will be seven-tenths the distance run between the first and second bearings. The seven-tenths rule and bow-and-beam bearings are two of the most valuable methods of determining position that are available to the navigator in coastwise navigation. For small boats not equipped with a pelorus, satisfactory results can be obtained if the 22½-degree, 45-degree, and 90-degree points are marked in some manner, both port and starboard. Thumbtacks in the railing, precisely placed, can be used. It's not absolutely necessary to plot the estimated positions.

Danger Bearing. The danger-angle method is used to avoid

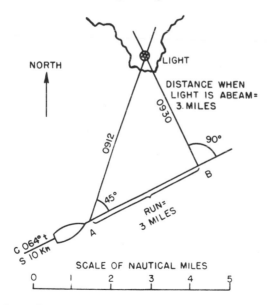

Figure 5-6: The bow-and-beam method of finding your position.

sunken rocks or shoals or other dangers marked on the chart. There are two kinds of danger angles: the horizontal and the vertical. The former requires two well-marked objects indicated on the chart and the latter requires an object of known height. As shown below, the desired course line is CD. A and B are two prominent objects shown on the chart and S and S′ are the danger points through which the

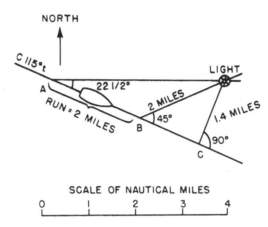

Figure 5-7: The seven-tenths method of finding your position.

ship wishes to pass. Describe a circle around the danger nearest the beach, well clear of the danger. From E, the outermost tangent of this circle, draw lines AE and BE to the objects ashore. The angle AEB is the greatest angle which can safely be reached in making the pass. Describe a similar circle around the outlying shoal. Lines GB and GA are joined, forming the AGB which becomes the minimum angle that can be attained to safely pass the outlying shoal or danger.

The same rule is used in the vertical danger-angle method as in the horizontal danger-angle one, except that an object of known height and distance, such as a lighthouse, is used. Lighthouses are measured from mean high water to center of the light. Allow for the stage of the tide if there is much range.

Ranges and Their Use. When two beacons (or any two objects) appear to be in line as seen from your boat, that is, when one object is directly behind the other, you're located somewhere on the straight line through these objects. Such a line is called a *range* and is the same as a line of position. Frequently two objects are placed so as to form a range that will mark the center of a channel. Your craft is then steered so as to keep the markers in line. As I stated previously, ranges have been established for specific navigational purposes along the coast and within harbors.

Electronic Bearings. Possibly the most valuable aid to foul-weather navigation is the radio direction finder. This electronic device obtains its bearings in a manner similar to a pelorus, but the bearing lines found by operating the RDF are laid out on the chart in the same way as bearing lines determined by eye.

Radio beacons, maintained by the government at frequent intervals all along both coasts and throughout the Great Lakes, operate,

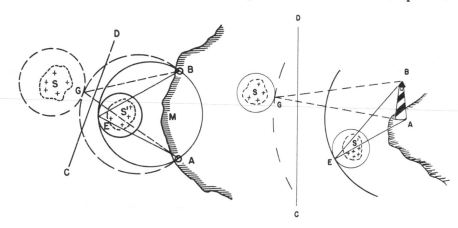

Figure 5-8: The horizontal (left) and vertical (right) danger angles.

in general, for two ten-minute intervals every hour during clear weather and continuously during fog. Operating schedules, wave lengths, and signals are listed in the United States *Light Lists,* and special charts showing their locations are issued by the Coast Guard. No knowledge of code is necessary to use the radio beacons, as the signals are easy to distinguish.

To take a radio bearing, you first set the compass rose on the direction finder's compass to read the same as the course you're steering. Turn on the equipment and allow it to warm up for at least 30 seconds, then tune in the beacon frequency you have selected. Swing the antenna loop until the beacon signal decreases to minimum strength or, perhaps, fades out altogether. This is the "null" point and can be heard by ear with a loudspeaker or headset. Some RFD gear have electrical meters to give a visual indication of the null point. The center of the null area constitutes the bearing

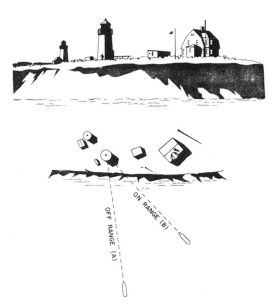

Figure 5-9: A typical range.

line and is indicated when the loop is at right angles to the bearing of the beacon and the indicator on the compass card is pointing directly at it. Extreme care should be employed to make certain that the helmsman is on his course while the bearing is being taken. Because radio beacons in the same area transmit on the same schedule and often on the same wave length, it is possible usually to take several bearings in rapid order and obtain a "fix" position. The deviation of your boat's compass must, of course, be applied to the bearing before laying it on the nautical chart.

An extremely valuable part of radio navigation is *homing,* whereby the boat's head is swung so that the null point of a beacon is just over the bow. If the craft wanders off course, the radio signal will pick up in strength, and the boat must be turned to restore the signal to the null point. By repeating the bearing every time the beacon is transmitting it's easy to run up the beam to the beacon.

Actually this system is so accurate that lightships with beacon-transmitting equipment on board have been rammed by vessels homing on them.

There are four other pieces of gear that often are used in electronic navigation, especially on ocean-going sailing vessels. They are loran, consolan, radar, and the depth finder. (The latter was described in Chapter 1.) In some sailing circles, there is a deplorable insistence on barring electronic equipment—except radio receivers, direction finders, and depth finders—in ocean racing. But for ocean cruising there's no reason why these aids to navigation (loran and radar) shouldn't be employed to their fullest advantage. It is a great deal easier than celestial navigation.

A loran chain consists of two or three radio stations, a "master" and one or two "slaves." These transmitters are located from 200 to 400 miles apart and transmit short pulses simultaneously or offset by a precise time interval. The pulses are repeated between 25 and 35 times per second. The difference in arrival time of signals from a group of loran stations is measured by a loran unit aboard ship. To get a "fix," it is necessary to take readings on two pairs of loran stations or a single three-station loran chain. The ship is located at the point where the hyperbolic curves or distance lines on the loran chart intersect. The daytime range of loran is around 700 miles over water; at night the effective range is about 450 miles, using the direct ground wave from the loran stations. At night, the reflected sky wave permits use at distances up to 1400 miles, but the results are less accurate.

The newest long-range radio navigational aid is consolan, known as "the poor man's loran." Unlike loran, it requires no expensive equipment; unlike RDF it provides a bearing accurate to from 0.3° to 0.7°, and an effective range of 800 miles. (It is not usable within 50 miles.) There are at present only a few stations (Miami, San Francisco, Atlantic City, and Nantucket Island) in or near operational status. In operation, for example, is Nantucket Island which provides an excellent single bearing source from Nova Scotia to Delaware (and is particularly helpful in the Bermuda race). To use it you must have a radio or RDF capable of receiving 194 kc. and an *Airman's Guide* (available from the Hydrographic Office), or HO-205 *Radio Navigational Aids–Consolan.* You then tune in, count the dots, look in two tables, and plot a bearing from Nantucket. A better approach is to take United States Coast and Geodetic Survey Chart 70 and preplot on it a number of consolan lines.

Radar, which could be considered a "weather-penetrating eye," hasn't been fully accepted by sailing men as a piece of their navigating gear. The reason for this may be that this piece of equipment requires quite a bit of room and needs a large special antenna. This would be a source of trouble as far as the sails are concerned. While the gear itself is seldom found on board sailing craft, it's a good idea to carry a radar reflector on the mast of your boat.

Dead Reckoning. For the sailboat enthusiast, the less accurate, and possibly the most difficult, method of determining your position is by a procedure known as "dead reckoning." Here, knowing that you have started from a given point of departure and have traveled in a specific direction for a given length of time at a certain speed, you can lay off a line on the chart from the point of your departure, in the proper direction, for a distance which is supplied through calculation of the speed and the time on your course.

Night Navigation

There are not many yachtsmen who sail at night, but there are numbers who are afraid to. The majority of those who do are men who are forced to stay out, and would, if they could get there, rather be in port snug at anchor and enjoying a good sleep or visiting a new yacht club. But outside of these there are a few who, like myself, enjoy night sailing, and will take a dose of it every chance they get.

In well-charted and well-lighted waters there is little risk of running ashore or of striking shoals or reefs, as the lead or depth finder and the compass or radio direction finder tell the same story by lamplight as they do when the sun is up. The great advantage of night sailing is that it increases your self-confidence as skipper. After a passage through the darkness, when by use of your knowledge you have safely brought your craft into harbor, you feel that you do know something about navigating. Sailing in the daytime, you're constantly able to correct your course by eye, and the compass becomes a mere auxiliary upon which little value is placed as a guide. But at night the compass is at times your sole resource, and must be watched and followed implicitly. Having once followed the needle, and having found that it led you truly to your port, you'll have a strong confidence in its guideship, and a firmer and better opinion of your own ability to use its directive powers.

Before darkness falls a thorough check should be made of all necessary clothing, equipment, and navigation aids. All material not necessary for the night run should be stowed to prevent stumbling over obstacles in the dark. Those things you need should be made accessible, ready for use, preferably in an area which can be lighted without interfering with the helmsman's vision. See that the running lights are in good condition and meet navigational requirements, and remember to turn them on before you start. Have your compass light ready and keep a flashlight or cabin light prepared for use if necessary, but don't plan on going along with all cabin lights blazing or with any lights other than navigation lights showing above deck. This might confuse skippers of other boats as well as impair your own vision. Keep in mind that red utility lights will preserve your night vision. Coat bulbs over chart table or compass with red fingernail polish or use red lamps.

Being able to interpret the lights you see around you is as important as making sure that your craft has the proper lights and that they are in good operating condition. Quick recognition of navigational lights will warn you of possible danger and whether you should swing your boat to port or to starboard. For instance, a red and green combination light or a pair of sidelights, without any white light showing, indicates that you're directly in front of another sailboat. A red and green combination light with a white light above indicates that a powerboat of less than 26 feet in length is approaching. On inland waterways when a pair of red and green side lights and two white lights are seen, the approaching vessel is in excess of 26 feet. In such cases, the white lights can be used as a range, since they are mounted on the centerline of the vessel. Keeping in mind that because the after light is the higher, it's possible to judge the craft's direction by their vertical alignment. When the white lights are in a straight line, the approaching vessel is coming directly toward your boat. When the higher light is to the right, the craft is heading toward your port side; when the higher is to the left, she is bearing toward your starboard. Other possible light arrangements that may be seen can be found on page 21.

When relating the Rules of the Road with the position of an approaching vessel, whether you are under sail or power, remember that when you see a red running light, you're heading into another craft's danger zone. In other words, even when you are under sail and have the right-of-way over a powerboat, it's just good sense to remember the comparison of navigational lights with traffic signals: green means go (right-of-way) and red means stop. When under power, of course, you must follow the Rules of the Road as you do in auxiliary operation during daylight. This includes meeting situations when both craft should veer to the right, or starboard, so each can see the other's red light.

If you see only a moving white light, it means one of two things: either you are approaching the other vessel from the stern (you're both traveling in about the same direction), or the other craft is a rowboat, which isn't required to carry navigation lights. (On the Great Lakes, it could be that you're being approached by a sailboat from abaft the beam.) A steady white light by itself means that a small boat is at anchor. Larger vessels at anchor show more than one white light (the higher one forward). When passing an anchored vessel, remember that the anchor chain may extend out some distance across your course.

Our country's navigational system employs lights in three different colors—red, green, white—to mark obstructions or channels. The night sailor can determine from the chart what light he wants to find, then search in the appropriate direction until he spots it. This is not always easy. Neon store lights on shore, auto headlights, or street lights reflecting off the water or shining through trees can cause confusion. Since perspective is different at night, use a stop watch to identify lights by their characteristics marked on the chart, and stay in the marked channels.

The compass can help you in channels and rivers as well as in open waters. A good sailor uses the compass to check his boat heading when on large bodies of water even in daytime with land in sight. At night the compass is a necessity on oceans or large bays or lakes unless you are an expert at celestial navigation. The stars can be a help, though, even if you're not an expert. Polaris, the North Star, is the sailor's guide, but you can also use other stars by checking your compass reading and then lining up a star with some point of your boat and keeping it in the same relative position. This is easy on the eyes and does away with the necessity for a continuous light on the compass. You must remember, however, that stars do change their apparent position in the heavens, and every ten or fifteen minutes you should check the compass and change your point of alignment or follow another star.

In a channel or river you may not need the compass if you can see the channel markers, buoys, or banks at all times. But if a marker does not appear when you feel it should, a check on the compass can tell if you are still heading in the right direction or if the current or wind has somehow turned the boat so you are heading for danger. If the compass reading is right for your course, then proceed slowly and the marker will probably appear. Remember that lights sometimes get out of order or are obscured by other objects. This may be the case with the one you seek.

Another method of using the compass in rivers or channels is to chart the courses between buoys and then run this course until the buoy or marker is in sight, always keeping in mind the effect of current and wind direction and those little points of land. If you are in shallow water or think you might be, take soundings, or use a depth finder if you have one on board.

Use your ears as well as your eyes. Listen for engine noises from other boats which might be running without lights; for whistles, horns, bells, breakers, water noises of unusual nature, or any other unusual sound. A good hearing aid for listening for night or fog sounds is a megaphone, when the mouthpiece is pressed against your ear. When you can't hear a distant bell buoy because of wind and sea, go below, press your ear to the hull—listen on each side for the stronger sound.

Radio direction finders are a valuable aid to night cruising. They are easy to operate and can be used to take bearings, fix positions, and to "home in on the beam." If you plan to do much night cruising in open waters they are certainly worth their price.

The skipper who always comes to port at sundown misses one of the most exciting and pleasurable parts of sailing. And the sailor who *must* be tied up before dark because he's not prepared for it is taking a serious chance, in case circumstances delay his port-coming. With a little preparation and practice, night navigation can be just as accurate as daylight piloting. And the pleasure of a sail under the stars can be unforgettable.

6

The Lure of Cruising

Whether you own a small or a large sailboat and have a couple of days or a month to spend afloat, you'll get more pleasure and enjoyment from your craft by taking a cruise in her during the sailing season. No other form of vacationing can compare with it for healthful sport and relaxation as well as freedom from worrisome details. There's no need of wiring ahead for reservations, riding in crowded trains, buses, or airliners, or putting in a long stretch at the wheel of the family car. You don't have to worry about poor food or sleeping accommodations at hotels or motels. With a boat, all you have to do is get your equipment aboard and, with your family or friends, shove off for any place that looks good on the charts. You may only get ten miles away from your home port, but you'll be in strange waters and when you drop anchor in some quiet cove and enjoy a delicious meal before turning in, that day will be long remembered.

Types of Cruising

There are basically two types of cruises: short and distance cruises. The former may be for a day, overnight, or a weekend, and may be in either a day-sailer or a cruising-style sailboat. Usually, day-sailers have roomy cockpits, and some have a cuddy cabin which provides a wonderful arrangement for overnighting, protection from the weather, and storage space for gear. If you wish more covered area, especially when at anchor, boom tents are available. Your local marine dealer will be glad to show you the type that is best for your boat and tell you how to install it. You can also rig an awning over the boom, with one end supported by the mast. If you plan to use such an awning, you should test it thoroughly beforehand, as it's not easy to rig one in such a way that it will stand up to wind and rain without letting in drafts and drops of wet. As for sleeping accommodations, there's room generally for one to four persons, depending on the size of the craft. Waterproof sleeping bags generally are recommended, but if you are the rugged type, rolling up in a blanket will provide all the luxury you will need. The fresh air and exercise of the day will make any bed feel soft. If you wish, you can sleep ashore under a tent or in a sleeping bag on the ground. In a pinch, you can empty the boat of all gear, drag her ashore, turn her over, prop up the leeward side, and sleep underneath. This hardly spells comfort, but at least it assures one of shelter in the worst of weather.

In a true cruiser-style sailboat, all the comforts of home (or almost all) are available. They have berths to sleep in, galley space, toilet (head, as it is called at sea) facilities, and stowage lockers for clothing and gear. For example, let's look at the "livability" features of a 28-foot cruiser. To enhance the cheerful convenience and comfort below decks (six feet of headroom in the main cabin), the lady of the family frequently has a choice from a wide selection of decorator colors. Actually, she can personalize the interior to reflect her individual tastes, blending combinations to best advantage. With her interior decorating skills thus displayed, the mate will thrill to her beautiful home at sea season after season. During extended cruising, the following features, as shown in the next illustration, add to the comfortable "livability": a stainless steel sink; a fully insulated, self-draining icebox accessible from cockpit or below; large hanging locker; six electric lights; stowage space under and behind bunks; linen locker; dish rack; four shelves. Bilge may be used for canned goods stowage. Three large stowage areas in cockpit area for life jackets, lines, winch handles, sails, and other gear.

Generally, as the cruiser-racer becomes larger, and more expensive, the features of "livability" also increase. A typical 41-footer, for instance, has over six-foot headroom throughout; six berths; convenient hanging lockers, drawers, and cabinets; large, roomy en-

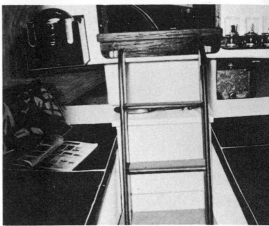

Figure 6-1: The 23-foot sailboat (left) has the fine living accommodations shown looking aft (top, right) and forward (bottom, right).

closed head with basin, mirror, and room for optional shower; a spacious galley with large fiberglass icebox; stainless steel two-burner alcohol stove; and beautiful, stainless steel sink and drainboard. Bulkheads are luxurious, wood-grained laminated plastic. I could go on describing various features of cruisers for the rest of the pages allotted to me, but rather than do this, I'll just say that the size of your boat has nothing to do with the amount of fun you and your family can have. Even small open prams have a world of possibilities for young fellows who don't mind roughing it a bit. Many teen-agers have cruised for hundreds of miles along sheltered waterways, sleeping under a cockpit tent and cooking their chow on the beach.

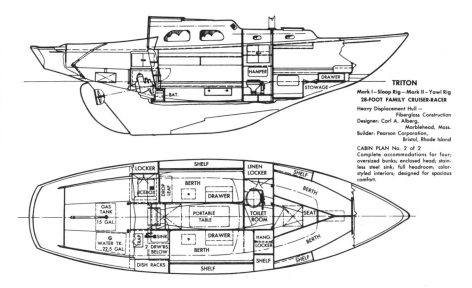

TRITON

Mark I – Sloop Rig – Mark II – Yawl Rig
28-FOOT FAMILY CRUISER-RACER

Heavy Displacement Hull –
Fiberglass Construction
Designer: Carl A. Alberg,
Marblehead, Mass.
Builder: Pearson Corporation,
Bristol, Rhode Island

CABIN PLAN No. 2 of 2
Complete accommodations for four;
oversized bunks; enclosed head; stainless steel sink; full headroom; color-
styled interiors; designed for spacious
comfort.

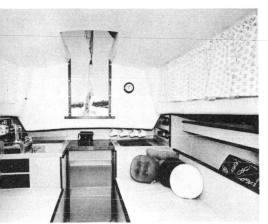

Figure 6-2: The cabin plan of a 28-foot racer-cruiser (top) and the interior—aft (bottom, left) and forward (bottom, right).

Planning a Cruise

Getting down to the mechanics of cruising itself, the main idea is to plan the cruise *most* carefully. All members of the family should engage in all of the cruise planning, and plans should incorporate the widest possible variety of things to do so as to include interest for each member of the cruise party. But, don't try to cover too much distance or plan too rigid a schedule at the sacrifice of leisurely cruising. More cruises have been ruined for the crew by the skipper's insistence that the boat arrive in a certain place a particular day. Don't spoil everyone's fun by doing this. Remember that you're out for rest and recreation. Otherwise you'll probably arrive back home dead beat and in need of a second vacation. And don't feel that you have to spend every minute of those two weeks aboard the boat. Lay over in some friendly little harbor for a day or two and go ashore to see the local points of interest, have dinner, and maybe take in a movie or summer stock production. You'll find that such a procedure will keep everyone happy on a long cruise.

Where to go, at least in part, will be determined by the amount of time at your disposal. But, as I just stated above, distance to be covered by the entire cruise and for any given day should be kept flexible. These two statements are not contradictory. Plan ahead, but also expect to change your plans somewhat to conform to items of interest that arise and other factors, including weather and water conditions. Remember that with a sailboat, it is sometimes difficult to judge your speed and time of arrival. However, unless you have an auxiliary on board, you'll want to be certain of a harbor within sailing distance before sundown. You should keep in mind that the wind has a general habit of dropping with the sun, and frequently if you have not made port by that time, you'll find yourself becalmed for the night within tantalizing view of shore. If you don't make it to the desired port, you should be able to select, from your United States Coast and Geodetic Survey charts, unfamiliar harbors with good assurance of what to expect in the way of approach, anchorage, and even dock facilities.

If it's vital that you receive mail, as it is in my case, check in advance for the names of major marinas or yacht clubs along your cruise route and have mail addressed to you care of these locations. Ask senders to mark envelopes "Please hold for arrival." Also, a number of the major gasoline companies offer mail port service to the cruising yachtsmen. Contact the marine division of the firm whose products you generally use, and ask for a list of their marine service stations on your cruise route. Be sure to inform those writing you to include a return address and the number of days the letter should be held pending your arrival. Yachtsmen expecting mail after their departure from a mailing location may leave their estimated arrival dates at points ahead and the mail port operator will usually be glad to forward letters to meet them.

Since most of our pets are land-based animals, they generally don't care too much for cruising. There are, of course, exceptions. I have a dog that just loves to sail; and the longer the cruise, the better. But, unless you have had previous experience in carrying small pets aboard your boat and the animal is used to and enjoys cruising, you are better off to board pets with your local veterinarian.

Since the real success or failure of a cruise can often depend to a great degree on the personnel of the crew, it is worthy of some discussion. When a person first takes up the fine sport of cruising, he regards his yacht as a source of entertainment for all, and invites his friends without discretion. Sometimes he even invites business associates and uses the craft for business purposes or functions that may prove helpful to him in business. For afternoon sailing or an overnight afloat, it may be a desirable policy; but a long cruise is a different story. As one gets more experienced in the art of cruising, the more it becomes evident that cruising companions must be selected with the greatest of care, and that by no means everyone is capable of going along on a cruise. There is no more searching test of character than a cruise, since it seems to bring out abnormal traits in most people. For instance, that bright sunny soul from the office may turn out to be a chronic grouch after you've been out a few days. He may want to sleep late when you'd planned to start at the crack of dawn each day; or he has his own ideas about where you should cruise, and if you don't follow them, you may get the old "silent" treatment. There's nothing like the close quarters of a 28-foot sailboat to bring out the good and bad points of your friends and relatives. So play safe and choose your cruising companions with care if you expect to remain on friendly terms after a junket of a week or two.

If your boat runs to any considerable length, you'll have another problem involving people, and that is how large a party to take on a cruise. There's no hard-and-fast rule for this, but one thing is certain. Don't think you've got to fill every berth you have aboard as well as sleeping people on the cockpit cushions. Too many members in the crew will slow up working the boat, besides making too much work for the first mate—your wife—bending over a hot stove below decks.

There's an old saying that for every day you're at sea the boat seems to get smaller. It's a good one to remember when you're planning a cruise.

Cruising Gear

A good deal of the success of any cruise depends upon having the proper equipment on board. For instance, if you're prepared for it, rough or rainy weather will be part of the adventure. If you're not prepared, the first cold, rainy day can easily douse the spirits of your crew. I'm not one of those who believes in the old theory of "traveling light." I don't think that it's the best approach. There is more danger that you'll take too little than too much; there's more likelihood that you'll neglect your comfort than be ever-thoughtful of it. But because every pleasure craft has its limitations for gear storage, the experienced yachtsman knows that what to leave behind is just as important as what to take. The newcomer to cruising should make an inventory of all items he would like to take and should then go over the list several times, eliminating those items not wholly essential to the safety, comfort, and pleasure of those taking the cruise. The gear required by law and for safety was mentioned in Chapter 1, while the navigating equipment was fully discussed in Chapter 5.

Cruising Clothes. While I'm not a believer in the "minimum amount of clothing" theory, it's not necessary to have a full wardrobe aboard your boat for every member of your crew. The growth of automatic laundries along popular cruise routes has been little short of phenomenal lately, and this will allow you to keep clean with a minimum of clothing. I usually hunt up the laundromat as soon as we hit a port, let the stuff wash while my crew and I explore.

To tell a woman what to wear is no task for a man, so I asked my wife, Virginia, for her advice, and she claims that sportswear manufacturers have made it easy for the first mate to prove to the skipper that she's no landlubber. No need to lose your femininity when you leave the ruffles and frills at home. Sleek lines, bright colors, and wrinkle-free fabrics will keep you looking as crisp and pretty at the end of the day as you did when you climbed aboard that morning—despite the effects of wind and spray. Boat wear now being made is a blessing for the comfort-minded young woman with an eye toward practicality. Unhampered by full-skirted dresses, you'll move about the craft with ease in boy-pants ranging in length from above-the-knee Jamaica shorts to long slim-jim slacks. A pair of well-fitted, rubber-soled boat shoes are probably the most indispensable item in a woman's sailing wardrobe. If you can't find them at boat dealers, try city department stores or suburban shops in boating areas. Boat shoes come in pumps and oxfords, and in a choice of colors. They can be worn with socks, peds, or over bare feet, as you prefer. In addition, be sure to bring along a sweater or light windbreaker in case of a sudden change in the weather. Chill bumps are no fun, and you'll be far more attractive buttoned up in a jacket than huddled under an old blanket. Also, as you know, a boat isn't the place for showing off your newest coiffure, so hide those unruly curls under a scarf or one of those popular straw hats that serve a dual purpose of also protecting you from the sun.

When going ashore to eat out or to go to a dance at a visiting yacht club, the first mate will wish to dress up. According to Ginny, she says she seldom has found an occasion to wear anything more elaborate than a nylon tricot dress. But make certain that it has a full skirt—tight skirts and teetering heels have no place on a boat or a dock. Carry a dressy white sweater to wear over it in air-conditioned restaurants and movies. The dress and sweater can also serve as a go-to-church-on-Sunday outfit. Bring a pair of white heels, but carry these shoes ashore in a plastic bag, and, once on land, change into them. When you get back to the dock, put on your boat shoes. Take plain summer jewelry to wear with shore clothes, but don't wear it while under way. If you wish, carry a small, crushproof hat in a plastic bag; tuck a pair of white gloves inside a flat purse, and you'll be ready for less informal emergencies.

While the first mate can be a fashion plate—a seaworthy one, however—if she desires, we males have no clothes problems. All we need is a pair of denim pants, Bermuda shorts, a couple of sport shirts, a sweater, a windbreaker, a long-visored boating cap or hat, underwear, socks, and a pair or two of rubber-soled boat shoes, plus one shore outfit—sport jacket, trousers, tie, shirt, and shoes. Formal yachtsman's dress is discussed in Chapter 10.

All members of your crew—and this includes the children—should have a suit of foul-weather gear on board. But, when selecting the suits, consider the type of sailing you're going to do and the locale.

In general, fabrics used in the better foul-weather suits are light to wear, pliable in varying degrees, don't crack or peel in sun or salt, don't stiffen in cold climates; are odorless; and are impervious to the effects of fuels and most chemicals. The zipper and other fittings on a good suit are made of either noncorroding metal or plastic. In spite of long-wearing qualities of the fabric in the suit you select, the foul-weather gear deserves to be properly dried after use and the salt rinsed off before prolonged storage.

As for the style of your foul-weather gear, this is a matter of preference. Some yachtsmen like an attached hood; others like sou'wester hats, claiming that the hood impedes hearing and view. The slip-on style of jacket is preferred by many as being the most water-shedding, while others prefer a fly front closing jacket, as easier to get in and out of. Trousers come either with suspenders or waist tie, and most suits have wrist and ankle fastenings of some type to keep water out. Boots, half- or full-length, may be worn as foul-weather footgear. But, regardless of the style, be sure that it is large enough to accommodate heavy clothing underneath when needed for warmth, and still allows plenty of freedom of movement. This means less wear and tear on the seams and provides the necessary insulation and ventilation within the suit. By the way, most suits have ventilation holes to provide some circulation of air so that the wearer will perspire less in warm weather. It is a good idea to have a couple of cheap clear plastic suits on board. They make fine auxiliary suits for occasional guests and for limited activity.

You must also guard against the sun. As a matter of fact, sunburn can quickly spoil a sailing weekend. The best protection comes with treatment before exposure and moderation of exposure early in the season. New oils, creams, and lotions are reported to completely block out the direct burning rays plus the severe water reflections, or screen them so that tanning progresses slowly. Another point to keep in mind is that every member of the crew should have a pair of good sunglasses.

Before leaving the subject of clothing, remember that suitcases are awkward to store aboard a boat and good luggage may also be damaged by the dampness. Save weight and space by packing all clothing gear in sea or duffel bags. An extra duffel bag or two will be handy for storing soiled clothing and will serve to lug groceries or carry laundry to laundromats.

Figure 6-3: A family all dressed up in their foul-weather gear.

Galley Gear. When the anchor is down or you're tied up to a pier, you and your crew will suddenly discover that everyone is hungry. Out in the open air with the wind and motion of the boat, appetites build to enormous proportions. A good galley stove is the key to wonderful meals afloat. But, like so many other things marine, the stove is somewhat different from its shoreside counterpart. Actually, the only stove that should ever be used on a boat is one of the types approved for marine use.

While some cruising sailboats use bottled gas, and a *very* few have electric ranges, the most popular by far with sailboat people is the alcohol stove. While alcohol stoves are available in several different types and styles, all burn gum-free, denatured ethyl alcohol. *Never* use methyl (wood) alcohol because it will clog the burners and give off highly poisonous fumes. The alcohol should be stored in metal cans because glass containers could break, spilling the contents into the bilge. Most marine stores package it in metal containers. When filling the tank, be sure to carefully use the filter-equipped funnel, which not only helps prevent spillage, but also traps dirt and lint, which might clog the burners. It goes without saying that the flame should be out and the burners cool when filling the tank.

The maintenance of most marine stoves is an easy task. Keep the outside clean, so that you won't have an unexpected grease fire from the surface accumulation. Occasionally tighten the fuel-line connections. Should an alcohol stove start to kick up a little trouble, the first thing to do is to clean out the generator brush. This is a long spiral-wound wire brush through which the fuel passes on its way to the valve. On some models, the brush comes out the front and on others it can be removed in the rear. In either case, the cap is removed first and the brush worked back and forth a few times, then taken out and immersed in a container of clean alcohol, shaking to remove the dirt. Don't slap the brush against any hard surfaces to knock the dirt loose, for this will bend and damage it. Replace the brush and tighten the cap and you'll generally find that you have cured the trouble.

No galley is too small for a refrigerator. Regardless of the stowage problem on your sailboat, there's a food-cooling arrangement that will suit your needs. There are two basic types:—mechanical and nonmechanical. The latter—the kind you fill up with natural ice or chemical "ice"—are adequate for most of us and is the type installed by most sailboat builders. In such iceboxes, generally three or four cans of patent sealed refrigerant that has been prefrozen in your home refrigerator, plus a fifty-cent piece of ice, will keep it cold enough to preserve anything for a three- or four-day period of time. To keep iceboxes smelling sweet and to prevent various foods from picking up the flavor from other foods stored with them, add a mesh bag of charcoal to the box. Periodically replace the charcoal in the bag with a fresh batch. Charcoal can be deodorized and refreshed by heating at high temperature over a stove or in an oven.

While the icebox is still the most popular with sailboat people, the increased use of alternators and generators has made mechanical refrigeration possible. If your kind of sailing justifies mechanical refrigeration, and it's within your budget, there are several such units

Figure 6-4: Alcohol-burning galley stoves: a two-burner model (top) and a three-burner type (bottom). Note how both are set on gimbals. This is almost a requirement if you plan to cook while under way in a sailboat.

available, and there is a good possibility that one can be installed in place of your present icebox. A mechanical refrigeration system has two basic components. One is the evaporator, which is located in the cold compartment. The other is the condensing unit, which is the compressor, condensor, and other parts such as the receiver. This component is located outside the cold compartment and has the moving parts.

Your pots and pans should be of stainless steel, since they are more easily cleansed and are far easier to maintain than other types. (Aluminum is cheaper and is a good second choice.) A pressure cooker will save fuel and, once mastered, will also save cooking time and thus give the first mate more chance to be on deck. If you like toast you can have it readily by getting one of those collapsible top-of-the-burner toasters at any good hardware store; this type of toaster is inexpensive but efficient. If your stove is equipped with an oven, or should you have one of the new portable stove-top burner ovens, there will be many times when cooking while under way will be less of a burden than otherwise. A casserole or other dish placed in the oven is less liable to get into difficulties because of balance problems than if perched on top of a stove. Use plastic glasses and plates and you have eliminated broken glass and crockery, which can be such a hazard on the water. There are also all sorts of plastic containers for your refrigerator stowage.

When you selected your boat you gave thought, of course, to a fresh-water tank of adequate capacity. The abundance of docks and marinas where fresh water is available in the modern age of the sail almost completely eliminates the possibility of a water shortage except when far offshore or when ocean-racing. Pressure and water-heating equipment is also no longer the problem it was to sailing yachtsmen even a few years ago. Pressure systems, if not already aboard your boat, are easily installed and are not overly expensive. There are several hot-water heating systems available, too. In our boats we generally use a system in which the water is heated by electricity while tied up at a dock and is heated by the auxiliary engine while afloat.

The heart of the cook's galley outfit is a kit of essentials that might, in your case, include toothpicks and bromo. Among the items that ought to be in your do-all kit are a good clamp-on screw-type hand can opener; metal foil for pan lids, cooking and food wrapping;

paper toweling for pan cleaning, drying, and, in a pinch, beach-fire starting; salt, pepper, and matches, each stowed in a small plastic or break-resistant glass bottle (try your drugstore for these); sugar, in a tight-closing, gasketed can or jar; detergent, also in a tight-closing plastic container; plastic dishpan; bottle opener; a Thermos jug or other similar vacuum bottle; a copper or plastic mesh pan scraper, and ice tongs or ice-carrying bag. Speaking of bags, you'll need various sizes of paper bags on board. For the garbage, the waxed bags are best. You'll want a plastic garbage can into which the garbage bags fit snugly, preferably one whose cover closes automatically either by gravity or a spring mechanism. You'll think of other items that should be in the galley: patent oyster opener; ice pick; combination fish scaler, corkscrew, olive fork, and carrot peeler.

For the boatkeeping (housekeeping) tasks, be sure to keep on hand a supply of chrome cleaner and polish, copper wool, stain remover, turpentine, grease solvent, bleach, and furniture polish and oil. But the basic requirements for an efficient galley afloat are to keep things reasonably simple, to keep a careful check on your gear, and if you must cook an elaborate meal, do it while you are safely moored in a harbor or tied up at a pier rather than under way in unpredictable conditions. Ideas on seagoing provisions and menu-making can be found in the next chapter.

The Dinghy. One essential part of your cruising equipment will be the dinghy or tender—whichever you wish to call it. The dinghy can be employed to run errands—to a dock to buy supplies, to take the family crew to a beach for a swim or cookout, to a lobster or fishing boat to buy the makings of a gala dinner, and to go fishing at a good location that may be a short distance from the anchorage. Also, if your boat goes aground, the tender can be used to carry an anchor out so the boat can be kedged free (see page 296). When equipped with a small outboard motor, a dinghy becomes an auxiliary. If the engine on your auxiliary conks out—or if powered only by sails, should the wind depart—the tender can tow her into a harbor or up to a dock. If the dinghy is equipped with a sail, it is an extra source of pleasure, especially for the youngsters. But, whether rowed, powered, or sailed, the tender widens the horizon for exploration. It can go into little creeks and inlets where larger craft can't venture. It also provides excellent basic training in seamanship. If the tender is of fiberglass, it will require little maintenance.

On the debit side, any dinghy can be somewhat of a nuisance to tow, and equally a nuisance to stow aboard. In towing, your boat's speed can be cut down as much as half a knot. In running before a following sea, a tender will sometimes try to climb aboard, and the rest of the time there's a yanking strain on the painter and the tender's stem. In maneuvering around a dock, there's always the chance that the painter will get wound around your prop. At anchor,

Figure 6-5: A dinghy is almost a must while cruising. It has the advantage of being a source of pleasure for the junior members of your crew as well as being a means of getting ashore. It can be rowed (left), powered by a small outboard, or sailed (right). It makes a fine tender when the sails are taken down and stored on the cruiser sailboat.

with the wind and current in any conflict, the dinghy is always fighting the big boat. The towing problem can be solved to a degree if you purchase a tender that is especially designed for this purpose. There are a couple on the market that are made for use with cruising sailboats and they have proven quite successful.

The best place to "tow" your dinghy is on deck; but if you haven't the room nor facilities to stow it on deck, or atop the cabin roof, it has to be towed. The following rules apply to towing the average round-bottom tender:

1. Your dinghy will tow best when the painter (towline) is made fast to the stem just above the waterline. Always lash your oars and

rowlocks in the boat before towing. If you employ a motor, bring it aboard the towing craft.

2. Pay out the painter to get the dinghy riding on the down side of the second wave. Hold the line in your hand and adjust its length until you feel the least amount of strain. A small boat towed incorrectly will reduce your speed a good deal.

3. See that your painter is renewed now and then, and in good shape for towing. In heavy weather bend on an extra line. And should the dinghy fill, haul her alongside on the lee side. Put a man into her with a line around him. Bail it out. Then try towing her on a short painter close under the stern, where the water may be smoother and where the upward pull of the line to the larger boat may keep the bow up high enough to stop the dinghy from shipping water. If the dinghy tries to climb aboard your boat in a following sea, give her a docking line to trail in a loop from her stern. The drag of the line will stop the tender's rushes before they begin.

When loading your dinghy, first have someone sit amidships, preferably yourself if you're rowing from amidships; then place your heaviest person forward and the two lighter ones in the stern, always keeping a little more weight aft than forward. Distribute supplies and luggage in the same manner, but don't overload her with either people or supplies. After loading your dinghy take careful note of the amount of freeboard she has. Just because she is still afloat doesn't mean the tender isn't overloaded. There should be sufficient freeboard to allow for the pitching or rolling of the dinghy as a result of the action of the waves and current or of passengers shifting their weight. Remember that no one should be permitted to stand up or try to walk around in a tender. Once your dinghy reaches her destination, there are two things that you should keep in mind. First, don't let anyone in the tender lean out and grab for the boat or dock and upset the balance. Second, unload in the reverse sequence from that in which you loaded.

Other Cruising Gear. The choice of materials is important for any boat accessory. For curtains, for example, the only fabric that should be used from a safety standpoint is fiberglass, because it is noncombustible. It is also easy to care for and can be had in a number of designs and attractive colors. Curtains are useful for filtering hot sunlight and are indispensable for privacy. With any but very short curtains you get the trimmest, neatest effect by using rods at

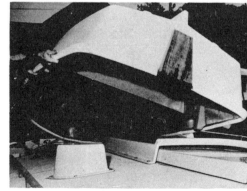

Figure 6-6: A tender can be towed, but note how low the towline is tied (top). A dinghy can also be stored aboard the mother ship (bottom left). Here are special mounting blocks that make the job much easier (bottom right).

both top and bottom. (Methods for installing curtain rods are given later.) Materials are also important in the choice of the ubiquitous seat cushion. This is probably the most common boat accessory, but it's seldom exploited to full advantage. Nautical quarters are at best compact, and more often crowded, and no accessory that's capable of performing two functions should be allowed to perform just one. It's pretty redundant to sit on nonbuoyant cushions and stuff the probably-insufficient storage space that's available with the life preservers required by law and good sense.

The type of bunk that you'll sleep on will be predetermined for you by the boat you have purchased. Built-in bunks today are generally equipped with foam-rubber mattresses. (A few sailors—I'm not one of them—like air mattresses because they also serve as sunbathing platforms, swimming rafts, and even aquaplanes.) The bedding should include at least two mildew-proof synthetic or wool blankets (I prefer the latter) per person. Take along sheets—single-bed size—and small pillows and pillow cases. A few cruising people that I know like to sleep in sleeping bags in bunks rather than to bother with sheets and blankets. Always air and dry your bedding on deck the first thing in the morning. Dampness has a habit of getting entrenched aboard a boat—and can become almost incurable unless caught early. Dry all damp bedding and clothing at every opportunity; never stow anything that's wet.

In addition to all the equipment you must have on board for safety and comfort, you may want hobby gear, cameras, fishing tackle, sketch pads, musical instruments, record player, portable TV, and games. Keep them as compact as possible and try to quarter them together. The tackle box for lures, gadget bag for photographic items, etc., is the best arrangement. Also bring along a supply of games to occupy children passengers. More on this can be found in the next chapter.

For a long time, I had difficulty with the ship's office. Registration papers, travel checks, credit cards, canal permits, customs, stamps (including special delivery and air mail), and stationery were always getting wet or lost until I thought of those plastic briefcase envelopes. Reading is another pleasure in the relaxed atmosphere of a cruise. Thus, your boat should have a bookshelf—for a few necessary nautical books like the tide and pilot books, for a good first-aid book, for some instructional books on navigation or the techniques of racing, and for general reading.

Fall Cruising

There is a day—in September or October, depending on the latitude—when the sky breaks hard and clear in the morning and a west wind rattles the first drying leaves down onto the streets of waterfront towns. It's at about that time that many sailors reckon that the sailing season has come to an end. Likely the first real fall day is the day they unload their craft and take them around to the yard to be

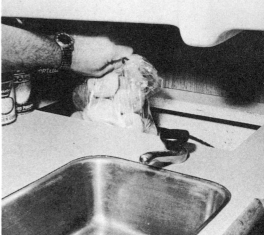

Figure 6-7: A well-designed sailboat uses all available space for storage—especially for food. The bilge—which in a fiberglass hull is always dry as compared with a wooden one—can be used (left) or behind the sink (right).

hauled out for the winter. It's always a rather melancholy occasion, the end of the sailing summer. But there are yachting families who have found out that, for them, this is the finest season of all. The days start crisp and cool, the nights really call for blankets—and in between, there is often some of the finest weather you'll find on the water from one end of the year to the other.

Living tends to be worthwhile at this time of year. It can blow and rain, and the wind has more of an edge to it. But with a little extra thought for changed conditions, you may find that you can extend your sailing into this new season with unexpected rewards—with new depth in the pleasure of your cruising. The responsibility of the skipper, however, begins with the safety of his boat, as always. Any sailboat skipper watches the weather carefully before and during the time he is on the water. In the fall, there are special conditions to watch for. For example, while quick thundersqualls are uncommon in the fall, a clear northwest day may develop into a howler with stinging winds and crested seas. Such weather may follow a blue sky, with no warning dip in the barometer. In fact, such an overwindy day (sometimes, but rarely, you meet something like them in summer) usually comes with a clear sky and rising barometer. You won't want to start playing with such a day on the theory that the wind will go down at midday or die with the sun. Such winds rarely do this. They stop in their own good time, and not until then. Beware of the clear breezy morning in July or August; it only heralds a cooler and livelier day.

The strength and persistence of autumn winds compared with normal summer winds are the two changed weather elements that the skipper of a sailboat must watch and weigh most carefully against the capabilities of his craft. As pointed out, what might be a clear breezy day in summer may turn out altogether too breezy for your craft in the fall. This is because the increased air density in cooler weather makes whatever wind is blowing act with greater force against your boat. As wind speeds get higher this difference between cool autumn winds and hot summer winds gets more pronounced. Keep in mind, when you form your opinion of the day's conditions, the fact that fall winds keep blowing more briskly and don't die so easily. Winds of about 10 knots or over, which begin to make occasional white crests on waves away from shore, are winds to watch. If they get harder during the morning it's quite likely that they will go on getting harder in the afternoon. Winds of 18 to 20 knots or over, which hum in wire rigging, are a signal for real caution to any open-cockpit sailboat. The frequent crested seas you will see in the morning at wind strengths of about this speed may well turn menacing if the wind pipes up another 5 or 10 knots during the course of the day. Thus, while you should trust the weather reports for a general indication of what you may reasonably expect, add your own personal observation of local conditions (see Chapter 4).

Since fall winds are often chilly winds, you and your crew should dress to be warm in the weather that is to be expected. When chosen with care, and with the selection based on well-established principles, clothes will provide maximum warmth with minimum weight. And it should be kept in mind that even on those prespring or post-autumn days of high-noon warmth and pellucidity, early mornings and late afternoons will offer sharp temperature contrasts, and chal-

Figure 6-8: While one of the oldest methods, the small stove at the left is still one of the best ways of taking the chill off a cabin.

lenge the versatility and adaptability of the seagoing wardrobe. At one time the accepted rule for warmth was to pile on as much clothing as possible, the heavier the better. Now it is known that bulk is not synonymous with warmth. A few thin layers, which can be peeled or put on according to changing temperature, are a great deal more efficient. The secret is to use the right materials, and modern manufacturers have come up with an array intriguing enough to warm the heart as well as the blood. Men may not care how they look, but if the mates can keep cozy without looking like refugees from an igloo, they will be a lot more enthusiastic about extraseasonal sailing.

Fall boating, north or south, is more enjoyable with a small amount of heat in the boat, particularly during the early morning or late afternoon hours. Since there are almost as many kinds of boat heaters as classes of boats, it is usually possible to select a heating arrangement suited to your particular needs, and some can double as air conditioners as well. The heating arrangement can be simple and cheap, or complex and expensive, according to your desires and needs. Check with your local marine dealer for the one that is best for your yacht and budget.

Group Cruising

Most of us cruise alone. We are content with family or invited guests aboard when we "get away from it all." This may be fine if we truly need separation from others. But often we most need relaxation in the presence of others. For this try organized group cruising; not just two or three boats but a gathering of ten or fifteen. Such mass cruises are gaining popularity. Why? The exhilaration of flotilla movement on a selected course, the evening comradeship at moorage or anchorage, the fun of sharing an experience from advance planning to final tie-up—these are the basic pleasures of group cruising.

The increased safety factor, and new formation of lasting friendships—these are the bonuses. Group cruising, incidentally, is a fine activity for weaning the timid skipper from day cruising only, to the adventure of extended cruising. Often veteran yachtsmen and qualified skippers, many of them graduates of several sailboat-handling and navigation courses, hesitate to embark upon an extended cruise alone. Yet extended cruising is to sailing as the onion is to hash and as the olive is to a martini: something that can't be explained, only savored.

In general, the group cruise is arranged under the auspices of a yacht club or a sailing club, and is open to all the members of that club. Not infrequently such cruises are also invitation affairs, and members of other clubs and sometimes sailboat skippers who are

Figure 6-9: A group of boats under way (top), and the fun at the end of a day's run (bottom). Triton owners, as a class, do a great deal of group cruising.

members of no club at all can arrange to be invited. Sometimes group cruises, are organized in races from port to port, as described in Chapter 9. In such cases, however, the essence of a cruise is the really important thing, and the racing merely adds a touch of interest.

While group cruising is usually delightfully informal, a well-organized cruise may have such affairs as clambakes, dinners, dances, and all sorts of pleasant festivities arranged at the different ports. When the anchor is down there is always a great deal of visiting between the different boats, too. All in all, the organized group cruise forms one of the most attractive phases of yachting activities.

7

Living Afloat

When your adventurous spirit moves you to pack up the necessary gear, get the whole family on board, and shove off for a real cruise, then you will have experienced the most pleasure and satisfaction that your sailboat can offer. But, to make any cruise a real success, everyone on board must cooperate; your home afloat is somewhat like a small efficiency apartment—some boats are like a very small one—in that to some degree privacy and freedom to move around are temporarily curtailed. While all the taken-for-granted comforts aren't built into your boat, this is more than offset by the wonderful new experiences shared by everyone on board and relived in many animated conversations.

Cruising Routine

One of the most essential things on any cruise is that the work of your vessel shouldn't be neglected, and it is the lack of the day-by-day boatkeeping and care of the craft that can quickly negate all the enjoyment of cruising. There is no question about the fact that cruising offers a splendid opportunity for long, lazy hours of sheer relaxation and physical comfort, but when the lazy hours dominate all and the care of your boat is neglected, you make more work for yourself in the end. The easiest way to keep up with the task of boat-keeping, as well as the other duties about the boat, is to conform to

186

an exacting routine. This routine will make the work seem easy and makes the boat much more livable. Thus, before starting out on any cruise, set a routine for yourself and your crew (this includes the children). This will make the voyage easier, smoother in operation, less demanding, and safer. Assignment of shipboard duties—anchoring, cooking, boatkeeping, and the like—beforehand gives each crew member time to understand his particular job and prepare for it.

For the average family vacation cruise the routine may be divided into two general departments: navigating and steward's. The navigating department, under the command of the skipper, is responsible for operation of the craft while under way; speed and course; handling of sails and helm; operation of engine (if an auxiliary); and anchorage. The steward's department duties, under the command of the first mate, should include maintaining sufficient food supplies; preparation of meals; obtaining fresh food, ice, smoker's supplies, and liquid refreshments; boatkeeping below deck; making-up of berths; replacement of galley and cabin gear; laundry or laundry service; stove maintenance; and ship's mail.

Cruising Records

Keeping a log is considered a dull, dry chore by the majority of yachtsmen who bother with it at all. And yet it can be made a very interesting and even instructive part of cruising if you go at it in the proper way. The failure of most yachtsmen to keep logs is due in part to the nature of the very log sheets themselves. They are, for the most part, either too blank or too cluttered up with a lot of columns for meteorological data which will never be used, and present such an imposing appearance that they scare the amateur skipper off. Many are too small for proper handwriting space; many are too big for convenient handling. Some are too frivolous and have no room for proper navigational data, being disfigured with drawings of anchors, mermaids, and blocked off squares for photographs and the vaporings of idle guests. A good log, which can be purchased at most marine dealers, should be a combination of space for navigational notes and room for more informal stuff. The most satisfactory form as far as I am concerned is one with a page for entries on one hand and a blank page opposite for additional notes, comments, sketches of landmarks or interesting shore scenes, notes on the doings of the party, and photographs of ships, men, and ports encountered at the time. There should be only one log sheet for every twenty-four hours and one opposite blank "sketch page" to correspond. A logbook should be printed on paper reasonably water resistant and should not include much over fifty pages. The hourly data sheet should be at the left as you open it up, and the blank page on the right. When not in use, keep the log wrapped in a neoprene bag.

Keeping a log is like everything else. You have to get into the swing of it before you find much fun in it. But there is fun to be had, and the more you learn about handling a boat, the more value you will place on a well-kept, accurate log. There are many reasons why a good log should be kept, even if you don't find any amusement in it. It eliminates guesswork in piloting and navigation. It affords a record of the boat's course and distance that is necessary for correct estimating of position if you are out of sight of landmarks, or caught in fog. It forces one to observe wind, weather, and the state of the sea, and gradually learn to predict conditions. It makes one more conscious of the need for careful steering. Over a season it constitutes an invaluable record of the boat's performance. It also provides fascinating winter reading after the boat is laid up and you are stormbound far from the water. A well-kept log is a character witness and proof of the boat's position and maneuvers if you are ever involved in a collision or other accident which may come to the attention of a court. Who knows? It may be worth its weight in gold some day for such use.

Eating Afloat

Part of the magic of the age of sailing that contributes to the joy afloat is what I like to call the food phenomenon. The average land-lubber turns into a ravenous, famished creature the minute he puts a toe into a dinghy. We do not know of one sailor who doesn't hold a SA—sailing appetite, of course. But, no matter what type your sailboat is, a luxurious cruiser or the most modest day sailer, good food can always be presented happily and pleasantly. To be sure, one doesn't always have the facilities of a home kitchen, but it seems out of place to carry ultra-gourmetism over the sea.

Meals for long-time cruising can be managed with ease if there has been sufficient prior planning. Day trips can be provided for with little strain on the hurried morning of setting out, and even parties can be arranged to impressively entertain the most landlubberly friends. One of my family's favorite foods afloat is chicken. This, of course, can be cooked the day before at home and reheated before serving. Poultry has the great advantage of eliminating knives and forks—a blessing when a crowded cockpit won't accommodate sawing elbows. The bones can be thrown overboard (on an outgoing tide, only). With this chicken you can serve "finger salad"—carrot sticks, celery, olives, canned white asparagus, and small tomatoes. If you feel like getting out your best stainless steel and hand-blown plastic glasses, you might accompany this with a tossed salad and white wine. Chill it in the bilge if you don't have icing facilities. Buttered French bread is nice to add. Plain is probably the most judicious; breathes there a man with stomach so dead that he can eat garlic in a seaway? Finish this off with small covered tarts, or rich, filled cookies that will answer as a complete dessert, all in the palm of your hand. Cupcakes are another good "hand dessert"; bake them in paper cups and ice them inside, like layer cake, to keep frosting off the tiller.

Meat can pose a problem if you don't have sufficient refrigeration space. Smoked meats like hams, bacon, pork butts, and the like can be carried in cool, dry places and will last a reasonably long time. However, you should inspect meat carefully before using it, while on a cruise of any length. Salted meats travel best. They must be cooked or soaked in fresh water before the final cooking. You can also utilize the new prefabricated dishes, for example, pot roast, potatoes, and vegetables all cooked on heavy foil plates that can be heated in the oven or on the stove with asbestos mats. Take some heavy pads with you to protect the dining table, or your lap, for these containers are plates as well.

In the last few years, a number of prepared meats with no waste have been produced, frozen via a new vacuum process. They come sealed in foil and only need to be soaked in a small amount of fresh water for a matter of minutes before being reconstituted. Then they may be treated like any fresh meat. The Armour Company and the Wilson Company have developed a line of these meats which are fine, especially if you are contemplating a long cruise away from good supply ports. Canned meats are very good, too, under such cruise conditions. For instance, canned hash is always rib-warming, and may be garnished with anything from tartar sauce to catsup.

Actually, canned food is the most important food category for meals afloat, which explains why a boat's can opener wears out so frequently. They are easy to prepare and when dressed with imagination can also be as delicious as any sophisticated taste could wish. For instance, a short cut to some of the most celebrated recipes can be achieved with a can of soup: condensed soups double for sauces or gravies, can be heated for hot sandwiches, add the flavor and vegetables to a hot stew, as as binder for one-dish main courses, and can be used as dressing for salads and vegetables. Quick lunches can be surprisingly palatable via the can opener. One dish that went to sea after years of apprenticeship at the children's lunch table is melted cheese over heated canned beans, on toast or rusk. But, in picking canned goods, don't go overboard; or rather, don't pick foods that should go overboard. Exotic sauces, artichoke hearts, and other fancy foods are best saved for home. Stick to old "stomachfuls"— canned beans, spaghetti, canned hamburgers, pressed meats, thick soup, etc. You'll also want juices and fruits (you can't have any scurvy aboard your ship); and a can of brown bread will come in handy to stretch out the beans when the crew is really hungry. But, remember to label any cans stored in or near dampness; the old stand-by for this purpose is an indelible pencil, but you can get more fancy with new waterproof labels that can be purchased at stationery stores. One other trick, which is easier and can be used if the cans are being stored where they won't bang around, is to put them in plastic bags that can be tied or closed up tightly. Also make a list of staples you can't do without. Then buy them in small sizes and pack those that are affected by moisture in tight jars.

When choosing fruit and vegetables such as tomatoes, it is best to select those that are slightly underripe and in firm condition. They need not be refrigerated as long as they are well-covered and protected from buffeting. Carrots, peppers, apples, onions, potatoes, cabbage, and produce of this type will keep for a week, or even two weeks if kept in a cool place. Buy lettuce in firm heads, leaving the tough outside leaves on for protection. Try to keep produce from being buffeted about. Bruises develop into soft spots that will rot easily.

Desserts should be simple, such as canned fruits, cookies, and packaged puddings. A cake may be made at home and brought aboard, or your first mate can make it from a package cake mix. A preheated pie is another welcome dessert. These pies need only fifteen minutes to a half hour in an oven before serving.

One of the most important factors in cooking afloat, as previously stated, is that you plan carefully for it. By this I mean that you should put the menu for the cruise (an example is shown below) down on paper, then count the crew and guests, and make out a grocery list. When making out the grocery list be sure to add one or two extra items for extra guests, changes in plans, or emergencies. The skipper, of course, may take his first mate and crew ashore for a meal or two while on a cruise.

TYPICAL MENU FOR VACATION WEEK

Day	Breakfast	Lunch	Dinner
Sat.		Soup Sandwiches Fruit, cookies Beverage (every day)	Roast beef (precooked) Mashed potatoes String beans Pie Beverage (every day)
Sun.	Frozen orange juice Cereal, rolls Eggs Coffee or cocoa (every day)	Macaroni and cheese Cold beef Fruit, cookies	Lamb chops Baked potatoes Spinach Cake
Mon.	Canned fruit or juice Cereal Coffee cake Eggs	Chicken soup Sandwiches Jello, cookies	Chicken Rice Julienne carrots Fruit, cookies
Tues.	Canned fruit or juice Cereal Coffee cake Eggs	Soup Tuna and tomato salad Fruit, cookies	Ham steaks Pineapple rings Sweet potatoes Asparagus tips Salad Cake
Wed.	Fruit or juice Cereal Toast, eggs	Beef stew with peas Fruit, cookies	Corned beef hash and poached egg Stewed tomatoes and corn Chocolate pudding

TYPICAL MENU FOR VACATION WEEK (*Continued*)

Day	Breakfast	Lunch	Dinner
Thurs.	Fruit or juice Cereal Toast Pancakes	Soup Sandwiches Fruit, cookies	Roast ham (canned) Sweet potatoes Peas Cake
Fri.	Juice Cereal Pancakes	Clam Chowder Tuna salad Fruit, cookies	Fish Mashed potatoes Peas Rice pudding
Sat.	Fruit or juice Hot cereal Biscuits	Beef stew with peas Jello, cookies	Baked beans and frankfurters Brown bread Asparagus tips Danish pudding
Sun.	Fruit or juice Cereal Toast and eggs	Ham steaks Spanish rice Beans Fruit, cookies	

Boatkeeping Afloat

It is essential that the boat be kept clean and shipshape at all times. This means not just the accommodations quarters but the entire boat. The first rule of good shipboard housekeeping is to have a place for everything and have everything in its place. This means you must have storage space, something most boats—regardless of size —don't have enough of. To make the most of the room available, there are several things you can do. For instance, a shelf can often be near the ceiling, under the deck, along the inside of each sleeping berth. This shelf should have a good high rail and, if space permits, should be wide enough to hold spare clothing, oilskins, and other miscellaneous articles. If impracticable to fit a shelf, pullman-berth hammocks make an excellent substitute. Instructions for adding shelves, racks, etc., to your cabin can be found in Chapter 11.

A well-kept craft calls for a regular daily boatkeeping routine. But, the actual cleaning aboard ship is the same as at home and generally requires the same techniques. The tools are the same, too. While attending to daily boatkeeping routine, you should also make a maintenance check. While cleaning, carefully inspect the plumbing, electrical appliances, stoves, rigging, etc., and take immediate steps to repair any faulty items.

To make your (or your first mate's) boatkeeping tasks simpler, you and your crew should develop good habits while afloat. Make certain to clean up messes as they occur, ·and you'll never be faced with accumulated work, which can spoil the entire voyage.

Lighting. Most modern sailboat cruisers have an electrical system consisting of a 12-volt alternator and battery. Such a system allows for sufficient interior cabin lighting fixtures, plus the navigational and anchor lights required by law. But remember that the battery must be kept charged, and if you don't use your auxiliary's engine, you must use your lights sparingly. Many sailors who don't like to use their engines when cruising will run them while at anchor to recharge the batteries. By reading the specific gravity of the battery with a hydrometer, it is easy to tell at a glance its state of discharge. A battery is fully charged when the hydrometer reads 1.275. It is fully discharged when the hydrometer reads 1.100. Also make sure that the battery's electrolyte is checked at regular intervals. Even in the dry-charge batteries, where the electrolyte is coated on the internal plates, the distilled water level must be maintained. And, no matter what type of battery you buy, it is eventually going to wear out. The internal plates deteriorate naturally due to chemical action.

It shouldn't be necessary to state that the voltage of the lamps and other electrical items used should be the same as the voltage of your power source. At one time, this had to be the same as the battery. However, power converters, inverters, and rectifiers are now used to match your primary power source to a group of electrical units which do not all require the same input voltage. A good example of this is where you have a radiotelephone which requires a 12-volt DC input, and you want to use it with a depth sounder requiring 115 volts AC. If your power source is a 12-volt battery, it can be connected directly to the radiotelephone, but must be converted (or inverted) into 115 volts AC for the depth sounder. Should you reverse the situation, and use a main power source of 115 volts AC, this must be rectified into 12 volts DC for the radiotelephone. In other words, power units can change one type of power to another. The most commonly used inverter is one which changes DC into AC. A practical application of this is to change 12-volt battery power into 115-volt AC power so that you can operate TV sets, broadcast radios, or electric razors from shipboard batteries. Power converters change 115-volt AC into 12 volts DC. Most sailboats don't have an AC generator, though many powerboats do. It is generally just a case of not enough room for this handy unit. Many sailboats do have an arrangement whereby the 115-volt dockside source can be used while tied up to a float or pier.

Insect Control. Insects are often a problem while on a cruise. Insect screens, which are generally available as an accessory with most stock cruisers, are usually the best way to cope with this problem. DDT bombs, spray guns, mosquito repellents, and fly swatters are other means of fighting this problem.

The Marine Toilet. The head—to use a sea term that has become a popular euphemism—or marine toilet is one of those luxuries that the habits of civilization have transformed into a necessity. Few items of equipment aboard a sailboat are so misunderstood and so fre-

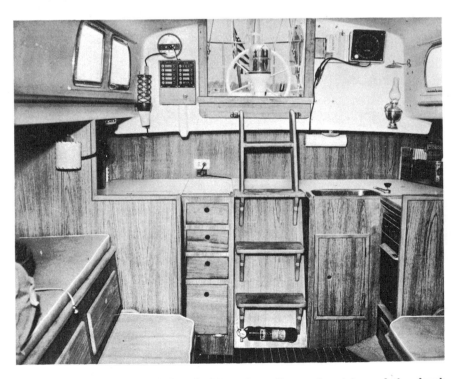

Figure 7-1: A view toward the aft. Note the galley at the right and the depth finder and emergency kerosene lamp. The boat's electrical panel board can be seen at the left.

Figure 7-2: Bunk arrangements. Top: as can be seen at the left, this system permits extra drawer space because of the step arrangement of the two single bunks. Center: the canvas pullman-type bunk arrangement. When not in use, the canvas is stored in back of the cushions. Then, when needed, the canvas is stretched out by placing the attached pole into special holders on the bulkhead (wall). Then the cushions are placed on the canvas to form the mattress for the bunk. Bottom: a convertible-type bunk. The folding dining table can be dropped to seat-height level and the cushions placed on it to form a bunk.

quently mistreated as the marine toilet. If properly installed and carefully maintained, it can be a joy forever; but if neglected or abused it will grow sullen, and is likely to react in unpredictable ways—and at the most inconvenient times.

Basically, a marine toilet consists of a bowl and pump, with suitable supply and discharge valves and the necessary fittings. To a harassed owner fumbling about with a worn cup leather this may seem like an oversimplification. There are additional parts, of course. Principal among these are the two through-hull connections, one for intake and the other for outlet, by which sea water is drawn into the system to flush the bowl and the waste is discharged from the bottom of the fixture. It must be remembered, however, that a marine toilet is totally different in design and operation from the common house toilet on shore. The boat toilet must be made so that it can pump flushing water in controlled quantities into the bowl and pump out the bowl contents against the pressure of water outside the hull. Check valves must be provided in both the intake and discharge lines to prevent sea water from leaking into the bowl and eventually flooding the boat.

The system of valves and piping required to accomplish this smoothly and in a dependable manner may look complex. But for all its formidable appearance when confronted for the first time, a marine toilet operates on a very simple principle. To operate, make sure that both sea cocks and the inlet valve on the toilet are open. Then just pump some water into the bowl before use. After use, pump until the bowl is flushed clean. If the boat will be left unattended for a period of time, the sea cocks should be closed and a few drops of good machine oil applied to the piston rod to keep the "O" ring soft. Periodic application of vaseline on the piston rod will keep the toilet operating more easily. The modern toilet is designed so that lubrication is not necessary; it was, with the old-fashioned leather-washer type. Maintenance consists merely of good shipboard practice. When running in rough seas, or when the boat is to be left overnight, close the inlet valve. Be sure to open it before using the toilet. If your toilet pumps hard, one of three things may be wrong:

1. A foreign object is in the pump.
2. The piston rod is dry.
3. The inlet valves or the sea cocks are closed.

If a foreign object becomes lodged in the toilet, close the sea cocks and remove the flange and discharge pipe. Most small objects will be caught at this point by the joker valve. Acids or harsh alkalis should not be used in cleaning the bowl.

When you haul your boat for storage, spend a little time to make sure your toilet will continue to give excellent service:

1. Fill the bowl, pump, and discharge lines with fresh water and pump overboard several times. Fill the bowl again and let stand for several days to dissolve the salt in the housing and lines. Then pump dry.

2. Apply vaseline to the piston rod and work it down.

3. Before freezing weather, remove the base plug.

Before you recommission your boat, inspect your toilet. Soaking and softening are not necessary to make the pump operative. Don't forget to replace the drain plug. Periodic checks after your boat is overboard will help to make certain that all connections remain tight. Don't place undue strain on the outlet flange, because breakage can occur. All parts necessary for the maintenance of your toilet are usually included in the repair kit, which can be ordered from your local dealer.

Electrical pumping toilets operate and discharge waste in much the same manner as the manual units, but have eliminated manual pumping. Usually these units have some type of a push-button control switch that incorporates a timing device which can be set for as long as a minute, depending on the amount of time needed to satisfactorily treat the waste. The switch can be placed in any convenient location on the bulkhead or wall.

While most cruising sailboats don't utilize chlorinating devices, it is very possible that in the near future they may be required by law. Some local inland waterway laws now require them. As a rule, chlorinators can be attached to most marine toilets, electrical or manual. They are easy to install. The only problem to be encountered on some boats would be the matter of space for the chlorinator box, which should be on the same level as the base of the toilet and within three to four feet of its installation. These units macerate waste, and automatically inject chlorine, destroying more than 99 percent of all bacteria. No matter how much most units are used, waste is reduced to a harmless liquid state before it is discharged, thus eliminating unsightly floating matter and obnoxious odors. Any household disinfectant or bleach containing 5 percent sodium hypochlorite by weight—such as Clorox—can be used. Normally one-half gallon is sufficient for two months. In many states and waterways chlorinators are now required by law to work in conjunction with the marine toilet.

Children on a Cruise

The care and feeding of small fry on a cruise can present some acute problems on any trip longer than an afternoon. Yet there are interesting challenges and real rewards for mothers and fathers who wisely begin to plan the children's hours the minute they've decided where they're going and when. As a matter of fact, even an infant need be no more a problem on a sailboat than at home (once you get all the necessary equipment aboard). They want to sleep most of the time anyway, and what better way to be lulled to sleep than by the gentle motion of a boat under sail or at anchor? Even the feeding won't be a problem if you think ahead. For example, my wife always mixed the canned milk formula directly into the sterilized bottle. By making up one bottle at a time, as needed, there was no danger of the formula spoiling if our ice supply ran low.

As your child grows out of the "eating-and-sleeping" stage, he'll want to be on deck with the rest of the crew when he is awake. So while you're under way he can be put in his car bed, which can be put down into the cockpit well. The car seat can be securely fastened to the cockpit and the baby strapped in the bed. In rough weather he should stay in his crib-bunk below, whether he likes it or not. Such a bunk can be made in several ways. Some have used fish netting successfully. You can borrow one side from a portable crib and attach it to the sideboard of the bunk, which doubles as a playpen. For a more permanent arrangement, you can install the whole crib in a bunk, by removing the bunk mattress and securing the crib (with legs removed), so that it can't slip out of position. This simplifies the job of changing baby's bedding, and leaves a handy space at the end of the bunk for stowing his clothing, diapers, etc.

When a baby reaches the crawling and climbing age, the age of exploring everything he sees, he must be watched constantly (whether afloat or ashore!). The main thing is to keep him from climbing out on deck, and to guard him from the dangers of anything that might be within reach of his busy little hands. A gate at this stage is an excellent idea. They are easily installed. One can be put up temporarily to keep him away from the companionway ladder and out of the galley.

It is a good idea to get him accustomed to wearing a child harness. Although the thought of putting him on a leash may not appeal to you, it could very well save your baby from a dunking or a bad fall. (And it saves a lot of wear and tear on the one who would otherwise have to keep a constant hold on him.) On deck the leash can be hooked to something secure so that the baby will have some freedom to move about, yet be safe from falling overboard or into the companionway.

When at anchor, the baby can spend much time playing happily in the cockpit well. He has room for toys and crawling around, but he can't climb out, so it is a perfect outdoor playpen until he is past a year old. It is also a wonderful "swimming pool." On warm days he can plug the scuppers and pour in a couple of buckets of water so that he can splash to his heart's content. It can keep him happy and cool on many a summer day.

Even the youngest tots should be made to feel completely at home in their life-preserving equipment. Above decks, the children and their life jackets should be inseparable. Life vests for children come in two sizes, depending on the child's weight. It's a good idea to give them several "dunk tests" in the water before setting out, to make sure the fit, adjustments, and performance are all they should be. Treat the wearing of these admittedly cumbersome vests as a game. The sight of your child romping around on the deck in his life jacket, far from giving you the dismaying suggestion of disaster, will have a beneficial effect on your peace of mind and your blood pressure after a voyage or two. Soon the wearing will become second nature and everybody can relax and enjoy the trip.

Here are some tips for keeping the children amused, content, and (let's admit it) quiet on a trip that's a real pleasure for all hands:

1. Books. Make an exception, if you have an anti-comic-book rule at home, and lay in a supply of them, at least the less offensive ones. They can be a holiday treat for the bored on board. Picture books of oceans, rivers, beaches, big and little fishes, will not only help to pass the time for the very young, but will provide some subtle indoctrination as well. Take along a couple of honest-to-goodness book-books for the children who are old enough to read. These ac-

complished elders can also help you keep a happy ship by reading aloud to the too-little-for-literacy set.

2. Toys. If you have a girl in your crew, she will want to take along her favorite doll. Let her. Rigging up a mock life jacket for Dolly is a good way to teach a safety lesson without resistance, by the way. Building blocks, with a big plastic dishpan as their home port, can keep any number occupied for a long time, and are easy to stow under a bunk. Cutouts aren't nearly so messy as they can be at home —you can tidy up by tossing the scrap paper over the side. Coloring books and crayons are also seaworthy companions.

3. Games. Above decks, "spotting" is fun for everybody and doesn't require equipment. Whether it's other boats, lighthouses, fancied shapes in cloud formations, buoys, markers, signs—whatever meets the eye in the line of the country where you do your sailing— suggest that your youngsters spot 'em and count 'em. A prize, from a cookie to a supervised turn at the helm, will permit you to prolong the game.

4. Taking the helm. This is especially good as the children grow older. While a child can't be allowed to drive a car or airplane, he can take the wheel or tiller of your boat—provided the skipper is on the spot. Never in crowded quarters, narrow channels, basins or docking areas, of course. But on the open water a youngster can be allowed to experience the thrill of handling the wheel or tiller with a sharp eye on the horizon and the world at his feet. This is the best time to launch his habits of respecting the proper handling of boats, the rights of others, and automatic observance of the Rules of the Road. Sailing is a family responsibility as well as a family sport. By this early training—and your own good example—you can help to develop a generation of safe and self-confident yachtsmen.

5. Allow for shore time. With children on board, it is well to plan for some shore stops so that they can have a soda, go to the movies, look at store windows, or just walk or play on terra firma. Also allow some time on a cruise for swimming, rowing or sailing in the dinghy, fishing, or even skin or scuba diving.

6. Make assignments. As suggested earlier in the chapter, mix a little responsibility or routine sailing tasks with the recreation— reading the charts, helping to handle lines, stowing toys, policing the galley, keeping lookout—all play and no work makes Jack a restless boy. Jill, too. Any or all of these pastimes will serve, whether you

have one chick or a brood. It's the advance planning that does the trick. If you can keep your head when all about you are pleading in chorus, "What can we do next?"—if you can come up with the answers with ideal parental calm and confidence—then you and your first mate are bound to have a successful cruise.

Cruising Activities

Since having a good time is the principal objective of a cruise, the wise skipper will take into account the kinds of things along the way in which he and his crew are interested. Are they especially interested in scenery; and if so, what kind—restful or the more spectacular? Are they interested in visiting places of historic interest, or do they want to fish? Would they like to visit friends or relatives en route? Are excitement and adventure a primary consideration, or is it just plain relaxation? Often it is possible to plan a cruise which will provide a balanced mixture of all of these things.

Swimming. Swimming from a sailboat can be very enjoyable, but it requires a little common sense. Under no circumstances should a group go swimming in deep water from a boat without leaving at least one member on board. It's extremely difficult to climb aboard a sailboat without a helping hand from inside or without the aid of a boarding ladder. (A dinghy can be used as a base for swimming.) Even when using a boarding ladder, one should stay aboard to act as a lifeguard and be able to take off after anyone in need of help. Also, never dive in unfamiliar waters. Slip over the side of the craft into the water until you are sure of its depth.

Skin Diving and Scuba Diving. If this sport interests you, it can be accomplished very nicely from a sailboat or her tender. Equipped with breathing apparatus, the swimmer can move below the surface with the balance of a bird in flight. Whether your interest is spearing fish, collecting shells, taking photographs, catching specimens for your home aquarium, or just plain sightseeing, you'll find the world down under your yacht a fascinating, ever-changing panorama of life and color.

Complicated equipment isn't required for the beginner; snorkel, face mask, and fins can provide an introduction to this thrilling water sport. Once you have mastered this phase, you can graduate to self-contained underwater breathing apparatus (scuba, for short).

But for the diving novice and expert alike, certain safety rules are basic. The following are seven of the more important ones:

1. Never skin dive alone. Take a safe, dependable companion.

2. Know the waters where you are diving, especially if they are influenced by tides or currents.

3. Have an operating base, preferably a tender, for a rest platform.

4. Know your own physical limitations and do not overextend them. Practice emergency procedures.

5. Have a skin-diving flag clearly visible to avoid danger from passing boats.

6. Be familiar with the sea life of the region.

7. Do not dive in areas where others are fishing.

Fishing. In this book, it would be impossible for me to go into the various techniques of catching fish. There are many good books available on fresh-water and salt-water angling. The important thing to remember, however, is not to leave home your fishing gear when going out on a sailboat cruise. The average sailboat is ideal for fishing.

Photography. The yachtsman can obtain a great deal of fun by taking pictures of his boating activities. Actually, hot-stove sailing picture sessions that are held during the winter months make photography almost a necessity. While you may be able to take only a few friends on your boat during the sailing season, you can be a skipper for many on a picture cruise during the off-months. Many yacht clubs schedule picture programs during winter hibernation.

In most cases the type of camera isn't as important a factor as the speed of the lens. A rapid shutter speed is helpful, but not essential. Actually the major problem is the motion of the boat you're shooting from. If your boat is under way, for example, be careful not to rest the camera on any part of the craft, and don't prop the camera with your elbows. Instead, stand with your feet widely spread, knees slightly flexed to "ride" with your boat's movement. Don't let the camera touch your body, either.

When taking photographs of other moving boats try to shoot from a high level down onto the subject, since this will show more of the boat and the people on her. Pictures taken from near the water level will reveal only heads above the boat's sheer line, while spray from your own boat or the boat you're picturing may block out the subjects. Always be conscious of both the direction of the light source and the wind when shooting marine pictures. Avoid aiming your camera into a stiff breeze; otherwise your lens will become coated with spray. Even a single drop of water striking the lens may diffuse the light entering the camera and may alter the exposure or distort the picture.

To make really good pictures, you must study the composition carefully before you shoot. When the horizon is part of the picture be sure to position the camera level so the subject doesn't seem to be sailing up or down hill. Pictures taken of perfectly calm water with no reflections are generally rather uninteresting. If the sun is such that you get no reflections, toss a stone or similar object into the water so ripples add pattern to the picture. Your camera will capture water texture best if the subject and water are side- or back-

Figure 7-3: While taking a picture afloat, steady the camera as shown above.

lighted so as to cast shadows. Marine pictures usually offer better water texture if taken when the sun is low.

Speaking of water reflections, remember that water reflects far more light than do ground surfaces, and many beginning yachting photographers overexpose many pictures taken on the water. In general, if you don't have a light meter to establish an accurate reading, close down one *f*-stop smaller for marine photography than you would shooting under similar light conditions on shore. However, an exposure meter is a tool of real importance to the marine photographer. When using it be sure to take into consideration the filter factor, for the use of the filter will increase the required amount of exposure and the factor will tell how much. A medium yellow filter will enhance sky, clouds, and water, rendering artistic effects. For color film, no filter will be required most of the time except on extremely clear days when the sky is a deep blue almost to the horizon. Then a skylight filter will help prevent an excessive bluish cast. A polarization filter will help darken the sky for better contrast between sails and background on a slightly hazy day. It also makes objects under the water's surface clear from above.

Taking good sailboat photographs requires a little knowledge of sailing techniques. For instance, before starting to shoot a sailboat, check for proper trim of the sails. Make sure that the halyards are tight and everything is shipshape. Wind of at least 10 to 12 mph will fill the sails sufficiently to give a good appearance of action. Try to expose when the boat is in a wave cycle, which will show her bow neither too high nor buried in the water. If the boat is racing, have the crew in the cockpit or along the windward rail. Sailboats look best when they are heeled toward the camera; there is more excitement then and masts look taller. With small sailboats, it adds to the picture if the crew is hiking.

Motion pictures are even easier to make than stills. With automatic cameras, one has only to wind the spring and press the release button. Several automatic movie cameras don't have to be focused and are completely self-setting. They tell you when you can't make a picture. Wide-angle, regular, and telephoto lens are permanently attached to the camera, and any can be selected with a simple twist of the fingers. If your motion-picture camera is fitted with a speed adjustment, increase the number of frames per second from 16 or 24 to 32. This will eliminate much of the jerky action from motion pictures taken under way, which is caused by shooting from an er-

Figure 7-4: An action picture like this is always desirable.

ratically moving platform. In motion-picture-taking you will create a greater feeling of action if you follow the subject coming toward you and pan more slowly than the subject, allowing it to move out of your field of view as you stop panning and hold your camera static.

A Pliofilm bag, lens hood, light meter, and haze filter are all the extras required for surface marine photography. A watertight camera case is required for submarine picture-taking. Salt-water spray and intense sunlight are two particularly damaging elements against which the boatman must protect his camera gear. A camera left carelessly in an exposed position on your craft may suffer lens damage, for the lens is made up of a number of separate elements glued together. Heat may melt the glue or hot sunlight may melt film emulsion and ruin properly exposed shots. When it's not in use, keep your camera gear and spare film protected from dampness in a Pliofilm bag.

Emergency Procedures at Sea

It's never pleasant to look forward to trouble, but a little planning in advance—old-time seamen called this "to be forehanded"—does a tremendous amount to minimize it when it does arrive. When an accident occurs, possession of the knowledge and equipment to deal with it can be lifesaving, no matter whether the damage is to the boat or to a member of her crew. In this chapter, we'll concern ourselves primarily with the well-being of the crew; we'll go into emergency repairs to your yacht in Chapter 11.

First Aid. As I stated in Chapter 1, every boat should have some type of first-aid kit on board. For cruises, you'll probably want a rather complete setup, while for inshore sailing in local waters, bandages, burn ointment, antiseptic, and soda may suffice. But, the more you know about first aid, the more secure you'll feel while out on the water. I strongly recommend that you buy and read one of the several fine medical books now available for yachtsmen, and keep it on board at all times, located where it can be found immediately when needed. It is also a good idea for one member of your crew (the skipper could go, too) to take a first aid course. Such a course is available at many Red Cross chapters. Remember, however, that as important as knowing what to do, is knowing what not to do, for the amateur cruising doctor has his limits.

Seasickness. The first indication of seasickness is usually a greenish pallor, followed by yawning, drowsiness, salivation, weakness, loss of attention, deep breathing, cold sweat, giddiness, inability to function, occasionally hiccoughing, dizziness, and vomiting. Following the vomiting the victim may feel a little better temporarily, but this relief is short-lived, and he soon becomes prostrated and continues to be nauseated. He may even think he is going to die, and in most cases probably wishes he were dead.

There are several motion sickness remedies on the market—Bonine and Dramamine are the most popular. These are frequently effective and need only be taken in doses of one or two tablets a day. If you're susceptible and planning a sail or cruise, consult your doctor. He'll recommend one for you. The important point is to take the medication for a day or two in advance of the outing. Almost all medical authorities agree it does little good to begin taking medication after you're aboard.

There is conclusive medical evidence that overindulgence in food or drink just before getting afloat will make you much more susceptible to seasickness. A recent survey showed that approximately 70 percent of the people that were seasick on fishing boats had orange juice or bacon and eggs for breakfast, or both. It is generally believed best to put to sea on an empty stomach or having partaken of grapefruit and a bit of dry toast. Then when the pangs of hunger attack you about noon, try some good hot chicken broth and rice or consommé, and a tongue, peanut-butter, or chicken sandwich. Such a snack should carry you through the rest of the day, or at least to the point where you have forgotten the threat of *mal de mer*. For dessert, if you crave it, fresh pears, peaches, or apples are the best things you can eat. Above all, stay away from anything fried or high in fat and fluid, avoiding prepared salads, cold eggs, meat and fish, mayonnaise, milk puddings, and pastries with moist fillings. If the soup betrays the least trace of grease don't touch it. Coffee, in the estimation of most experts, is a poor drink for anyone subject to seasickness. Ginger ale, club soda, or similar soda drinks are far better. Chewing gum between meals and swallowing small chunks of ice is also good. Remember that liquor of any kind is *never* a preventive or cure for seasickness. Save your drinking for shore. If you "hang one on" the night before a cruise, top off the evening's tippling with a hearty buffet, then wind up with a minimum of sleep, you are a candidate for seasickness.

While the following statement isn't very delicate, it is something you should know: the odor of regurgitated material also can be a factor inducing seasickness, as can be the various sound effects—those haunting tunes caused by the rapid intake of air into the larynx (a sort of organ pipe in reverse) during vomiting. It is believed that the throaty melodies played by a mamboing stomach can be quite a factor in causing seasickness in otherwise unaffected spectators. In other words, many people have been made ill by watching others with the high heaves. Speaking of seeing, it is a very good idea for those prone to seasickness to constantly wear sunglasses—the best procurable—and always have an extra pair along. Doctors are convinced that a great deal of motion sickness is due to eyestrain. Once under way, reading on board a boat is bad for the eyes.

It is generally agreed that the seasick individual probably benefits most by lying supine with his head flat or just slightly raised. The nearer amidships he stays the better. Sudden movements should be avoided. The victim should not go below, if possible, because fresh air is helpful to him.

Man Overboard. While sailing it's altogether conceivable that one of your crew members may fall or be knocked overboard. If this should occur and the person doesn't have a life jacket on, throw him a life preserver, a life ring, a seat cushion, or an oar, but make sure of your aim if you toss anything made of wood. Even if he's a good swimmer, one of these items will reduce the effort he must put forth to keep afloat, and it will also mark his position. Immediately assign one member of your crew to point at the person with an outstretched arm and to keep pointing while your craft is being maneuvered for the pickup.

If a person goes overboard while the boat is sailing with the wind abeam or forward of abeam, the quickest way to get back to your man is by jibing. But sail far enough away to avoid coming upon him in the middle of your turning circle. Approach from the leeward side so that if he is in difficulty, the boat won't drift down on top of him. The mainsail sheet should, if at all possible, be trimmed, then eased off to prevent the boom from slamming violently across, possibly injuring someone in the cockpit or damaging your boat's rigging.

If the accident should occur while the craft is sailing before the wind, you have the choice of two maneuvers to execute the pickup. In the first maneuver, you bring the wind abeam, sail away for a few boat-lengths, then bring the craft about and reach back on the other tack and head into the wind. The second procedure is to continue sailing before the wind for a short distance, then tack back. You'll generally reach the person in the water on the second tack. The distance you sail before the wind will depend upon how your boat responds and the condition of the water and the amount of breeze. Through practice and experience in sailing your boat you'll be able to obtain the answer to this question. By the way, it would be very wise to practice the pickup maneuvers so that when an accident of this type occurs—which is seldom—you and your crew will know exactly what to do.

Approach your man in the water slowly, spilling the wind from the sail as you go. The sheets should be loose so that the boat is almost dead in the water, and the centerboard should be all the way down during the actual pickup operation to give your craft full stability. Then throw a line to the person overboard and help him in over the stern. Make the rescued party as warm, dry, and comfortable as possible.

The person who falls overboard should concern himself with three important objectives while in the water. First, *keep calm, don't panic.* Second, *keep himself clear of the rescuing craft.* Third, *keep himself afloat the easiest way he can.* If you should go overboard while out by yourself, tread water until you see the boat round into the wind, guess where it will stop dead in the wind, then swim for that point.

Distress Signals. Searching for a vessel in distress can be a rather quick and easy job or a difficult and lengthy procedure, depending upon the amount and accuracy of the information given to the rescuing ships. Thus you must know the recognized distress signals and have the proper gear on board to send them. This signaling equipment isn't a minimum legal requirement; your needs of this type must be based upon the waters in which your boat sails and the size of your craft.

As mentioned in Chapter 1, more and more cruising sailboats are being equipped with radiotelephones. This is possibly the best way to summon aid since merchant vessels, pleasure craft, Coast Guard ships and stations listen on 2182 kilocycles on the radiotelephone band. This is a calling and distress frequency. A vessel calling "Mayday" (code word for needing emergency assistance) stands an excellent chance of receiving help quickly. Though 2738 or 2638 kilocycles may not be busy and may bring assistance sooner, in an emergency you may use any available frequency to indicate your need for help. The Coast Guard has available a 4-inch by 5-inch cardboard placard called *Distress Information Sheet* for posting near your radiotelephone. These placards, which gives the information desired by rescuers, can be had at most Coast Guard units, or from their headquarters in Washington, D.C.

Since many searching craft today are equipped with radar and because boats made of fiberglass don't make the best radar targets, the locating of a radar reflector such as the small collapsible type (available at most marine suppliers) high on the mast of a disabled boat will increase the chance of radar detection and rescue. While almost any signal that will attract attention and bring help is a satisfactory distress signal, there are known or recognized distress signals that will greatly enhance your chances of obtaining assistance. There are, however, new signals coming along all the time. For example, the latest recognized one for small boats on waters of the United States is that of slowly and repeatedly *raising and lowering arms outstretched to each side.* This is a distinctive signal that is not likely to be mistaken for a greeting. To be as effective as possible, this signal should be given from the highest vantage point on the boat, with consideration given to color contrasts. Other recognized signals are given below:

RECOGNIZED DISTRESS SIGNALS

Signal	Inland Rules	Great Lakes Rules	Western Rivers Rules	International Rules*
A gun or other explosive fired at intervals of about a minute	Yes (day and night)	Yes (day and night)	Yes (day and night)	Yes
A continuous sounding with any fog-signal apparatus	Yes (day and night)	Yes (day and night)	Yes (day and night)	Yes
Rockets or shells, throwing red stars fired one at a time at short intervals				Yes
Signal made by radiotelegraph or by any other signaling methods consisting of the group ... −−− ... (SOS) in Morse code				Yes

RECOGNIZED DISTRESS SIGNALS (*Continued*)

Signal	Inland Rules	Great Lakes Rules	Western Rivers Rules	International Rules*
A signal sent by radiotelephone consisting of the spoken word "Mayday"				Yes
The International Code signal of distress indicated by N. C.			Yes (day)	Yes
A signal consisting of a square flag having above or below it a ball or anything resembling a ball		Yes (day)	Yes (day)	Yes
Flames on the vessel (as from a burning tar barrel, oil barrel, etc.)	Yes (night)	Yes (night)	Yes (night)	Yes
A rocket parachute flare showing a red light				Yes
Rockets or shells, throwing stars of any color or description fired one at a time at short intervals		Yes (day and night)		
Rockets or shells, bursting in the air with a loud report and throwing stars of any color or description, fired one at a time at short intervals			Yes (day and night)	
Reverse the ensign so that it flies upside down			Yes	
A continuous sounding with a whistle			Yes (day and night)	

* International Rules do not distinguish between day and night use of signals.

8

The Lure of Racing

Everyone who sails has probably thought at some time or other of racing just to test himself out against the other fellow. Actually sailboat racing requires more pure sailing skill and nerve than any other branch of the sport, and if you can prove yourself able to hold your own as a skipper, you can with confidence undertake any other kind of sailing.

As discussed in Chapter 1, there are various types of races, and a sailor who might be a champ on an inshore course race event may be a chump in an offshore distance contest where basic seamanship and navigation is much more vital. Really, one of the many wonderful lures of sailboat racing is that there is a race to suit the taste of every sailor. There are races for male and female, young and old, summer and winter. The boats, as stated earlier, vary in size and style. For example, the Yacht Racing Association of Long Island Sound schedules regular races for more than thirty-six different styles of sailing craft, while we in the Narragansett Bay area have well over thirty. But, regardless of the many types of hulls, there are two major classifications of sailboat racing:

Class boat racing—between boats of the same class, racing on even terms.

Handicap racing—between boats of different types handicapped by some type of time-allowance system to make all boats as evenly matched as possible. With the resulting handicap rating, sloops, cutters, yawls, ketches, and schooners would be able to compete evenly against each other regardless of size (see Chapter 9 for further details).

Racing Courses

Most one-design class boat races, and a few handicap races, are held on a definite course. The majority of local regattas are held around triangular courses. Such a course is a good test of skill since it requires sailing to windward, reaching, and sailing before the wind. Boats start the race by crossing the starting line between a white flag on the committee boat or station and the starting mark, and they finish by crossing a line formed by a white flag on the committee boat or station and the starting mark. Generally the race course is so arranged that the first leg requires a beat to windward. This spreads the boats out a little and minimizes, to some degree, traffic jams at the first mark. Some courses are twice around the triangle.

One of the most popular courses, especially for class national championship, is the "modified Gold Cup" course, which consists of five legs, with starting and finishing at the same mark. The first three legs are generally around a triangle, starting with a windward leg followed by two reaching legs; the fourth leg is usually a repetition of the first leg to windward; while the fifth leg is a return downwind to the finish line at the starting mark. A typical modified Gold Cup course is as follows: The triangle laid out for this course should be an equilateral one not less than 2 nautical miles on a side, making a total course length of not less than 6, or more than 7½ nautical miles. This course can't be changed under any conditions, and cannot be shortened after the start of a race.

In the America's Cup races, two courses are usually sailed: the windward-leeward and triangular, on alternate days. The windward-leeward course is twice around two buoys placed 6 miles apart, for a total of 24 nautical miles. If wind conditions permit, the first leg of the course will be to windward. A triangular course, which tests a boat on all points, consists of a beat to windward, a reach with wind abeam, and a run before the wind. The legs in the America's Cup races are 8 nautical miles each for a total of 24.

In the 1964 Olympic Games, courses were employed with eight buoys spaced evenly around a circle, and numbered clockwise in succession with the northeast buoy being No. 1, the easterly one being No. 2, etc. The windward legs of the course are always full diameters, i.e., from No. 4 to No. 8 in a northerly wind; from No. 5 to No. 1 in a northeasterly wind, etc. The start is always a windward start, at the beginning of such a leg, and the first round constitutes a triangular course; i.e., No. 4, No. 8, No. 6, and back to No. 4. The

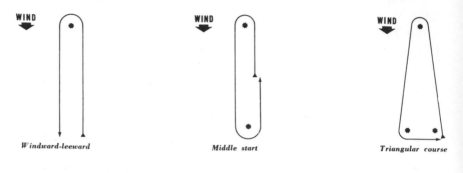

Windward-leeward   *Middle start*   *Triangular course*

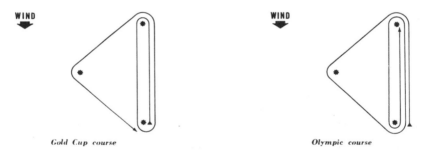

Gold Cup course   *Olympic course*

Figure 8-1: Typical racing courses. (Courtesy of Yacht Racing Association of Long Island Sound)

final leg of the course is a third windward leg with the finish at its completion; i.e., No. 4, No. 8, with the finish at No. 8. Thus, barring major wind shifts, the racing will constitute 61 percent windward sailing, 24 percent broad reaching, and 15 percent directly down-wind. It is unfortunate that the reaches are both rather broad instead of one being fairly close—especially in very light air conditions, when they may prove as tedious as the leg of the course that is directly downwind.

Usually there are four bases for the establishment of yacht-racing courses:

1. Government marks (buoys, beacons, lighthouses, lightships).
2. Permanently moored, or located, club marks.
3. Combinations of government and private marks.
4. Temporary marks located in position especially for a specific race.

Under the first three classifications, two types of courses are usually possible:

1. Prearranged or preselected courses arbitrarily laid out from different combinations of marks properly identified on the racing instructions by assigned letters of the alphabet (see previous page). The course combinations carry numbers.

2. Flexible courses using the same buoys in varying combinations depending upon the whims of the weather, or committee, or both.

When temporary marks are set out (tall, moored flag stakes, or inflatable rings and pylons in the new high-visibility colors are best), their locations are indicated by flag hoists giving compass directions to the first mark, from there to the second, and thence home—assuming the course is triangular; if it is windward-leeward, the direction of the first mark should suffice.

Some races, due to geographic reasons, can't be sailed over a triangle. Such courses may be modified triangular or a variation of the windward-leeward courses such as a middle-start windward-leeward course. But should you ever have anything to do with the arrangement of a course, remember that the most successful sailboat races are sailed for the benefit of the skippers. It's the one sport in which the spectator isn't considered and a great many of the biggest regattas are held far away from shore solely with the idea of making the race a fair test of skill and not a matter of knowing all the little slants and vagaries of winds and currents along the shore. Sailboat races are to be won by fair sailing and superior seamanship, and the idea is to give the visitors every possible chance at fair sailing.

Sailing Instructions

The sailing instructions contained in the race circular and the advertisement of the race, if one is made, may contain valuable information that may be profitable to study, especially when the race is being sailed at unfamiliar locations. These sailing instructions, prepared in writing by the race committee, include the following matters: the starting signals and their scheduled times; starting line; finish line; the order in which the turning marks of each course are to be passed and the side on which each mark is to be passed, with a description of each mark. The instructions also cover such of the following matters as may be appropriate: the date and place of the races; the classes to race; possible courses; eligibility and entry requirements; measurement certificates; the signals used to designate courses other than the only prescribed or regular course; any government buoys or other objects required to be passed on a specified side; whether buoys will bound the starting area (if so, they don't rank as marks); special method of recall; time allowance; special time limit; prizes; the scoring system; special time limit for protests; and any special provisions and signals. These written instructions make it possible for you to form a mental picture of the race course and to lay racing plans in advance.

Racing Rules

Racing rules were invented to keep boats out of trouble with their competitors. Therefore, make certain that you know your class and right-of-way racing rules thoroughly so that you won't be disqualified before you even start, or lose valuable ground having to ponder these rules during the race. A complete set of the Racing Rules of the International Yacht Racing Union may be obtained for a small fee from the North American Yacht Racing Union, 37 West 44th Street, New York, New York 10036. Class rules can be obtained from the secretary of the class. By following all the rules, you'll stay out of serious trouble. Briefly stated and with exceptions that are covered in the complete racing rules of the Union, the following basic rules of right-of-way may be summarized in this manner:

1. Before starting, a boat that is clear ahead, or a leeward boat, may alter course, but only slowly, if the change would affect another boat.

2. When approaching the starting line, and about to start, a leeward boat does not have to give a windward boat room to pass between her and the starting mark.

3. A boat crossing the starting line ahead of the starting gun must turn and recross the line and start properly. During this maneuver the boat must give way to all boats that have started properly. While returning to restart, the boat has no rights whatsoever.

4. After starting and when on parallel course, the overtaking boat must give way to the overtaken boat.

5. When two boats are converging on opposite tacks, the boat on a starboard tack (wind over starboard rail, with boom to port) has the right-of-way. In other words, a boat on a port tack must give way to a craft on a starboard tack.

6. When courses converge on the same tack, the windward boat must keep clear.

7. Boats tacking or jibing must keep clear of those on a tack.

8. When making a turn, an overtaking boat may demand buoy room—if she has established an overlap on the overtaken boat. This rule does not apply at the starting line.

9. When on a reach, or when running, a boat must not bear off to prevent a leeward boat from passing. Or if a boat that is clear astern is steering a course to pass you to leeward, you cannot bear off to interfere.

10. Under the proprieties of yacht racing, when a serious collision is imminent, all boats involved must do their utmost to avoid it, regardless of any rule or right-of-way situation.

The start is a specific time. The race committee starts the boats by visual signals, but calls attention to these by audible signals (horns, whistles, or guns). The starting signals (display of warning signal, white shape; preparatory signal, starting signal for the first class to start, red shape) are hoisted usually at five-minute intervals. Each signal is lowered thirty seconds before the hoisting of the next. In starting boats by classes, the start signal for each class is the preparatory signal for the next class. The hoisting of a starting signal, even if improperly timed, controls the start.

The race committee on the committee boat judges the finish, particularly when boats are fairly close at the end of the race. The committee must also act as judges for any protests which may be filed. The only requirements for finishing are that the boat must cross and clear the finish line, and that the first boat must finish within a prescribed time limit, usually designed to get boats home before sundown.

Races Are Won at the Start

Not only must the boat be in the best possible condition and tuned up to peak form, and the sails the best obtainable, but the skipper's skill in sailing and getting the last ounce of speed from his boat must be developed to the highest possible degree. One of the first things to remember is that many a race has been lost because of a poor start. It is therefore worth concentrating on the three main

Figure 8-2: Start of a race.

essentials which go to make a good start. These essentials are: (1) To cross at the right point on the starting line; (2) to arrive on the starting line, ready to cross it, not more than three seconds after the starting gun; and (3) to be moving at a good speed when crossing.

The most important factors in good starts are speed and proper position. Speed means full boat control, the ability to alter your course quickly with the least loss of time. It is usually best to cross the line on a starboard tack in order to have the right-of-way. There are two exceptions to this: 1) When the number of boats permits a safe port tack start and port tack is advantageous; 2) and when arriving late intentionally or accidentally will preclude the possibility of fouling. In the latter case, however, you must have full headway, travel fast, and be prepared to give way to other boats coming up on a starboard tack. Don't take chances on the port tack when trying to clear a starboard-tack boat.

As to position, the starting line should be squared to the wind, but it may not be, and you must therefore determine which end of the line, or which spot, will be most favorable for a good start. If several races have been run off before the one in which you're entered, watch the boats in them closely and see what their behavior is at the windward or leeward end of the starting line. Watch the champion of the class (if you can pick him out) and try to remember from which end of the line he starts. Sometimes the starting line is badly laid out, so that by starting from one end of it you sail a shorter course. If this is the case, you'll know it by the number of boats jamming up at the favorable location. (Other things being equal, the favored end of the line is the one nearer the wind—the port end on most courses.) When this happens, either try to get a perfect start and be a few feet ahead of the rest; or, if you're not so sure of yourself, start a little farther down the line to clear the crowd. While the boats in the crowd are fighting it out for position, the lone wolf sometimes gains enough lead to decide the outcome of the race right then and there.

It's a good idea to get yourself a stop watch and set it with the ten-minute advance signal. (Ideally, one crew member should keep time and call off the remaining time. If there is a second crewman, he should watch the visual signals.) Then check it again with the five-minute gun and maneuver your craft so that it goes across the line on the second of the start and under full way. Some skippers get up to the starting line and then luff their sails there, waiting for the gun. When it fires, they're caught flat-footed without any way whatsoever while other boats with all their sails drawing cross the starting line. Remember that it takes time to get your boat under way. Therefore, work on being on the starting line at the second of start, even to the point of running a risk of being premature and being recalled. A good start gives you an unobstructed wind and the freedom to go where you wish rather than being forced to tack to gain clear air. There are two factors, however, that may upset your timing. One is the current; when it is running at right angles to the starting line, it may be necessary to either speed up or slow down your final run back to this line. Several practice runs down to the starting line and back just before the race, timed with a stop watch, will help you determine the current's effects. The second factor is that the wind may not be constant. Should it suddenly decrease or go light, your run away from the line should be shortened, or if the wind picks up, your sails should be luffed to slow the craft down.

On some days, if the wind is right and there happens to be no tidal current, you can sail away from the starting line 60 seconds before the last gun, come about and then hit the line right on the nose. However, this takes skill and practice to avoid hurrying the move and losing valuable time. If you do try this maneuver, make a wide sweeping turn and keep your boat moving all the time.

Racing Pitfalls

On the weather leg you must be on a continual alert to the trim of your sails. As a general rule, the mainsail should be sheeted in hard and the jib should also be trimmed in flat, but take care that it isn't too flat. While on this leg, keep these two simple rules in mind: 1) When the wind permits you head up, stay on that tack; and 2) when it heads you, change your tack. Always tack to keep your wind clear; you should make a quick tack right after the start if it appears to be to your advantage. But under no circumstance should you head too high into the wind. By doing this you may slow your boat to the point where no amount of sailing skill will make up for it later on in the race. Quite frequently a boat will pass another faster if she's permitted to fall off a bit and pass to leeward of a competitor that is heading too high. If the tacking leg is long enough, this boat may gain enough so that the other craft may never come near again. You'll learn with experience just how much to let your boat fall off to accomplish this maneuver.

It's wise to keep in mind that, except in a variable wind with pronounced wind shifts, it pays to avoid frequent tacking. Tack as little as possible. In other words, two long tacks are better than six short ones, because every time your boat goes about, valuable distance will be lost until the boat regains headway on the other tack. Unless in a hopeless position, don't tack away from the fleet if their course is the logical one. The odds of getting a wind shift way over there are against you. While such a gamble may bring a first, the chances are more often a last. In fleet racing the best course to windward is usually the collective course.

When on a tack, remember that other boats affect your wind. Of course, the ideal condition is to keep clear air and avoid the turbulence in the air and on the water caused by other boats. Sometimes, however, this is not possible and you must engage a foe at close quarters, taking away his air (blanketing), or sailing so that he can't pass (backwinding). The blanket zone, or wind shadow, of a boat's sails extends about three mast lengths, depending on the strength of the wind, and seems to trail along in the direction of the apparent wind. You should make every effort to keep clear of your competitors' sails to prevent their blanketing yours. Conversely, if you can blanket the wind from competing boats, you'll have a definite advantage. While on the windward leg your craft will blanket another, not only when directly upwind of it but also when off a competitor's leeward bow. In the latter position, wind striking your sails will be deflected aft and toward the boat astern, effectively backwinding it and slowing it down. You're in the "safe leeward position," a good place to be. But if other boats get this position on you, either tack or pinch-up in an effort to gain clear wind.

Generally, passing another boat to leeward is a rather difficult maneuver; but it can usually be accomplished by bearing off a little, plus running at increased speed through the tip of the blanket zone of the boat you're passing. Once clear of the covering effect and wake of the antagonist's craft, you can immediately pinch a little and make a full effort to work up to windward. While you may lose a little distance during this maneuver, it will generally place you in a safe leeward position, where it's possible to give your antagonist a taste of backwind.

When leading, try to stay between the fleet and the mark. But, whether or not you're in the lead, attempt to fetch the mark on a starboard tack. This will give the right-of-way, and you can round it without tacking. If you pass the mark to starboard, it will be necessary to fetch it on a port tack. While this may sound rather contradictory, it's a fact, because if several boats are coming up on the mark on the port tack, and you're on a starboard tack, you can't tack unless you're far in front of them. All they have to do is merely to bear off slightly, go under your stern, and round the mark ahead of you.

When approaching the mark, make certain not to overstand. This

Figure 8-3: Getting ready to round the windward mark.

means pointing too high above the mark so that your craft has to sail back down to the turn at the end of the windward leg with sheets eased. When making the actual turn, attempt to do so as smoothly as possible, because if your boat becomes jammed around with a quick thrust of the tiller, she loses both speed and headway. While the turn should be close to the buoy, it shouldn't be too close, for any boat that strikes a mark of the course is immediately disqualified. For this reason, a good rule is to steer wide of the mark on its near side, then head up smartly on the far side as the turn is completed. A boat finishing a turn close to the mark may be able to slip inside to windward of someone ahead who has sagged off. When a turn is begun too wide, however, it is an open invitation for a trailing boat to sneak inside, closer to the mark. Should current be a factor on the course, be sure to use it to your best advantage when rounding a mark.

On a reach or run many skippers consider that these legs have little effect on the outcome of a race, but very often it's during these portions that there are real opportunities for ground-gaining. On a reach, keep your wind clear and head no higher than the next mark. If possible, steer to leeward of it so that you're in a good position to gain speed by heading up, but make sure to compensate for any current taking you off course. Avoid getting entangled in a luffing match that might permit other craft astern to go ahead of you. When passing boats, be sure to allow enough clearance so that they'll have trouble in covering or luffing you.

The boom vang is very valuable in this leg of a race. It should be set up before reaching the weather mark. With the boom vang, the boom and sail swing as a unit and the sail is held in one plane. This allows the sail to be eased further off than would otherwise be possible. Without the downwind pull of the vang, the mainsail will luff first aloft, and the entire sail must be trimmed to meet this condition. With it down, the luff occurs simultaneously along the entire hoist. A spinnaker can also be employed effectively on broad reaches. While quite often it may be hard to judge on the prior leg if your boat should carry the spinnaker on the next, prepare to set it anyway, and save the actual decision until the turn has been made and the angle of the wind on the new course can be fully determined. The latter is most important. For instance, on a close reach, a spinnaker is generally more of a liability than a help because it will drag the boat to leeward, off the proper course.

When a spinnaker is used on a reach it is set the same way as described on page 67—at right angles to the wind—which means that the pole goes forward on the windward side, right up to the headstay if necessary. Keeping one's wind clear is again a must and therefore there is little profit in mixing with competitors. All too often skippers have become so interested in luffing matches that they

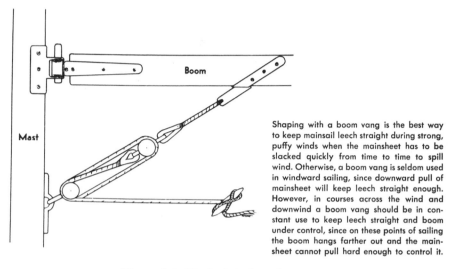

Shaping with a boom vang is the best way to keep mainsail leech straight during strong, puffy winds when the mainsheet has to be slacked quickly from time to time to spill wind. Otherwise, a boom vang is seldom used in windward sailing, since downward pull of mainsheet will keep leech straight enough. However, in courses across the wind and downwind a boom vang should be in constant use to keep leech straight and boom under control, since on these points of sailing the boom hangs farther out and the mainsheet cannot pull hard enough to control it.

Figure 8-4: Typical rig for a boom vang.

have forgotten that the main idea was to be first around the mark. Concentrating too much on the luffing business, they have sailed far, far away, only to find that some tailender has seized the opportunity of making for the buoy and is well on the way home. Before the battling strategists can abandon their private naval war and recall that they are supposed to get across a finish line, the tailender has won the race.

The boat should usually be set on her best lines at a slight heel. In light air, the crew sits to leeward to give the boat this heel. But in heavy weather the leeward rail should be clear of the water, with the crew riding to windward and perhaps the mainsail luffing to spill a little unnecessary wind. Long before reaching the mark, you should plan to be the inside boat at the buoy, and sail the course accordingly. You should try to establish an overlap on the boat nearest you, so that you'll be entitled to buoy room, and in addition, be the windward boat after you have rounded.

When racing downwind the use of the spinnaker is most important. But, to obtain the most from it, you must know how fast the spinnaker can be set up at the beginning of the leg and how long it can be kept aloft before dousing at the end. When this big sail is pulling, it adds so much speed that the crew which get its up first has an excellent chance to pass others. Actually this leg of the race presents opportunities to run up on those ahead, blanket their wind with the spinnaker, and perhaps pass them. In other words, you should try to blanket others ahead and avoid being blanketed by those behind. In most instances, try to sail a straight-line course. Compensate for the leeway made by the current. Remember that more and more skippers have come to conclude that races can easily be won or lost downwind.

When the wind is light and spotty, watch out for the smooth spots where there's a dead calm. If you sail into one of these you may sit there for what seems like hours, watching the rest of the sailing fleet go around the course. Skill in observing weather conditions and interpreting them correctly plays a very important part in winning a race. The experienced sailboat skipper will recognize these smooth, glassy spots as traps to be avoided. He knows that even a light breeze will leave small ripples or cats'-paws on the water and he'll try to shape his course for these spots. During the summer months particularly, breezes are apt to be light and variable, and it requires a lot of sailing know-how to take advantage of every puff of air that comes along. Watch wind direction in puffs. It may indicate the direction of a permanent shift. A weather-wise skipper will watch other boats, some of them far away, to see if the wind is blowing there. Flags ashore or perhaps a large factory smokestack are also good indications of wind conditions. Even a small wisp of smoke may give an advance warning of a shift in the wind. Usually, the darker the color of the water, the stronger the wind is. It's actually possible to sail a longer course in more of a breeze and travel around a fleet of becalmed racers. And don't forget about tide and currents. Know when it will turn, and study your local current charts to determine where it's strongest. You can then alter your course to compensate

Figure 8-5: Charging downwind toward the finish line.

for its effect and to gain the greatest benefit. Above everything else, remember that the shortest distance between two racing marks isn't always the quickest course to the winner's cup.

In this chapter I've touched only on the basic techniques of sailboat racing. But if you follow them and get plenty of practice, you'll go a long way toward success in racing. Later, with added experience, you may become a real champion. In any event, you'll surely have plenty of fun in sailboat racing.

Class Association

As stated previously, if you plan to race, membership in a class association is a must. While all class associations vary to some degree in their rules, I selected the Ensign Class Association's rules to show the organization of a typical class. (Part II, which is not included, covers specifications and measurements.)

ENSIGN CLASS ASSOCIATION

CLASS RULES

Part 1: ORGANIZATION

1. *Name.* The name of this organization shall be the Ensign Class Association.
2. *Object.*
   A. To promote and develop Ensign Class racing under uniform rules and to maintain rigidly the one-design feature of the Ensign.
   B. To promote the use of the Ensign as a family boat for recreational sailing.
3. *Emblem.* The emblem of the Class shall be the red block letter "E" and six blue stars.
4. *Class Design.* The boat shall be the 22½-foot sloop keel type, with fiberglass hull designed by Carl A. Alberg, manufactured by Pearson Yachts, introduced in 1962 as the Electra Day Sailer, and subsequently renamed the Ensign.
5. *Organization and Membership.* Any owner or bona fide charterer of an Ensign may apply for membership in the Association. He shall join, if possible, through an Ensign Fleet on whose waters he normally sails. The power to accept or reject applications for membership is vested in each Fleet, but any application is subject to refusal, for cause, by the Governing Committee.

   The Fleet, a territorial branch or unit open to all eligible individuals, shall elect its own officers, always to include a Fleet

Secretary. It shall be self-governing in all local matters that do not conflict with the Association's Rules.

6. *Fleet Charters.* The Governing Committee may grant Fleet Charters to each Fleet consisting of three or more owners upon application to the Class Secretary. Charters shall be revoked by the Governing Committee upon failure of a Fleet to maintain a minimum number of members in good standing or other adequate cause.

7. *Dues and Membership.*

   A. Regular membership in the Ensign Class Association shall be extended to owners, part owners and charterers of Ensigns registered upon payment of dues. However, in all matters requiring representation and voting, each boat shall be limited to a single vote.

   B. The organization may accept as Associate Members all persons interested in the Class, but no Associate Member shall be entitled to representation or voting.

   C. The dues shall be $2.00 for the Calendar Year 1965 and in future years shall be determined by the Executive Committee.

   D. Applicants who are not members of local Fleets shall remit dues directly to the National Ensign Class Treasurer. Fleet members shall remit both national and Fleet dues to their Fleet treasurers, who in turn shall remit national dues to the National Treasurer.

8. *Executive Officers and Duties.* The Association shall be governed by the following officers, who shall be elected at each Annual Meeting or until their successors are elected at a special meeting.

   The President, who shall preside at meetings, shall rule on procedure and appoint special committees. He shall be empowered to call all meetings and shall designate the time and place, excepting only the Annual Meeting.

   The Secretary, who shall, as the Secretary, keep minutes of the meetings, reports on Fleets, records of membership registration of boats, issue all Fleet Charters and, in addition, shall perform all other duties pertaining to such office. The Secretary shall preside in the absence of the President.

   The Treasurer who shall, as Treasurer, deposit all funds,

keep financial books, make necessary disbursements and render a report at the Annual Meeting.

9. *Governing Committee.* The powers of the Association shall be vested in, and administered by, its Governing Committee.

   The Governing Committee shall consist of the three officers as designated, and four other members of the Association elected at the Annual Meeting, or until their successors are elected at a special meeting. An affirmative vote of four of the seven members of the Committee shall decide all questions, and such votes shall be final. The Committee shall interpret the Class Rules, grant or revoke Charters, sanction or ban Association races; fill vacancies in office; conduct all business and determine the policies of the Association.

10. *The Rules Committee.* It shall be appointed immediately after each Annual Meeting by the President and its members shall hold office for one year. It shall pass on all questions relative to eligibility of boats and equipment, interpret the Rules and Specifications, and recommend to the Governing Committee any advisable alterations or additions to the Class Rules.

11. *Meetings and Elections.* Annual Meetings shall be held in January of each year at a time and place to be designated by the Governing Committee. The Secretary shall mail a notice of this meeting to all Fleet Secretaries at least thirty days in advance of the date selected. A quorum shall consist of the presence of at least 5 Regular members. Voting shall be by Regular members who shall be entitled to one vote for each boat enrolled and the majority vote of those present then in good standing, in person or by proxy, shall be sufficient. A proxy must be in writing.

    The order of business at an Annual Meeting shall be as follows:
    1. Call to Order
    2. Roll Call
    3. Reading of Minutes
    4. Reports of Officers
    5. Ratification of Governing Committee Rulings
    6. Other Business
    7. Election of Officers and Governing Committee
    8. Adjournment

A Special Meeting shall be called by the President upon request of the Governing Committee or upon written request to the Class Secretary by Fleet Secretaries of at least twenty-five per cent of the total number of Chartered Fleets.

A Class Secretary shall give to all Fleet Secretaries not less than two weeks' written notice of the purpose, time and place designated by the President for any special meeting.

12. Amendments: The Class Rules may be amended only at an Annual or Special Meeting by two-thirds vote of the total number of boats represented at the meeting in person or by proxy provided, however, that the proposed amendment shall be set forth in the notice of the Meeting.

In addition to class associations and yacht clubs there are racing associations which are made up of either or both class association and yacht-club members. The purpose of a racing association generally is to foster and develop the interests of one-design racing craft through the supervision of boat regattas for recognized one-design classes.

Another sailing organization you may wish to join is the United States International Sailing Association. In 1964 the Association paid all expenses of the United States Olympic sailing team. (Our company donated the five hundredth Triton which we made—she was a golden one—to USISA and they auctioned her off to their members. While the actual sale price was just under $13,000, many sailors joined the Association to place bids for the golden Triton.) The USISA also plans to meet expenses of certain international competitions in the future. The necessary funds come solely from membership dues and contributions. Dues range from $10 up, depending on category, and they are tax deductible. For further information, write United States International Sailing Association, 37 West 44th Street, New York, New York 10036.

9

The Lure
of Ocean Racing

The lure of ocean racing can only be explained by the perversity of man, because it is a tough pastime, a form of masochism or self-torture imposed in the name of sport and good fellowship. But, there are people—namely the ocean-racing yachtsmen—who live just to come to grips with the sea in her many moods. These hardy racing sailors of the high seas are ever mindful of the words of an old French abbé in his blessing of a fishing fleet: "The sea will always be wild and untamed. A sweetheart to those who love her. A mother to those who earn their bread upon her bosom but an avenging angel to those who hold her in contempt."

While the sea has her violent moods, the organizations that run ocean racing events have attempted to keep her in bounds by placing heavy emphasis on safety. And this preoccupation with safety at sea has paid handsome dividends. For instance, the Cruising Club of America, which sponsors the Newport to Bermuda race, has held this event twenty-five times. In these, over one thousand yachts and approximately eight thousand men have competed. The total number of casualties are insignificant when you consider the dangers inherent at sea during a race of this type: One vessel burned at sea, one yacht wrecked on Bermuda's reefs, one man lost (in 1932).

While several of the sailboats illustrated in this book could have or have taken part in the Newport to Bermuda, San Pedro to Diamond Head, San Diego to Acapulco races and others (the Invicta

Figure 9-1: Two popular ocean racers: the 37-foot sailboat (top) and the 41-footer (bottom).

Class, *Burgoo,* was over-all winner of the Bermuda race in 1964), I will confine my discussion to such offshore events as one-day affairs, overnighter or rendezvous or group races. Such racing generally takes place over courses of varying lengths from a few miles to several hundred, raced by cruising-racing craft under some type of handicap system.

Handicap Systems

As was stated in the last chapter, racing can be done either even-up or handicapped. As was mentioned, most one-design class races are sailed without handicap, although some yacht clubs and racing associations work out a system of some type by which a boat that wins a race incurs a handicap penalty in the next. Actually, in the waters where I usually sail, when such a method is used, the skipper is handicapped rather than the boat. Handicaps, however, become necessary when boats of different sail area and hull size race against one another. When this occurs there are two main systems employed: 1) Handicaps by "time-on-time"; and 2) handicaps by "time-on-distance."

In the time-on-time system the allowance is calculated at a given number of seconds or minutes per hour of the finishing time either of the leading boat, or more often, of the individual boat which is receiving the handicap. According to the time-on-distance system, the allowance is calculated with reference to the length of the course. Both handicap systems have their faults and under some weather conditions each may favor one boat over another boat. For example, the time-on-time system generally gives an advantage to the small boat should the race be sailed in light air conditions with periods of calm; for its time allowance over the larger craft increases while both are becalmed. In a time-on-distance race, on the other hand, no more allowance is given if the course is a dead beat against strong winds than if the course were a straight run in good weather the entire way.

Measurement Rules and Time Allowance

Whether a race is based on time or distance, many different rating formulas have been devised to establish what handicap one boat should receive against another. In general, they cater to a class of boats more or less uniform in design and sail area. With the North American Yacht Racing Union time allowance system, the scale is based on the rating and distance sailed, which gives a fixed time allowance regardless of the elapsed time of the race—a time which will vary under different sailing conditions.

While there are other, simpler rules in current use (the Storm Trysail and Off Sounding Clubs' measurement rules, for example), the measurement rule under which the large proportion of important races for cruising yachts are sailed is that of the Cruising Club of America. This rule has been considered the fairest by the majority of racing committees because it incorporates the refinements affecting the potential speed of a sailing yacht as well as the fundamentals. While the efforts of yacht designers, builders, and owners to develop boats which sail faster than their ratings call for continue, the existing CCA rule reflects periodic adjustments of measurements to compensate for the ingenuity of yacht designers in taking advantage of loopholes in the rules that preceded it. In the spirit of fair racing, all of us should vow to uphold the CCA's *Spirit of the Rule* statement, which reads as follows:

It is the intent of CCA Measurement Rule to make it possible for yachtsmen to race seaworthy cruising boats of various designs, types, and construction on a fair and equitable basis. The rules are not, and can never be, perfect. In order that the rules may serve this purpose, yachtsmen themselves must interpret them in keeping with the Spirit of the Rule. No infringement of the *Spirit of the Rule* nor any method of reducing the rating of any yacht by utilizing questionable, unreasonable, or unsafe methods will be acceptable; and the Club will not issue a rating certificate to any yacht owner who in any manner attempts to defeat the purpose for which this rule is intended. All Race Committees conducting races under this Measurement Rule are strongly urged to require that any unusual practice in rig, hull, ballast, or other factors not covered specifically within these rules, be reported to the Race Committee for a ruling, and in any case, be subject to protest. The test of said ruling shall be whether or not, in the opinion of the Race Committee, the practice would give unfair advantage or in any way violate or circumvent the intent of the rule.

In the comparing of the relative potential speeds of different-sized boats, the CCA rule starts with the accepted theory that the potential speed of a boat varies approximately in proportion to the square root of the waterline length (potential speed : $\sqrt{\text{LWL}}$). The time allowance tables contained herein are based on this fact. These tables, long ago standardized and used by the NAYRU, New York Yacht Club, and other organizations, give the number of seconds it

Here are some of measurements taken to determine C.C.A. rating: L.O.A.=length from aftermost part of hull to intersection of forward side of stem and top of covering board; O.H.F.=overhang length of stem from plane of flotation to forward L.O.A. point; O.H.A.=overhang length at stern; L.W.L.= load waterline length, which is L.O.A., O.H.F. and O.H.A.; 4% W.L.=length measured at point 4% of L.W.L. above the plane of flotation; Mes. Bm.=average of beams at L.W.L. and the 4% W.L. taken at fore and aft position of maximum beam of the L.W.L.; Mes. F.=average of freeboard measured port and starboard to top of covering board abreast bow and stern endings of L.W.L. plus half the average rail height at those points; B=length of foot of mainsail; P=length of hoist of a jib-headed mainsail; B_2=actual fore triangle base, spinnaker pole length, or a percentage of spinnaker measured width, whichever is greatest; P_2=actual fore triangle height, or height determined by spinnaker dimensions, whichever is the greater.

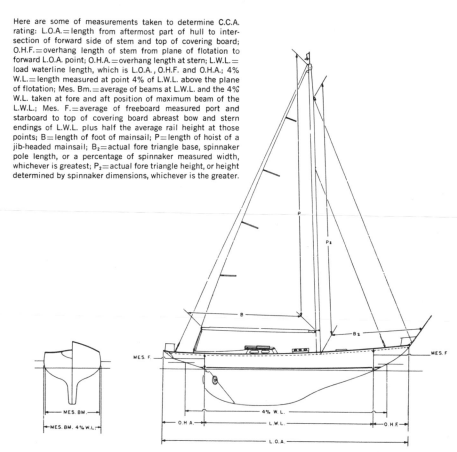

Figure 9-2: (Courtesy of Cruising Club of America)

will take theoretically for a boat of given waterline length to go one nautical mile under average racing conditions.

To use these time allowance tables in comparing the performance of boats of varying design and size required the development of a formula of rating rule which would provide corrections to the waterline length for size and design factors which vary from a standard. Such a formula would then correct the waterline length to a *rated length* (R) which could be used in the time allowance tables to determine the relative average racing-condition time per mile for varying types of boats. These times could then be used for determining a fair time handicap for all boats in a race—using the time for the highest-rated boat as the scratch or base time from which differences in time could be calculated for the length of the course—and thereby establish handicaps for all boats which would be relative to the scratch boat and all others.

The measurement rule of the CCA is a formula for correcting the waterline length of a boat to obtain a rated length. It takes into consideration the principal factors which affect the potential speed of a boat. It endeavors to correct for differences in design which tend to increase or decrease the speed of a boat in relation to a standard, so that in applying these corrections, all boats in a race will be on an equitable basis as far as these factors are concerned. For instance, the power to drive a boat through the water is obtained from the sails, and therefore more sail area, or a more efficient sail plan, will increase speed, while the reverse is true with less sail area or a less efficient sail plan. The formula endeavors to correct for variations in sails and to convert variations from a standard, or base, into a change in waterline length. However, displacement, or the weight of a boat, offers resistance to hull movement through the water, and therefore the rule endeavors to allow for variations from a standard or base displacement by giving a credit or reduction in waterline length when displacement is greater than a standard, and by giving a penalty or increase in waterline length when displacement is less than a standard. Similarly, beam affects the speed of a boat. As a general rule, an increase in beam increases wave-making resistance, and it also increases wetted surface, thus increasing skin-friction resistance. However, as explained below, it must be realized that if a boat has insufficient beam it cannot properly carry her sail and therefore will suffer when on the wind. The formula provides for a decrease in the waterline length for increased beam above a standard, or for an increase in the waterline length for decreased beam below a standard. Also, the draft of a boat has a considerable effect on speed. A boat with light draft may benefit by having less wetted surface, whereas a deep draft lowers the center of gravity, thus adding to stability and sail-carrying capacity, as well as perhaps giving a more effective lateral plane, or better performance to windward. Although corrections for these factors, plus corrections for freeboard, propeller type and location, centerboards, and iron versus lead keels are important and necessary; there are direct calculations by themselves as to their effect on speed and on rating. However, stability is a very important factor in determining the sailing qualities of a boat, as it involves the combined effect of many of the other factors. It is therefore necessary to devise a formula to take stability into consideration in order that variations in it may be properly evaluated. This results in some of the more complicated calculations of the measurement rule for translating stability into the effect on speed and rating. Ballast-to-displacement ratios and measured beam-to-beam ratios are needed from which is derived a correction factor to rating. For instance, more ballast or more beam increases the stability of a boat and results in a penalty correction to rating, but the corresponding increase in displacement or beam derived by their respective formulas increases the resistance of the hull through the water, and results in a credit correction to the rating; so that a loss in one adjustment may be offset to some extent by a gain in another. Therefore, in the final calculation of the rating, the plus-and-minus corrections for all the factors are summed up and applied in the rating formula to determine the rated length of the boat.

Time Allowance Tables
For One Nautical Mile, In Seconds and Decimals

Rating	Allowance	Rating	Allowance	Rating	Allowance	Rating	Allowance	Rating	Allowance	Rating	Allowance
15.0	381.35	21.0	294.98	27.0	239.33	33.0	199.65	39.0	169.52	45.0	145.61
.1	379.49	.1	293.87	.1	238.56	.1	199.08	.1	169.08	.1	145.28
.2	377.65	.2	292.76	.2	237.79	.2	198.51	.2	168.64	.2	144.92
.3	375.83	.3	291.65	.3	237.03	.3	197.95	.3	168.19	.3	144.56
.4	374.03	.4	290.56	.4	236.27	.4	197.39	.4	167.75	.4	144.20
.5	372.26	.5	289.48	.5	235.52	.5	196.83	.5	167.31	.5	143.85
.6	370.50	.6	288.40	.6	234.78	.6	196.27	.6	166.88	.6	143.50
.7	368.76	.7	287.33	.7	234.04	.7	195.72	.7	166.45	.7	143.15
.8	367.03	.8	286.26	.8	233.30	.8	195.17	.8	166.02	.8	142.80
.9	365.31	.9	285.20	.9	232.57	.9	194.63	.9	165.60	.9	142.46
16.0	363.64	22.0	284.15	28.0	231.84	34.0	194.09	40.0	165.18	46.0	142.12
.1	361.97	.1	283.10	.1	231.11	.1	193.54	.1	164.75	.1	141.78
.2	360.31	.2	282.07	.2	230.39	.2	193.00	.2	164.32	.2	141.43
.3	358.66	.3	281.04	.3	229.67	.3	192.46	.3	163.88	.3	141.08
.4	357.02	.4	280.02	.4	228.95	.4	191.92	.4	163.46	.4	140.74
.5	355.39	.5	279.00	.5	228.24	.5	191.38	.5	163.04	.5	140.39
.6	353.79	.6	277.99	.6	227.53	.6	190.85	.6	162.62	.6	140.04
.7	352.21	.7	276.99	.7	226.82	.7	190.32	.7	162.21	.7	139.70
.8	350.64	.8	276.00	.8	226.12	.8	189.79	.8	161.80	.8	139.37
.9	349.08	.9	275.01	.9	225.43	.9	189.28	.9	161.39	.9	139.04

TIME ALLOWANCE TABLES (*Continued*)
For One Nautical Mile, In Seconds and Decimals

Rating	Allowance	Rating	Allowance	Rating	Allowance	Rating	Allowance	Rating	Allowance	Rating	Allowance
17.0	347.52	23.0	274.03	29.0	224.74	35.0	188.76	41.0	160.98	47.0	138.71
.1	345.99	.1	273.06	.1	224.05	.1	188.24	.1	160.56	.1	138.38
.2	344.47	.2	272.09	.2	223.37	.2	187.72	.2	160.15	.2	138.05
.3	342.96	.3	271.13	.3	222.68	.3	187.20	.3	159.74	.3	137.71
.4	341.46	.4	270.17	.4	222.00	.4	186.68	.4	159.34	.4	137.38
.5	339.97	.5	269.22	.5	221.33	.5	186.17	.5	158.93	.5	137.05
.6	338.50	.6	268.27	.6	220.66	.6	185.65	.6	158.52	.6	136.73
.7	337.04	.7	267.33	.7	219.99	.7	185.15	.7	158.12	.7	136.40
.8	335.60	.8	266.40	.8	219.32	.8	184.64	.8	157.73	.8	136.07
.9	334.17	.9	265.48	.9	218.66	.9	184.14	.9	157.33	.9	135.74
18.0	332.75	24.0	264.55	30.0	218.00	36.0	183.64	42.0	156.93	48.0	135.41
.1	331.33	.1	263.64	.1	217.34	.1	183.14	.1	156.53	.1	135.08
.2	329.93	.2	262.73	.2	216.70	.2	182.64	.2	156.13	.2	134.76
.3	328.54	.3	261.82	.3	216.05	.3	182.15	.3	155.74	.3	134.44
.4	327.17	.4	260.92	.4	215.40	.4	181.66	.4	155.35	.4	134.11
.5	325.83	.5	260.03	.5	214.75	.5	181.16	.5	154.96	.5	133.79
.6	324.48	.6	259.14	.6	214.11	.6	180.67	.6	154.57	.6	133.47
.7	323.14	.7	258.26	.7	213.48	.7	180.19	.7	154.19	.7	133.16
.8	321.82	.8	257.38	.8	212.85	.8	179.71	.8	153.80	.8	132.85
.9	320.50	.9	256.51	.9	212.23	.9	179.23	.9	153.42	.9	132.54
19.0	319.19	25.0	255.65	31.0	211.61	37.0	178.75	43.0	153.04	49.0	132.22
.1	317.89	.1	254.78	.1	210.98	.1	178.27	.1	152.66	.1	131.90
.2	316.60	.2	253.92	.2	210.36	.2	177.79	.2	152.28	.2	131.58
.3	315.32	.3	253.07	.3	209.74	.3	177.31	.3	151.90	.3	131.27
.4	314.05	.4	252.23	.4	209.11	.4	176.83	.4	151.52	.4	130.96
.5	312.78	.5	251.39	.5	208.50	.5	176.36	.5	151.14	.5	130.64
.6	311.53	.6	250.55	.6	207.89	.6	175.90	.6	150.76	.6	130.33
.7	310.29	.7	249.72	.7	207.28	.7	175.43	.7	150.38	.7	130.03
.8	309.06	.8	248.89	.8	206.68	.8	174.96	.8	150.01	.8	129.72
.9	307.84	.9	248.07	.9	206.08	.9	174.50	.9	149.65	.9	129.42
20.0	306.62	26.0	247.25	32.0	205.48	38.0	174.04	44.0	149.28	50.0	129.12
.1	305.42	.1	246.44	.1	204.88	.1	173.58	.1	148.91	.1	128.81
.2	304.24	.2	245.63	.2	204.29	.2	173.12	.2	148.54	.2	128.50
.3	303.05	.3	244.82	.3	203.70	.3	172.67	.3	148.17	.3	128.20
.4	301.87	.4	244.02	.4	203.11	.4	172.21	.4	147.80	.4	127.89
.5	300.71	.5	243.23	.5	202.52	.5	171.76	.5	147.43	.5	127.58
.6	299.54	.6	242.44	.6	201.94	.6	171.30	.6	147.07	.6	127.28
.7	298.39	.7	241.66	.7	201.36	.7	170.84	.7	146.71	.7	126.98
.8	297.25	.8	240.88	.8	200.79	.8	170.40	.8	146.35	.8	126.68
.9	296.11	.9	240.10	.9	200.22	.9	169.96	.9	145.99	.9	126.39

(Courtesy of the Cruising Club of America)

The CCA rating formula is as follows:

Rated Length (R) = .93 (L ± BM ± Dra. ± Displ. ± S ± F − I) × Bal. R × Prop.

This (R) is used as "rating" in the time-allowance table to determine the seconds per mile or "allowance."

To find the allowance a yacht of any given rating should receive from a larger one, take the figure to be found opposite the small rating; from this subtract the figure opposite the measurement of the larger yacht; and the difference, multiplied by the number of nautical miles in the course, is the amount of time allowance due the smaller vessel, in seconds and hundredths of a second. For example, in a race between a Triton Class and Rhodes 41 Class boat, the allowance or time handicap would be as follows:

Triton—CCA rating 20.6

Rhodes 41—CCA rating 28.0

Course length—100 nautical miles

Triton allowance from table (for 20.6) = 299.54 seconds per mile

Rhodes 41 allowance from table (for 28.0) = 231.84 seconds per mile

Rhodes 41 allows Triton . . . . 67.70 seconds per mile

In the race (100 nautical miles), the Rhodes 41 allows the Triton (100 × 67.7) = 6770 seconds; or 1 hour, 52 minutes, 50 seconds.

The table is based upon the assumption that, under average racing conditions, a yacht of rating measurement, R, will sail one nautical mile in the number of seconds given by the formula

$$\frac{2160}{\sqrt{R}} + 183.64$$

The allowance per mile between yachts of different ratings will, therefore, be given by

$$\frac{2160}{\sqrt{r}} - \frac{2160}{\sqrt{R}}$$

in which R is the rating measurement of the larger yacht and r that of the smaller yacht. The theoretical number of seconds required to sail one nautical mile under average conditions (as would be encountered in a triangular race) is obtained by adding 360 to the figure in the table opposite the yacht's rating measurement.

Typical instructions for rendezvous race. (Courtesy of Yacht Racing Association of Long Island Sound)

Eligibility:

Open to auxiliary sailing yachts, with permanently attached motors, 24 ft. or greater L.O.A., rated under the current Storm Trysail Club rule.

Rules:

The current racing rules as adopted by the YRA of LIS except as modified herein shall govern the race.

Ratings:

Yachts will be rated under the current Storm Trysail Club measurement rule as amended effective May 1, 1963. A current measurement certificate must be submitted with entry blank unless it is on file with the Yacht Racing Association of Long Island Sound. Minimum rating for calculating time allowance shall be 15.0.

Time Allowances:

Time allowances will be based on the NAYRU tables for the ratings submitted and for the distance of the course selected.

Divisions:

Entrants will be assigned to two or more Divisions. Prior to the race the assignment to Divisions will be announced and each contestant will be supplied with a list of each contestant registered, together with ratings and time allowances.

Courses:

On the day of the race the Regatta Committee will decide on Course A if there is a fair breeze or Course B if the winds are light. The course selected will be signaled by the letter "A" or "B" on the Committee boat.

Course A (25.7 mi)

From Can 1, N of Execution Light, to Bell 15, N of Lloyd's Point, to Nun 2, SW of Great Captain's Island, and back to start.

Course B (15.6 mi)

From Can 1, N of Execution Light, to Matinecock Bell 21, N of Point, to Nun 2, SW of Great Captain's Island, and back to start.

All Divisions will race the same course.

Turning marks are to be left to port. Government marks, except if marks of the course, may be passed on either hand.

Starting and Finishing Line:

The starting and finishing line shall be between a white flag on the Committee boat and Can 1, N of Execution Light.

Starting Signals:

10:20 One White Cylinder—Warning

10:25 One Blue Cylinder—Preparatory Div. I

10:30 One Red Cylinder—Start Div. I and Warning Div. II

10:35 Two White Cylinders—Preparatory Div. II

10:40 Two Blue Cylinders—Start Div. II and Warning Div. III

10:45 Two Red Cylinders—Preparatory Div. III

10:50 One White Cylinder—Start Div. III

This pattern will be continued if additional Divisions are designated.

Postponement:

Postponements will be for five minute periods. They will be signaled by international code answering pennant "AP" and two guns. The next raised signal will be the warning signal for the Division scheduled to start.

Recall:

A recall will be indicated by a white cylinder with a red band and one blast of a horn for each yacht recalled. The number of the yacht will be called out. A recalled yacht that fails to return shall be penalized on elapsed time as determined by the committee prior to the first finish.

Time Limit:

If no yacht in any Division has finished by 7:00 p.m., the race shall be deemed canceled. If the committee boat is not on station, yachts will take their own time when Can 1 bears 180 degrees magnetic at a distance of no more than 150 yards, and report the time to the Regatta Committee.

Protest:

A protest must be in writing to the Regatta Committee according to the NAYRU rules and filed within forty-eight hours of the finish.

Prizes:

1st, 2nd, and 3rd prizes will be awarded in each Division.

We are pleased to announce that this will be one of the qualifying day races for the DeCoursey Fales Long Island Sound Distance Championship Trophy, conducted under the auspices of the YRA of Long Island Sound.

Entries:

All entries must be filed by July 18, 1964.

Guest Privileges:

The privileges of the Knickerbocker Yacht Club are extended to visiting Captains, their crews and families for the weekend of July 25.

Midget Ocean Racing Club

The Midget Ocean Racing Club was founded in the mid-1950's to promote cruising and racing among small boats under 24 feet in length. While this is still the Club's primary objective, an amendment to the constitution now gives each station (subject to the approval of the governing board) the option of raising the over-all length limitation for races in its locality to 29.99 feet. Although this expansion is subject to option by the individual MORC stations, the vast majority of stations have so optioned. All boats compete for open fleet prizes, but the fleet in turn is divided into two classes: Class B for boats up to 24 feet over-all length and Class A for those over that dimension and under 30 feet.

As with the other ocean-racing association, MORC instituted and rigidly enforces several safety requirements. Boats, for example, must be self-righting and outfitted with either a self-bailing or watertight cockpit. If the measurer is not satisfied as to a vessel's ultimate stability, he may insist on a stability test, which consists of placing the boat on her beam's end and observing whether she is capable of righting herself. Besides the addition of personal life lines for each member of the crew and a choice between either built-in flotation with a resultant positive buoyancy of 250 pounds or the carrying of a bottle-inflated rubber life raft, the balance of the MORC safety requirements are roughly equivalent to those of the United States Coast Guard for vessels of this size.

MORC racing at present can best be described as regional in nature. They certainly don't have anything like a Bermuda race or a Trans-Pac race, with the fleet being drawn from the four corners of the globe. Actually, MORC racing varies in character considerably from station to station. Geographical differences naturally contribute to this variance. Usually, private yacht clubs give ample opportunity to those interested in day racing or the port-to-port cruising sort of thing. In areas where this isn't true and there is interest in this type of activity, the MORC station has moved to accommodate. Where there is a lack of other organized activity a MORC station could very well have each weekend of the season earmarked for racing. Many stations also will have a purely social race or two, such as an affair known as the rendezvous where they will race to a given point on a Saturday, then raft up, have a picnic or clambake in the evening, and race back to Saturday's starting point on Sunday. Also where there is interest, day races are scheduled for MORC boats; and in certain instances MORC's safety rules are waived for such activities in the interest of capturing new recruits. Occasionally a novelty race also will appear in the form of a singlehanded race, a lady skipper's race, or the like. Most stations schedule *at least* one major overnight event annually. This event generally covers as much open water as local environs allow and normally requires something over twenty-four hours to traverse. After all, they have to justify the "ocean racing" in their name.

Tips on Distance Racing

While the sport of offshore distance or ocean racing has many things in common with inshore racing around the buoys, it has one major difference: the result does *not* depend solely on speed. Navigation, for instance, plays a most important part in it, for if the fastest craft misses a few marks or bearings, she might finish among the "also rans." For this reason, the navigator is perhaps the most important member of the crew, although the cook can't be considered to be far behind; for if—as Napoleon is supposed to have stated —an army marches on its stomach, the crew of an ocean (distance) racing yacht sails on theirs. For real long races, it's a great asset to have a dependable full-time navigator. But for the average offshore race it is best for the skipper to do all the navigation work, because both the strategy and tactics of offshore racing are closely connected with the navigation. Unfortunately, under this arrangement the skipper has no one to blame but himself if the next mark doesn't appear right on the nose.

Speaking of a crew, its choice and ability to work as a smoothly functioning unit are most important. While family crews, or ones made up of friends, are popular in rendezvous or group races, longer events require some experienced hands. This becomes more evident in the case of ocean races where the yacht must be driven as hard as possible from start to finish, day and night. Experience shows that a good crew (in which of course the skipper is included) can be of greater importance to the final result than small differences in speed between competing yachts. Thus, when entering such an event, a great deal of thought must be given to the tasks each member can perform.

It's not good enough, for example, when offshore racing, to have just one good helmsman amongst the crew. Presuming that the skipper knows how to sail his own boat, there should be at least one other good helmsman in each watch. (This is only important when the boat is sailed both night and day.) While it would be an ideal situation to have all members of the crew be equally good as helmsmen, this would be wishful thinking, and therefore the skipper must make sure that only the best helmsmen take turns at the helm. Remember, however, that a successful inshore racing helmsman isn't necessarily a good one for offshore events without special training. But I believe that inshore racing is necessary to anyone who wishes to become a good ocean-racing man. The difference in helmsmanship between offshore and inshore racing actually can be found in that the former is only done in daylight, when the helmsman can always watch the action of the sails. Since an offshore event may include racing at night, the helmsman must be able to sail his craft "by the feel." This requires some experience, and knowledge of the particular kind of skill which can only be gained by the experience of sailing in rough seas offshore. For example, when sailing close-hauled out at sea, the helmsman should feel free to steer the course that gives the best speed. Therefore the navigator should only give the helmsman the limits between which that tack will remain the favorable one. The helmsman should keep track of the compass course steered and make notes in the logbook. If he does find himself sailing outside these limits, he should either tack or ease sheets, depending on the circumstances.

When the skipper knows his crew before the start it is a great

Figure 9-3: The start of a rendezvous offshore race.

advantage. Sometimes this is impossible, and he must make a crew
from men recommended to him. But, even if the skipper succeeds in
finding a crew with considerable experience in offshore racing, they
should be trained as a unit before the race. If this isn't possible, the
skipper should make it clear how he wants things done. Each man
may know quite well how the job should be done, but the same thing
may be done correctly in several ways. The crew should, therefore,
be trained, or at least informed, as how each maneuver should be
performed to get good teamwork. Once they have learned that
method, no other way may be employed without first consulting the
skipper. The crew members, of course, should be good sailors with
strong stomachs. The question of seasickness was discussed in Chapter 7; here it need only be said that it is practically impossible to find

a crew that will never be seasick. But one should try to find a crew that will continue to work and race, even when seasickness takes its toll.

When planning the watches set them so that the proportion between rest and work enables all members of the crew to produce their best for all the twenty-four hours of the day and during the entire time of the race. The usual way to set the watches is to divide the twenty-four hours into four-hour turns, of which one is split in two (usually called the port and starboard watches) in order to avoid repetition. By this system the watches will change at 0400, 0800, 1200, 1600, 2000, and 2400. While the ideal crew should be made up of members with even tempers and free from complexes, this is not always possible. If two men's temperaments tend to clash, be sure that they aren't scheduled on the same watch.

Basically the same racing rules are used for offshore racing as for racing around the buoys. But it's seldom that incidents occur offshore, where the knowledge of how to use the rules to the best advantage is not of the same deciding importance as it may be when racing around the markers, at which time a few seconds' lead at a buoy may easily decide the entire race. This is generally not the case in an offshore race, although this doesn't mean that it is of little consequence to be a few seconds late, say, at the start. It should never be forgotten that a race may well be won or lost by a few seconds, even after a day or more at sea. A good position at the start is valuable for boosting the morale of the crew and it must be remembered that time lost at the start can never be recovered later. This may be of special importance when racing in a yacht that has a high measurement rating. From a racing point of view, it's wise to do what you can to reduce weight aboard during a race, without impairing the safety or comfort of the crew.

The actual sailing procedures of ocean racing are the same as those when cruising. Several excellent complete books have been written on the subject of offshore distance and ocean-racing techniques and tactics. While it may not be a bad idea to read a couple of them, it's my advice for you to practice your navigation and offshore cruising techniques, and sail in several group or rendezvous cruises. After several of these, plus some inshore racing experience, you'll be ready to try your hand in offshore distance races. There's another way to learn ocean racing—sign on as a crew member. There

Figure 9-4: Photograph of the Newport-to-Bermuda winner—the *Burgoo*—in 1964.

are opportunities for this. The most practical way to try for a berth is to seek out an opportunity in the shorter, coastal races. Yachting calendars can be studied for this. The owners belong to yacht clubs, and chances are that their craft are in *Lloyd's Register of American Yachts.* Skippers, looking for crew material in larger, longer, more important races, might well give you a try in the lesser ones.

No chapter on ocean racing would be complete without a word about the Corinthians. Whether you're a sailing enthusiast on the lookout for a berth or own a boat and need a crew, if you're a member of the Corinthians you just call up the crewing office and state your requirements. It's almost that simple. This remarkable group of amateur seafarers is dedicated to serving the needs of boat-less crews and crewless skippers, and its crewing committee is kept busy year-round matching men and ships.

The Corinthians were formed in 1934 by Carleton S. Cooke and Frederick M. Delano, who felt that there was a definite need for a different kind of yachting organization and were inspired somewhat by The Little Ships Club in England. In the 1930's, as now, more and more yachtsmen were finding it difficult to crew their boats with professionals; and at the same time many good amateur sailors, who were not yet in a position to own boats, had trouble getting afloat. To help solve the problem, the Corinthians were incorporated as a non-profit, member association in the State of New York. In the succeed-ing years they have more than lived up to the objective set forth in their constitution: "to promote sailing, to encourage good fellowship among yachtsmen, afloat and ashore, to assist yacht-owner members to obtain competent and congenial crews, and to assist non-yacht-own-ing members to obtain desirable berths." But, in addition to crew-ing their own boats and other people's, the Corinthians sponsor a spring and a fall rendezvous afloat, followed by a dinner ashore at a convenient yacht club. Recently the rendezvous has been preceded by a handicap race. This is not a racing club, however, and the events have been kept very informal. Wives and families are cor-dially invited to every rendezvous, and participate with enthusiasm.

The Corinthians have demonstrated that there is a real need for this type of crewing association, over and above the recognized func-tions of a regular yacht club. There are other similar organizations —one may be in your sailing area—and there is room for many more. In business, a good "sale" is one which benefits both buyer and seller. In boating, good "sails" are often the result of mixing crew-less skippers with boatless sailing enthusiasts. A club that accom-plishes this kind of an affiliation will always be popular with yachts-men.

10

Yachting Etiquette and You

A great many of our yachting customs—and even some of the rules of etiquette of the sea—are rather meaningless in this new age of the sail because they have been handed down to us by older generations who lived at different times and sailed under different conditions. But, one of the first things you'll learn about sailing is that while we're in the new age of sailing, our sport is steeped in tradition. It is this tradition that has set aside the yachtsman from the rest of his fellow man. (Remember that you don't have to be a member of a yacht club to be a yachtsman. It is your actions in observing the customs and etiquette that have been set down that stamp you as one.) Thus, as you go afloat, you carry with you the reputation of your fellow yachtsmen. It's a most precious charge and one that must be safeguarded.

Good Manners Afloat

Before actually going on to the subject of yachting customs, perhaps a word or two on courtesy afloat and general sailing etiquette is in order. A yachtsman must first of all be a gentleman, which means basically that he must have consideration for others. Thus, let's consider the points of etiquette and good manners afloat that rule you a better yachtsman:

1. Although you have the right-of-way over powerboats, don't

249

abuse this right by forcing them into a dangerous situation. Also, in the case of sailboats, never wait until the last minute to make clear your intentions of obeying the Rules of the Road.

2. Try to anchor clear of lines of traffic and outside of narrow channels. If forced to anchor in a narrow channel, take extra precautions should the tide or wind change. It's always best to anchor in an authorized anchorage or select an anchorage which allows room to swing without fouling other vessels already anchored. Always ask permission before picking up a buoy that doesn't belong to you. When sailing in a harbor, never have your tender on too long a line.

3. Navigate with care on well-known fishing grounds and keep well clear of fishing vessels. Don't run over fishing stakes or buoys.

4. Don't pass a vessel in distress. When you go out in your yacht, be on the alert and receptive to possible distress signals (see Chapter 7). In the case of small boats, it's a good idea to investigate any irregular motion or activity. It is better to know that you haven't passed up someone in trouble. Also, during the summertime most sailing areas are infested with young sailors who are attempting to learn our sport. Often they may be headed for trouble without knowing it, and it is your duty, as a yachtsman, to give them a word of advice or a helping hand. Remember that it's a tradition as old as the sea itself that mariners always go to the aid of those in distress.

5. Don't tie up to government buoys, or local navigation markers, except in emergencies. Actually, the law forbids any person to interfere with, remove, move, *make fast to,* or willfully damage any aid to navigation maintained or authorized by the Coast Guard. Violation of this law subjects that person to a fine up to $500.

6. Don't throw garbage or refuse overboard in harbors, or near beaches, or in lakes used for drinking-water supply. (Use shore disposal facilities.) Never throw cans overboard, even in open water, unless punctured at both ends so they'll sink.

7. Always be on the alert when passing dredges where divers may be at work and keep away from areas indicated by the skin diver's flag.

8. Never land at a private dock or float without invitation, except in an emergency. If your yacht is berthed in a marina or yacht club, other members have equal rights with you, so don't interfere with their berthing spaces. When visiting another yacht club, pull

up to the dock or float and inquire as to where you might moor your boat so that you're certain you don't interfere with some regular member's berth. Then properly moor your craft before going ashore. Avoid tying up across club floats. And when anchoring for a swim, or using the bathing facilities of a club, do so quietly, without screams or roughhouse.

9. Don't stare at other yachting parties or into cabins as you pass. If you see a beautiful yacht and wish to look her over, you may do so, but avoid being obvious about it.

10. Never anchor on top of another boat unless there is a good reason for such action. Don't caterwaul or permit your children to do so, and be sure not to keep your radio or phonograph going late into the night on quiet evenings in crowded harbors.

11. Always talk to other yachtsmen. Remember there is no snobbishness about our sport. Always greet other yachtsmen—and landlubbers, too—with a wave of the hand or a cheery "good day." Wish them luck and exchange opinions about the weather. To get the most fun from sailing you must enter into the camaraderie of the sport.

12. Never presume upon the courtesy of yacht clubs, unless invited, or unless they exchange courtesies with your club. If you desire to use the club facilities, inquire first of the steward or attendant as to the club rules and regulations. When you're coming in as a guest at a strange sailing club or yacht club, act as a courteous guest. In general, yachtsmen are quiet, gentlemanly folk. They don't call attention to themselves by loudness or rowdiness. Therefore, it's best not to make yourself obnoxious by being demanding, because even if their courtesy gains the upper hand and you are served as you wish, it will mark you for any future time you may wish to take advantage of the facilities offered by that club.

13. Visiting between yachts that are anchored within easy reach of one another is a common practice. But, there is a ritual to be observed about visiting. Never board another boat without a distinct invitation from the owner. If you don't know the skipper get close enough to his yacht and engage him in conversation, but don't attempt to board until he asks you. Never stay if you're interrupting the work of the vessel.

14. When you anchor in a small port, make friends with the local natives. Greet and talk with them while ashore. Their customs

and manners are a great deal different from the people of a large city, who make it a rule never to speak to strangers.

15. Don't give uncalled-for advice while a guest on someone else's yacht. Take your orders from the skipper and never try to interfere with the way in which he handles his craft. Courtesy and common sense are the basis of yachting etiquette. If this is kept in mind, the sailor is well on his way to becoming a true yachtsman.

Flag and Yachting Routine

To be rated a 100 percent yachtsman—in other words, a "seasoned skipper"—the owner or captain of a boat should know the proper etiquette of the various flags, what they mean, and how to fly them. In this connection, it has always been my feeling that most yachtsmen would gladly comply with the protocol associated with the display of flags if they understood it. In addition, there's no doubt but that flags make for a yachty appearance.

Flags. The ensign may be either the conventional fifty-star, thirteen-stripe American flag or it may be the special yacht ensign with the thirteen red and white stripes of the American flag and a fouled anchor encircled by thirteen stars. The latter yacht ensign was designed by the New York Yacht Club in 1849 at the request of the Secretary of the Navy to designate yachts, and exempted them from entering and clearing at customhouses. Although this flag in no way officially replaces the national ensign, through usage it has become the ensign commonly used aboard yachts sailing our coastwise waters. In entering a foreign country or in displaying flags on the high seas, it would probably be better to fly the regular American flag. But remember that no flag flies unless the ensign flies. The only exception is the signal of the flag officer of a yacht club. His flag, in place of a personal signal, flies day and night while the boat is in commission, while he's in his own harbor or with his own fleet.

When under sail and under way, fly either ensign at the leech of the mainsail, or when there's more than one mast, at the leech of the aftermost sail, approximately two-thirds the length of the leech above the clew. Under power alone, or when at anchor or made fast, the ensign should be flown from the stern staff of all sailboats. The ensign should be flown from morning to evening.

The owner's private signal, sometimes called the house flag, is usually swallowtail, sometimes rectangular. Any yacht owner, whether or not he is a member of a yacht club, may design and carry a private signal, and have that signal registered in *Lloyd's Register of American Yachts*. If you don't have a private signal and wish to design one, obtain a copy of *Lloyd's Register* and check to see if any of the flags illustrated therein resemble too closely the design you have

Figure 10-1: When at a mooring or at anchor, the national ensign should be flown from the stern.

in mind. Since the basic purpose of the signal is to identify your boat, it should be as simple as possible so that it may be recognized easily at sea. This means that it is best to stick to a simple design, employing no more than three colors. The traditional colors used are dark blue, red, and white. The owner's private signal flag is flown from morning to evening colors.

The club burgee is usually triangular in shape, but sometimes may be swallow-tailed. It is never proper to fly the burgee of more than one yacht club at a time. On any two-masted sailing craft the burgee is carried on the foremost mast and the private sign at the aftermost mast. For example, in a yawl, the burgee would be displayed at the mainmast and the private signal from the mizzenmast. On a sloop, a burgee is displayed at the mainmast when at anchor; the private signal is flown at the mainmast while under way. The burgee is normally displayed from morning to evening colors. However, the Cruising Club of America has a long-established tradition, only recently incorporated into their bylaws, permitting its members to fly the burgee day and night. This club has no official clubhouse, so each member's boat becomes an informal club station to which all members are welcome at all times, whether for social reasons or for necessity. A yachtsman may carry only the burgee of the clubs of which he's a member.

The flag officer's flag is rectangular, blue with a white design for a commodore; red with a white design for a vice-commodore; and white with a red design for a rear commodore. This flag replaces the private signal when it can be properly flown. In cases where the private signal can't be flown, such as a sloop under way, the flag officer's flag replaces the burgee. A flag officer never flies his private signal because he and his vessel now represent his club and not an individual. And when he pays an official call on another yacht whose owner belongs to the same club, then this owner should replace the club burgee with the flag officer's flag.

A fleet captain's flag may be displayed at the bow staff of a small boat from morning to evening colors when this officer is executing his official duties. Yacht routine regarding the fleet captain's flag may vary with the individual yacht clubs.

The absentee flag is a rectangular blue flag which is displayed from sunrise to sunset when the yacht owner isn't aboard. It is carried from the starboard main spreader and is hoisted the minute the owner steps off the boat, and is kept flying until his return. The purpose of the absent flag, of course, is to save a fellow yachtsman the long journey out to the boat to see the owner, when the owner isn't on board. It is part of the yachting tradition to lower away the absent flag the moment the owner comes on board and to hoist it smartly the minute he goes over the side.

The guest flag is a rectangular blue flag with a white diagonal stripe which is displayed when the yacht owner is absent but his guests are aboard. It is carried in the same manner as the absentee flag, but is displayed when under way as well as at anchor.

The owner's meal flag is a rectangular white flag which is displayed when the owner and his guests are at meals. It is carried in the same manner as the absentee flag, but only when the yacht is at anchor.

The crew's meal pennant is red and is displayed when the professional crew (or paid hands) are at meals. It is carried when at anchor from sunrise to sundown at the foremost port spreader.

The nighthawk or wind pennant is a blue pennant which is displayed at the mainmast from evening to morning colors, or at other times when no other flags are flown.

The United States Power Squadron flag with its thirteen vertical stripes may be carried as an ensign on yachts owned by members of this organization. If the national or yacht ensign is flown, then the USPS flag is flown from the main starboard spreader, except when the absent, owner's meal, or guest flags are flown.

Other flags, those authorized by naval, military, or recognized yachting authorities as well as those that may be displayed at option, should always be displayed according to their respective regulations. For instance, when a boat acts as a racing committee vessel, the race committee flag should be flown. This flag is displayed on the mainmast. During a race, all competing vessels should comply with pertinent sections of the racing rules regarding flags and any specific instructions of the race committee where these conflict with any provisions of yacht routine. Racing rules concerning the carrying of flags may vary, but most state that a boat should display her private signal on the leech of her mainsail, in the case of a sloop, or from her mizzenmast in the case of a yawl. The private signal flown in this way is often helpful to the race committee in identifying a yacht at the finish line when her racing number isn't visible.

Other special flags may include those that sports fishermen use to designate the nature of their catch. Also, boats accompanying scuba divers generally carry a special flag when the divers are below. This is a red flag with a white stripe. A wind indicator of solid color (which is usually interpreted to mean the nighthawk) or a telltale may also be carried. These are all considered "legitimate" yachting flags. However, battle-ax flags and cocktail or beer flags are in the poorest possible taste on board.

Sizes of flags are optional, but all flags should conform to the size of the craft and staff at which they are displayed. The New York

Yacht Club suggests the following dimensions: The ensign should approximate a minimum of an inch on the fly per foot of over-all length of the yacht, with a hoist of two-thirds the fly. The burgee, private signal, and flag officer's flags should approximate one-half inch on the fly for each foot of the height of the highest mast above the water of a sailing yacht. The hoist should be two-thirds of the fly. The wind pennant or nighthawk should approximate three-quarters of an inch on the fly for each foot of height of truck above the water. The hoist should be one-tenth of the fly. The USPS flag, when flown from the starboard spreader, should approximate five-eighths of an inch on the fly for each foot of over-all length.

Notice that the word "minimum" is used when referring to the size of ensigns. The ensign should be oversized rather than too small, and carried on an adequately long stern staff held as nearly vertical as possible. All other flags, burgees, and pennants are better under-sized than too large, with the exception of the "T" International Code flag (see page 258), which should be as large as possible.

Making Colors. This refers to the ceremony of hoisting or lowering flags. Morning colors are made at 8 A.M., evening colors are made at sunset. Time should be taken from the senior officer present. When in company of a vessel of the United States Navy or Coast Guard, or a shore station of these services, or in the home anchorage of another yacht's club, time should be taken from such vessel, station, or club. In making colors, a yacht always represents the rank of her owner, whether he is aboard or not. Also remember, when making colors, that all flags should be hoisted at the same time. When this isn't feasible, the ensign should be hoisted first, followed as rapidly as possible by the burgee and the private signal. Flags are lowered in inverse order. Colors should be hoisted smartly but lowered ceremoniously. Flag officers' flags normally carried night and day may be lowered and hoisted at colors. The nighthawk is hoisted at evening colors.

Half-Masting Flags. The ensign is half-masted only on occasions of national mourning. On Memorial Day, the ensign is half-masted from morning colors to noon. On the death of a yacht club member, the burgee and private signal only are half-masted on his yacht. The yacht club may also order mourning for a member, in which case the club, other members' yachts at anchor, and other stations should half-mast the burgee only. Custom dictates that such burgees be two-blocked after the funeral ceremonies. The owner's private signal and burgee are lowered and not rehoisted. If not previously hoisted, flags should be mastheaded and then lowered. Before lowering from half-mast, the flag should be first mastheaded, then lowered.

Flag Salutes. This is one tradition that has been almost completely lost, and one that would add immeasurably to the color of the modern yachting scene. All the following salutes are made by dipping the ensign once. The ensign should be lowered to the dip and hoisted when the salute is returned.

Vessels of the United States and foreign navies should be saluted. When a yacht in which a flag officer is embarked comes to anchor, all yachts should salute, except where a senior officer is present. Also, when a yacht comes to anchor where a flag officer is present, such flag officer should be saluted. A junior officer anchoring in the presence of a senior should salute, and the salute should be returned by the senior only. Yachts passing each other should salute, the junior saluting first. The ensign should be held at the dip until the yachts pass clear. All salutes should be returned in kind. On yachts displaying no ensign, or displaying an ensign which can't be dipped, the owner renders and returns salutes by doffing hat or cap.

Guns may be fired to call attention to signals, but their use otherwise should be avoided as much as possible. Guns should never be fired on Sunday. Whistles are never used in saluting.

International Code Flags. Hoists of the International Code flags may be carried at the starboard main spreader or yardarm or wherever they may be most easily seen. If they be the private code of a yachting organization, the burgee of such organization should be hoisted over the Code flags. The absence of the burgee indicates that the International Code is being used. While many yachtsmen don't carry a set of International Code signal flags aboard their craft, it is important that "Urgent and Important" flag hoists are understood when they appear. (All boats should carry Code flag "T.") The Code comprises forty flags: twenty-six alphabetic flags, ten numeral pennants, one code pennant, and three repeaters. The purpose of the repeaters is to enable the sender to transmit the same letter or number more than once in the same message. The code or answering pennant is used by the receiving vessel to indicate recognition and compliance with the message transmitted. Each flag has a meaning in itself which should be known to everyone who may come in contact

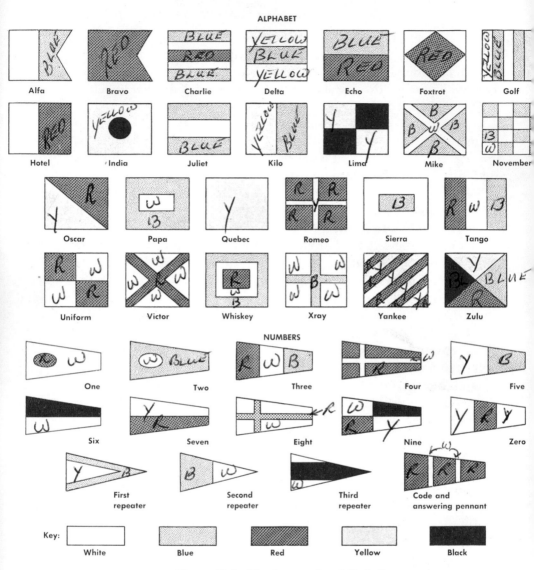

Figure 10-2: The International Code flags.

with this method of communication. For complete information on all the various flag hoists, we suggest that you purchase a copy of *International Code of Signals, Vol. I, Visual, H. O. Number 87* from the United States Government Printing Office. While it is a very good idea to have this aboard, here are the hoists that are important to the average yachtsman:

SINGLE FLAG HOIST MEANINGS. (Only those marked with an asterisk should be used by flashing.)

A: I am undergoing a speed trial.

B: I am taking in or discharging explosives.

C: Yes (affirmative).

D: Keep clear of me. I am maneuvering with difficulty.

E: I am directing my course to starboard.

F*: I am disabled. Communicate with me.

G: I require a pilot.

H: I have a pilot on board.

I: I am directing my course to port.

J: I am going to send a message by semaphore.

K*: You should stop your vessel instantly.

L*: You should stop. I have something important to communicate.

M: I have a doctor on board.

N: No (negative).

O*: Man overboard.

P*: In harbor: All persons are to repair on board as the vessel is about to proceed to sea. (Note: to be hoisted at the foremost head.) At sea: Your lights are out, or burning badly.

Q: My vessel is healthy and I request free pratique.

R*: The way is off my ship; you may feel your way past me.

S: My engines are going full speed astern.

T: Do not pass ahead of me.

U: You are standing in danger.

V: I require assistance.

W: I require medical assistance.

X: Stop carrying out your intentions and watch for my signals.

Y: I am carrying mail.

Z*: To be used to address or call shore.

TWO-FLAG SIGNALS—URGENT AND IMPORTANT

A D: I must abandon my vessel.

A M: Accident has occurred. I require a doctor.

A P: I am aground.

A T: I am aground and require immediate assistance.

D N: I am coming to your assistance.

D P: I am drifting and require immediate assistance.

D Q: I am on fire and require immediate assistance.

D U: I have parted towing hawser; can you assist me?

D V: I have sprung a leak.

E J: Do you require any further assistance?

E X: Bar is impassable.

F R: I require a boat. Man overboard.

F U: I require a water boat.

H P: Submarines are exercising; navigate with caution.

J D: You are standing into danger.

J T: You should follow me or vessel indicated.

J Z: I have a damaged rudder. I cannot steer.

L I: I am disabled.

L J: I am disabled. Will you tow me in or into place indicated?

L O: My engines are disabled.

L P: My steering gear is disabled.

L V: I am in distress for want of fuel.

M J: Have you a doctor?

N C: I am in distress and require immediate assistance.

P C: I am not in correct position. (Used by lightship.)

P Q: I have sprung a leak and require immediate assistance.

P T: I require a pilot.

Q W: I have mail for you.

R H: Message has been received.

R J: Have you a message for me?

R S: Is all well with you?

S	D:	I am short of lubricating oil. Can you supply?	V	C:	Your distress signal understood. Assistance coming.
S	E:	I am short of gasoline. Can you supply?	X	Y:	Can you take me in tow?
S	T:	I require a police boat.	V	B:	Signal is not understood though flags are distinguished.
T	H:	I have lost my propeller.			
T	K:	I require provisions urgently.	W	U:	What course should I steer to make nearest land?
T	Z:	My radio is not working.			
U	W:	I cannot distinguish flags.	X	Z:	Shall I take you in tow?
			Y	J:	I require water immediately.

The flags are hoisted, the first letter above the second on the same halyard, where they will be most visible. As a general rule, only one hoist should be shown at a time, but each hoist, or set of hoists, should be flown until answered. In answering a flag signal, hoist your answering pennant halfway up as soon as you see the signal, then all the way up when the signal is understood.

The Code flag "T," commonly known as the transportation flag, may be flown from the starboard spreader or yardarm, or where it can best be seen, to indicate a request for a club launch. It should be accompanied by three blasts of the horn.

On national holidays, at regattas, and on other special occasions, yachts often dress ship with International Code signal flags. Flag officers' flags, club burgees, and national flags are not used. The ship is dressed at 8:00 A.M. and remains so dressed from morning to evening colors (while at anchor only). In dressing ship, the yacht ensign is hoisted at the peak or staff aft, and the jack at the jackstaff. Then a rainbow of flags of the International Code is arranged, reaching from the waterline forward to the waterline aft, by way of the bowsprit end to the foretop masthead, then across to the main top-mast, and down to the main boom end, allowing several flags to touch the waterline from both the bowsprit end and the main boom end. To keep the flags in position, a weight should be attached to the end of each line. Where there is no bowsprit, flags will start at the stemhead. Flags and pennants should be bent on alternately, rather than in an indiscriminate manner. Since there are twice as many letter flags as numeral pennants, it is good practice, as in the Navy, to follow a sequence of two flags, one pennant, etc., etc., throughout. In order to effect a degree of uniformity in yacht procedure, the following arrangement has been proposed: Starting from forward, AB2, UG1, LE3, GH6, IV5, FL4, DM7, PO third repeater, RN first repeater, ST0 (zero), CX9, WQ8, ZY second repeater. The arrangement here proposed is designed to effect a harmonious color pattern throughout. If enough flags are not available for "full dress," the "up and down" dress may be used. The line of flags is strung from the after masthead to the water aft, or on a two-masted vessel it may be strung from the top of each mast to the water.

Some yacht clubs have adopted signal codes of their own, which are not in conformity with signals prescribed by the International Code Book. Furthermore, since the practice among the clubs may vary to a certain extent, the interpretation of such club signals depends largely on a knowledge of the local code as prescribed in the club's yearbook. The purpose of the signals prescribed in club codes is principally to provide a means of communication between boats of the club. Most clubs provide that yachts using their own club code should hoist the club burgee over the club code flags; otherwise, absence of the burgee would indicate that the International Code is used.

Lights. In addition to navigating lights that *must* be displayed by law from sunset to sunrise, the following lights may be carried from sunset to sunrise while at anchor to conform with yacht routine: Flag officers may display two lights, arranged vertically, in the same position at which the absentee flag is flown during the day. The commodore's lights should be blue; the vice-commodore's lights should be red; the rear commodore's lights should be white. A single blue light may be displayed in the same way when an owner isn't aboard. A white light may be displayed in the same way when the owner is at meals.

The Ship's Bell. It is perfectly proper to strike ship's bells every half hour while at anchor. It's by no means necessary to do this, but it is a very pleasant habit and should be encouraged. The time for the ship's bells should be taken from the senior boat in port just as the time is taken for colors.

A clock with ship's bells is an expensive item which many don't wish to acquire, but such a clock is found on many boats and in most yacht clubs. The meaning of the bells should be part of any yachtsman's vocabulary. The custom of telling time in this manner is one of the oldest traditions associated with the sea. Men aboard the naval and commercial vessels of long ago stood four-hour watches or turns of duty exactly as they do today. The first watch is from 8 P.M. to midnight, the midwatch from midnight to 4 A.M., the morning watch from 4 A.M. to 8 A.M., the forenoon watch from 8 A.M. to noon, the afternoon watch from noon to 4 P.M., and the dog watch from 4 P.M. to 8 P.M. The first half hour of each watch is designated by one bell, the second half hour, or first hour, by two bells, and so on. Thus one bell is rung at 12:30, 4:30, and 8:30, both A.M. and P.M.; two bells at 1:00, 5:00, and 9:00; three bells at 1:30, 5:30, and 9:30, and so on. Eight bells are rung at 4:00, 8:00, and 12:00. Bells are struck in groups of two; thus 6:30 would be ding-ding, ding-ding, ding.

In most instances in this book, as above, I have been guilty of using the landlubber's time system rather than the naval system, which is employed by most yachtsmen afloat. In the naval timekeeping system the hours begin with zero at midnight and run through 23. Thus 6:30 A.M. is simply 0630; noon is 1200; and 6:30 P.M. is 1830. In some long-distance ocean races, the navigator uses an accurate chronometer which runs according to Greenwich Civil Time (standard time of Greenwich, England).

Clothing for Yachtsmen

When it comes to clothing, most yachtsmen have pretty strong convictions as to whether or not they should, or must, abide by any arbitrary set of regulations. The spokesman of one faction argues that he goes afloat for pleasure and relaxation, and proposes to dress as he pleases—for comfort and practicability. Members of another group insist on strict adherence to all the proprieties, frowning upon those who can't be made to conform to the dictates of etiquette, whether it be in dress, the display of flags, or anything else. Actually, many yacht clubs have written regulations concerning the proper attire to be worn at official club functions. This uniform may also be worn at any time aboard ship. If your yacht club doesn't have such instructions, a yearbook of one of the larger yacht clubs, or the catalog of one of the prime yachting clothing suppliers can give you this information.

In general, the service coat or yachting jacket is basically the same as the navy officer's or chief's coat; of any desired navy blue material, double-breasted, with two rows of either three or four buttons. White coats with gilt or brass buttons are seldom worn except in the warmer climates. Designations of rank are worn on the sleeve of the coat, black stripes on the blue coat, white on the white. These stripes should be of three-eighths-inch lustrous mohair braid. The member wears one stripe with a trefoil; the captain (or boat owner), treasurer, secretary, measurer, fleet surgeon, fleet captain, and race committee, two stripes, the upper with a trefoil. Various gilt emblems are worn in the upper loop of the trefoil to designate each of these ranks except that of captain. The rear commodore wears three stripes, the upper one with trefoil, and one gilt star in the center of the upper loop of the trefoil; the vice-commodore, four stripes, the upper one with trefoil, and two gilt stars in the center of each of the lower loops; and commodore, five stripes, the upper one with trefoil, and three gilt stars, one in each loop of the trefoil. Former flag officers are entitled to wear the designation of rank on the sleeve, but without the star.

The coat may be worn with trousers of the same material and color as the coat; or gray, white, or khaki trousers with blue coat. The khaki trousers are the least desirable. A recently accepted, if unwritten, innovation is gray flannel or khaki-colored shorts instead of the long trousers. A soft, white, button-down collar shirt is traditional, and a black four-in-hand tie, or a club four-in-hand or bow tie should be worn. White buck shoes are often seen with this outfit, but almost any plain shoe is permissible, including sneakers aboard ship, and dancing pumps in the evening.

The yachting cap resembles the navy cap of the late 1800's, quite a different size and shape from the caps worn by the armed services today. It should be of navy blue cloth or white duck, with black lustrous mohair band one and five-eighths inches wide. Crown for size $7\frac{1}{8}$ cap should be $9\frac{7}{8}$ inches long by $9\frac{1}{4}$ inches wide. Quarters of the cap to the crown seam in front should be $1\frac{3}{8}$ inches, the same side and back. The visor should be of black patent leather, 2 inches wide and set at an angle of 42 degrees. The chin strap should be of black patent leather, fastened at the side with two black buttons. The complete description of this cap is given here to encourage all yachtsmen to favor this distinctive cap over the navy cap (with the grommet removed), which is usually used. The yachting cap should not look like a navy cap, because it isn't one. Not only does it look better with a yachting uniform, but it doesn't blow off so easily, and hence is more functional. It should not be forgotten that this is a civilian hat and should be removed and held over the heart when saluting the flag and on other such occasions. The cap is worn straight on the head, not at an angle, as is the navy chief's cap. It is never worn indoors, or below decks in a yacht. It is usually worn to complete the entire uniform, although its use is not obligatory. It may be worn without the coat or with more informal attire such as shorts and a plain shirt, but should never be worn with a bathing suit or similar very informal or abbreviated attire. A yachting cap is not worn by a lady under any circumstances.

The regulation uniform may be worn at the club at all times, but especially at all official functions, such as commissioning, decommissioning, or at yacht club sponsored events such as cocktail parties, informal dances, and so on; and also aboard ship at any time. The uniform should not be worn at the yacht club while attending events not sponsored by yacht clubs or private parties. If a man belongs to more than one yacht club, the insignia of one should not be worn at another. In no case should the insignia of different clubs be mixed, such as the hat insignia of one club, buttons of another, and officer's stripes of a third.

A boatowner may not belong to a yacht club, for reasons of his own, and still desire to present a proper appearance. A yacht club member may not wish to invest in the complete uniform. In either case, proper shoes or sneakers, trousers or shorts, and shirt and tie are easy to obtain. A dark blue blazer with plain brass buttons can be substituted for the yachting jacket to complete a very "yachty"-looking outfit. A cap is not necessary, nor should one be worn by those persons not members of the yacht club. The latter may also properly wear the inexpensive, yachting-type cap, or other caps with nautical-looking, nonyacht-club insignia. These are perfectly all right to wear with informal attire such as shorts and a plain sport shirt. They should not be worn with a bathing suit or other extreme-looking outfits. They should not be worn by women or children, but this idea is probably hard to enforce. In no case should a cap with the crossed anchor insignia be worn by the Corinthian sailor, since this denotes the professional crew member or paid hand.

11

The Care
of Your Sailboat

In the previous chapters of this book we have discussed sailing principles, sailboat living, cruising, racing, and so on—but unless you take care of your boat and her sails, all the "dope" given in these chapters may be for naught. For if your craft isn't in the best of condition, you can't expect her to perform her best.

Lay-up Time

Many boatowners have the mistaken idea that once their craft are hauled out of the water, they can forget about them until fitting-out time rolls around in the spring. These are the same fellows who usually are fitting out their boats when everyone else in the club has had his boat over for weeks and is enjoying the warm days that usually come in May. If you want to join them and spend more of your time afloat next summer, then put in a few days' work before the spring and save yourself weeks of sweating in the spring.

Most cruiser-racer–type sailboats are generally stored for the winter at boatyards, while often owners of day-cruiser or small craft trailer them home and keep them there for the off-season. In most good boatyards, particularly in areas where there is a well-organized marine trades association, storage and work done while the craft is laid up is done on a flat-rate basis. In other words, storage is so much per foot, winterizing the engine is a specific amount for the

Figure 11-1: Small day-sailer such as the Hawk Class boat (top) can be taken home and stored on her specially-built trailer (bottom) in a garage.

size and type of engine, and so on. There is a definite charge listed for nearly every possible job—painting, repairing damaged parts and sails, etc.—you could want done. Go over every detail with the yard-master and draw up a contract with *exact* details as to what is to be done and the cost. (In most yards, for the owner who is so inclined and who has the time, there are many things he can do to keep yard charges down.) When the contract is agreed to and signed by both of you, it's generally possible to budget accordingly, and you and the yard will know just where each one stands as far as spring accounts receivable. But, remember that there's one thing that no one ever guarantees, and that is the date your sailboat will go back into the water in the spring. This is controlled solely by the gods of the weather and the strange things that go on at all boatyards.

Proper Shoring or Cradle Supports. As in the case of boats built of other materials, it's important that fiberglass hulls be supported properly when stored ashore. Although the strength and monocoque integrity of the hull will make it highly resistant to strain and distortion, it is possible to injure the structure if poor procedures are practiced.

Most modern sailboats, especially those of fiberglass, are designed so that the hull weight can be supported by keel blocks while stored ashore. Exceptions to this rule are some hulls strictly for racing and a few centerboard boats that are stored in cradles built to conform to the special shape of their hulls. In preparing a conventional sailboat for hauling and storage, the boatyard's hauling master will first wish to know exactly where, under the stern, the aftermost keel-bearing timber of the hauling cradle must be located. This should be under solid keel or deadwood, not under the rudder or its skeg. He will also want to know the location of the radio ground plate and the depth finder so that these fixtures won't be damaged from contact with keel bearers or the hauling blocks that slide under the bilges, supporting the hull from tipping over once the keel is grounded. The mast is removed before the boat is removed from the water; in the case of larger boats this is generally done with a mobile crane. To make ready for this, release all standing rigging, tie to mast, and rig guy ropes for handling the spar from the ground. Pad the mast well where the crane's sling will take its hold, usually about one-third up the mast or just above the lower spreaders at the point where it will balance fairly evenly. Once the spar is out of the boat, set it level on horses and remove all standing and running rigging. Mark and store carefully all mast wedges. Mark the rigging with tags before you take it off or you'll forget what's what. Coil the rigging down, tie the coils with a piece of light line, and put a tag on each coil. The following spring you'll be surprised to find how easy it is to forget where lines and shrouds run.

Small sailboats that are normally transported to and from the water on towed trailers usually present no problem to amateur boat handlers. The hauling, moving, and blocking-up for storage of heavier craft, however, is not work for unskilled individuals, and is best done by skilled boatyard personnel. Remember that unless the job is done properly, damage to hulls may result from strain and distortion.

In any case, as soon as possible after hauling, your boat's bottom must be scrubbed clean. While most yards do this for you, it is imperative that she be thoroughly clean. Even if an antifouling paint has been used, it is likely that a film of scum has built up. This film is not easy to remove if allowed to dry. If any barnacles have fixed themselves to the bottom, knock them off with a scraper, and use a little sandpaper to rid the surface of the hard shell which may still hold fast. Barnacles seem to fuse tightly to a fiberglass surface which has not been protected by antifouling paint. They won't damage the fiberglass hull, but are a nuisance.

Algae or scum which will not come free in the washing procedure is easily removed with bronze-wool pads (use the finer grades). Scouring pads such as SOS are very effective. Fiberglass hulls which have been in dirty water for an extended period may show staining on an unpainted bottom, and perhaps up to a few inches above the waterline. It is naturally most visible on a white hull. A fine bronze-wool pad dusted with a kitchen cleanser will do the job in most cases. However, if this treatment doesn't yield satisfactory results, the owner will have to consider paint on the bottom and a painted boot top to restore the desired appearance to the topsides. Washing down the topsides, deck, and interior is an optional procedure, but if done when the boat is hauled out, cleaning in the spring will be easier.

The colored pigment finish on a fiberglass boat is designed to hold its luster and appearance for a number of years. Although it is quite durable it should receive reasonable care. Wash it with soap and water whenever dirt accumulates. Apply car wax to preserve the finish and make the surface easier to keep clean. Don't apply wax to those areas to be painted, as paint will not adhere to a wax film. It is also recommended that interior surfaces be given the same treatment. Any wood surfaces should be cleaned, too, to remove salt traces.

General Laying-up Procedures. One of the first tasks is the removal of all clothes, curtains, blankets, linen, mattresses, furnishings, etc. If any of these need cleaning, it should be done in the fall. All furnishing items that aren't being stored at home should be neatly folded and wrapped in paper with moth flakes before being placed in the boatyard's storage locker. It's also advisable either to wrap or cover the mattresses and cushions with plastic or canvas to protect them from dirt. Sails should also be washed, dried, and stored in a well-ventilated location (further details on sail care are given later in this chapter). Any sails that need repairs should be sent to the sailmaker in the fall. Also order any new sails you need at this time. You'll avoid delays in the spring.

Make certain to remove all bottled goods and food; bottled goods left aboard may freeze and break, while food will attract insects and mice. Wash out the icebox with soap and water and leave it open for the winter. Open all sea cocks in the plumbing system to let the water drain out. The toilet pump particularly requires special attention, as described in Chapter 7. All electronic equipment—depth finder, radiotelephone, direction finder, etc.—should be removed from the boat. If you are not thoroughly familiar with this kind of work, have the yard take off the instruments; they should be stored in a dry place, preferably in a heated room. Also be sure to remove all navigational gear, books and charts, lifesaving gear, and all similar items.

Ice resulting from frozen fresh-water accumulation in various parts of a fiberglass boat won't cause damage under normal conditions. Because the material will not absorb moisture and because it has a high degree of resilience, ice (except in considerable volume and under the most confining circumstances) will not cause injury. By way of example, I have allowed a sailing dinghy to remain inverted and uncovered every winter. The centerboard trunk is a closed unit. Water remains in it all winter long, freezing and thawing. The trunk has been exposed for seven winters without injury to the fiberglass laminate. However resistant the material is to such pressures, common sense precautions are best observed. Undoubtedly a full fiberglass water tank can expand to the rupture point, if the contents becomes a solid frozen mass. Such tanks should be drained. There is usually a joint for this purpose at the lowest part of the pipe connecting the tank to the plumbing. All fresh-water pumps should be taken apart and drained. Air chambers (flotation compartments) ought to be checked to see that water hasn't accumulated from condensation or as a result of a small pinhole.

Check all lines—ground tackle and mooring lines, standing and running riggings—for wear. Place any needed lines on your shopping list. Inspect all deck hardware, too, since it takes a beating from exposure to salt-laden sea air. Remove fittings with pitted chrome and have them replated. It's cheaper than buying new hardware each year. But if the deck chocks or cleats are chewed up or too small, replace them with new ones that will reduce chafe on the anchor or mooring lines. Set aside blocks, snap hooks, sail hanks, turnbuckles, and other working hardware for cleaning up, lubricating, and overhaul during the long winter evenings. Your dinghy can be taken home and kept in the garage.

Preparing Engines for Winter Storage. Neglect in preparing an engine for winter storage may lead to annoying or costly damage that will not be seen until the engine is prepared for use the following spring. The engine should be carefully covered to give complete protection from rain and snow. Drain completely to avoid damage from freezing.

1. Cylinder blocks. A drain cock is found on the distributor side of the engine. Leave the drain cock open.

2. Manifold. A pipe plug will be found in the right side and to the rear end of the exhaust manifold.

3. Water pump. Pumps are particularly susceptible to damage from freezing because of the restricted space and clearances. The pump should be carefully drained. A drain plug is provided on the bottom of the gear housing. Remove it to allow the gears to drain. The water will run out slowly from this hole since it must run through the clearances of the pump. The pump should be dry during the winter.

4. Lubrication system. The oil pan and lubrication system should be drained of old or contaminated oil so that any moisture or acid present in the oil will not cause corrosion during the winter.

Two or three quarts of new clean oil should be pumped through the system by turning the motor by hand or electric starter. This should distribute a film of clean oil to act as a rust preventive. Regular rust-preventive oils can be obtained.

5. Fog the engine. Run the engine at about 800 rpm, and slowly pour about 4 ounces of *Marine Care* into the carburetor to coat the combustion chamber and cylinder walls. Stall the engine by pouring the last two ounces in rapidly. Also coat the valves by removing the valve cover plate.

6. Electrical system. Remove the battery and store it at the boat-yard or at your local battery dealer. Loosen the distributor cap for ventilation and protect all other electrical parts from moisture.

7. Fuel system. All gasoline should be drained from carburetor, fuel pump, feed lines, filters, and tanks. This is to prevent development of sludge or gum in the system. The carburetor air intake should be covered by waterproof paper or cloth and sealed to prevent entrance of moisture into the engine by way of the intake valves that are open.

8. Exhaust system. Exhaust pipes should be drained free of water. Allow the exhaust pipes to dry out. Seal the exhaust pipe end to prevent entrance of moisture into the engine through exhaust valves that are open.

9. Rust prevention. Exposed metal parts liable to rust should be coated with grease or rust-preventive compound.

Winter Cover. If your boat is stored outside, she is now ready for her winter cover. The colored surface coat on a fiberglass boat will last many times longer if it is cared for and protected. For this reason, either inside storage or a winter cover is highly desirable. In actual fact, the intense rays of the summer sun take a greater toll on the plastic "gel" coat than the weak winter light. Nonetheless, adequate protection from winter weather is greatly beneficial to the long-term appearance of the boat. Larger craft should have a loose-fitting cover that protects the deck and superstructure and, since most sizable fiberglass boats have some wooden exterior or interior components, the usual provisions against water and dampness are important. Mildew may accumulate on fiberglass surfaces but won't cause damage and can be wiped away.

With most large boats, the first task is to set up the frame; if a new frame is built by the boatyard, be sure that it is marked immediately. Each rafter should be marked. A good system is to label them in numerical order, as Port 1, 2, 3, and so on. The ridge pole should be marked with a corresponding number where each of the rafters is to be placed. A frame that is properly marked will go together a great deal more quickly than one that isn't. Be sure to pad the lower ends of the rafters where they rest on the rail or rail cap, to prevent any possible chafing.

The best winter covering is one tailored by a sailmaker to fit the frame and shape of your boat. Since this is usually a rather expensive proposition, the cover most extensively found is a tarpaulin which simply covers the frame and the boat and is tied underneath to prevent it blowing away. While a big tarpaulin is pretty difficult to handle, one man can do it, however, if he goes about it the proper way. Stretch out the tarpaulin beside the boat, flaking it down so that it lies in accordion pleats with one edge uppermost. Then go to the bow and lift one corner aboard, then work along that edge, pulling the edge up and over the ridge pole of your frame, lifting it up little by little. You will have no trouble getting it up and in place. Don't try to take it all aboard at once. A tarpaulin should come well down over the topsides and extend at least slightly below the waterline. Never lash the cover down too tightly; allow for shrinkage when the canvas is wet. If you fail to do this, the grommets will tear out before the winter is over. Before lacing up the flap, make certain that the ports, hatches, and locker doors are open to assure thorough ventilation of the hull.

Wet Storage and Operation in Freezing Climates. Some people believe a boat doesn't belong on dry land and was built to be completely supported by the embrace of the surrounding water. Leave her in the water if you want to, since wet storage of fiberglass boats in a northern climate is relatively practical. The material will resist damage more than wood and, compared to metals, there will be no danger of corrosion. The laminate has a slick, hard surface very resistant to the cutting action of ice. By example I can point to the practice of sheathing wooden boats with fiberglass to protect them from razor-sharp skim ice. Molded fiberglass duckboats have been used successively for years in Wisconsin and Minnesota lakes that often freeze over early in the hunting season.

A molded boat, because of its impact resistance and resiliency, will break through thick ice without being damaged. Generally the determining factor is whether the engine has power enough to push through the ice formation. Surface scratches may occur to the plastic finish after repeated contact with sharp ice, but we have been surprised how minor the effects are. The plastic is very slippery and the hull yields and releases itself quite readily. If you decide on wet storage, follow the general laying-up and engine-care procedures given earlier in this chapter. Also check with local boating people for the best areas for wet storage and their specific tips for that region.

Spring Fitting-out

When you start, the spring fitting-out depends on three factors: how much work you plan to do, what amount of work you plan for the boatyard to do, and, of course, the weather. With the latter in mind, don't be in a rush to remove the winter cover completely. A great deal of the inside work can be done with it in place. When a portion of the cover is taken off to do a specific job, it should be replaced before nightfall or in the event of a shower. When the cover is completely taken off, make certain that it's thoroughly dry before you store it away. Gather up all the framework and be sure that it is correctly marked with the name of your boat so that it can be located easily in the fall. It should be stored in a location designated by the boatyard. If this isn't done, the chances are you'll never see it again.

Painting over Fiberglass. Almost any paint system can be used on a molded fiberglass surface. There is nothing complicated in doing a good job, but there are some points to observe. Three basic types of paints are popularly used today on fiberglass: the regular alkyd marine paint, the epoxy paint, and the very new polyurethane type. (The latter is what we use.) For amateur use, the epoxy types have been widely and successfully used on metals and fiberglass surfaces because of their superior adhesive characteristics. The epoxy paints have the advantage of surface hardness and adhesion without a heavy film build-up. They have good hiding power, and priming coats are ordinarily not necessary. The regular alkyd-base paints generally need a primer surfacer in order to establish proper adhesion to a fiberglass surface. It might be injected, however, that on aged glass boats (several years of weathering) alkyd paints without a primer seem to attach quite dependably. This is apparently due to the slight etching of the exterior, which contributes to a better mechanical bond.

Epoxy paints do seem to be the best answer for reconditioning glass boats at this time, but I would like to mention several points wherein they are inferior to the modern alkyds. They are more difficult to brush out, they must be applied at warmer temperatures, and they don't hold their original luster as long as the conventional alkyds. Polyurethane, when readily available, will be best.

The thought of having to paint a fiberglass sailboat may understandably bother some owners. However, paints stand up a long time on fiberglass, so one is not committed to seasonal reapplication. The reason is quite simple. The need for repainting wood or metal boats generally occurs because of working of the wood or corrosion of the metal, causing the paint film to crack and detach. The fiberglass surface substrata is completely stable and is without movement or deterioration. As an example, I have experienced more than three seasons of serviceable use on glass decks coated with alkyd or epoxy paint.

Obtaining proper adhesion of antifouling bottom paints on fiberglass has been a varying problem, more pronounced on powerboats than sailboats because of the higher speed and attendant friction of the former. The leading marine paint companies have lately developed special primers and paint systems to avoid the peeling that was commonly experienced a few years ago. In applying bottom paint it is very important to follow the instructions closely, not only to obtain maximum protection from growth but to get a proper bond. The cause for most bottom paint peeling off fiberglass is wax on the surface originating from the molding operation. This film isn't visible and consequently is difficult to be sure it has been removed. On a new boat, wash the bottom with a strong solution of warm fresh water and kitchen soap or detergent. Sand briskly to remove the surface glaze, then proceed with the antifouling paint system selected. Boats that have been in service for over a year and are then given a coat of bottom need less attention to surface preparation. By this time the wax film has disappeared and the surface minutely eroded from use, so a good paint bond will be obtained. I have found that such boats will "accept" bottom paint without the primer which normally is specified.

While the need for using paint removers should rarely arise, I have often had questions on the subject from owners who wish to take off several years' accumulation of bottom paint. It has been found that certain of the strong, paste-type removers will attack the plastic gel coat if allowed to remain on the surface for an extended period. In the case of one powerful type of remover left overnight on a test panel, I found the polyester surface coat severely enough etched so that some fiberglass fibers were visible. So it is best to allow the remover to remain only long enough to perform its function, then wash it out with fresh water. If there is any doubt about how the remover will function, first experiment on a small area.

Touch-up and Surface Repairs. These repairs are easy because only the surface of the boat is damaged. They fall into two categories: (1) damage to the gel coat colored outer surface, and (2) holes or gouges that are deep enough to penetrate the fiberglass reinforced area of the boat. The repair operations are similar.

For damage to the gel coat surface, you'll need a small can of gel coat, of the same color as your boat, and a small amount of catalyst. For deeper holes or gouges (⅛ inch or more) you will also need some short strands of fiberglass, which can be trimmed from a fiberglass mat or purchased in the form of "milled fibers." These materials can usually be purchased from your local marine dealer.

1. Be sure the area around the damage is wiped clean and dry. Remove any wax or oil from the inside of the hole or scratch.

2. Using a power drill with a burr attachment, roughen the bottom and sides of the damaged area and feather the edge surrounding the scratch or gouge. Don't "undercut" this edge. (If the scratch or hole is shallow and penetrates only the color gel coat, skip to step no. 8.)

3. Into a jar lid or onto a piece of cardboard, pour a small amount of gel coat, just enough to fill the area being worked on. Mix an equal amount of milled fibers with this gel coat, using a putty knife or small flat stick. Then add two drops of catalyst, using an eyedropper for accurate measurement. For a half-dollar-size pile of gel coat, this amount of catalyst will give you 15 to 20 minutes of working time before it begins to "gel." Carefully cut the catalyst into the gel coat and mix thoroughly.

4. Work this mixture of gel coat, fibers, and catalyst into the damaged area, using the sharp point of a putty knife or knife blade

to press it into the bottom of the hole and to puncture any air bubbles which may occur. Fill the scratch or hole above the surrounding undamaged area about $\frac{1}{16}$ inch.

5. Lay a piece of cellophane or waxed paper over the repair to cut off the air and start the "cure."

6. After 10 or 15 minutes the patch will be partially cured. When it feels rubbery to the touch, remove the cellophane and trim flush with the surface, using a sharp razor blade or knife. Replace the cellophane and allow to cure completely (30 minutes to an hour). The patch will shrink slightly below the surface as it cures.

7. Again use the electric drill with burr attachment to roughen the bottom and edges of the hole. Feather hole into surrounding gel coat, do not undercut.

8. Pour out a small amount of gel coat into a jar lid or onto cardboard. Add a drop or two of catalyst and mix thoroughly, using a cutting motion rather than stirring. Use no fibers.

9. Using your finger tip or the tip of a putty knife, fill the hole about $\frac{1}{16}$ inch above the surrounding surface with the gel coat mixture.

10. Lay a piece of cellophane over the patch to start the curing process. Repeat step No. 6, trimming patch when partially cured.

11. Immediately after trimming, place another small amount of gel coat on one edge of the patch and cover with cellophane. Then, using a rubber squeegee or the back of the razor blade, squeegee level with area surrounding the patch. Leave cellophane on patch for one to two hours, or overnight, for a complete cure.

12. Using a sanding block, sand the patched area with 600-grit wet sandpaper. Finish by rubbing or buffing with a fine rubbing compound. Some slight color difference may be observed. Weathering will blend touch-up, if properly applied.

When buffing the boat to restore her finish, care should be taken not to cut through the gel coat surface. This is especially true on corners and edges of the hull. A power buffer may be used or the work done by hand, using a lightly abrasive rubbing compound such as Mirro Glaze No. 1 for power buffers or Dupont No. 7 for hand buffing. Any high-quality paste wax may be applied after buffing.

Patching Punctures, Breaks, and Holes. A fiberglass hull has terrific strength and high impact resistance. Sometimes, however, damage will result in a break in the hull or decks. It is easily and economically repaired. Materials needed include fiberglass mat and cloth, polyester resin and catalyst, colored gel coat to match your boat, cellophane, and backing materials (cardboard or sheet aluminum). Materials are usually available from your local dealer. It is preferable to do repair work in a shaded spot, because the sun may speed curing the resin.

1. Be sure the area around the break is clean and dry. Damage to the hull should be repaired as quickly as possible, since water may weaken the hull around the break. Wipe any dirt or wax from around the break before repair.

2. Use a keyhole saw or electric saber saw to cut away ragged edges, even if you must enlarge the hole at the break. Be sure to cut back to sound material.

3. Working inside the hull, rough-sand the hole and the area around it, using 80-grit dry paper. Feather back for about 2 inches all around the hole. This roughens surface for strong bond with patch. (If hole can't be reached inside boat, see later in this chapter.)

4. Cover a piece of cardboard with cellophane. Tape it to the outside of the hull, covering the hole completely. Cellophane should face toward inside of hull. If the break is on a sharp contour, you may use sheet aluminum formed over a similar contour that is undamaged. The aluminum should also be covered with cellophane.

5. Prepare a patch of fiberglass mat and cloth. Cut about 2 inches larger than the hole.

6. Mix a small amount of resin and catalyst—about 10 parts of resin to 1 part of catalyst. Mix in small quantities as needed for each step, as resin will cure in 30 minutes to an hour.

7. Thoroughly wet mat and cloth with catalyzed resin. Daub resin on mat first, and then on cloth. Mat should be applied against hull surface with cloth on top. You may "wet out" both pieces on cellophane and apply as a sandwich.

8. Lay patch over hole on inside of hull, cover with cellophane, and squeegee from center to edges to remove all air bubbles and assure adhesion around edge of hole. Air bubbles will show "white" in patch and they should all be worked out to the edge. Allow patch to cure completely (1 to 2 hours).

9. Remove cardboard from outside of hole and rough-sand the patch and edge of hole. Again feather edge of hole about 2 to 3 inches into undamaged area.

10. Mask area around hole with tape and paper to protect hull

surface while you work. Then cut a piece of fiberglass mat about 1 inch larger than hole, and one or more pieces of fiberglass cloth 2 to 3 inches larger than hole. Brush catalyzed resin over hole, lay mat over hole, and "wet out" with catalyzed resin. Use a "daubing" action with brush. Then apply additional layer or layers of fiberglass cloth to build up patch slightly above surface of boat. "Wet out" each layer thoroughly with resin.

11. With rubber squeegee or broad knife, work out all air bubbles in patch. Work from center to edge, pressing patch firmly against hull. Allow patch to cure for 15 to 20 minutes.

12. As soon as patch begins to set, but while still rubbery, take a sharp knife and cut away extra cloth and mat. Cut on outside edge of feathering. Strip cut edges off hull. Do this before cure is complete, to save extra sanding. Allow patch to cure overnight.

13. With dry sandpaper (80-grit) on power sander or sanding block, smooth patch and blend with surface around it. If air pockets show up while sanding, puncture with sharp instrument and fill with catalyzed resin. Let cure and resand.

14. Mix colored gel coat and catalyst in small quantity, and work into patch with fingers. Smooth carefully, and work into any crevices or holes.

15. Cover with cellophane, and squeegee smooth. Allow to cure completely before removing cellophane.

16. For large areas it is desirable to spray gel coat. For one pint of spray, use ½ pint gel coat, ½ pint acetone, 5 cc. catalyst. After spraying gel coat, it must be covered to complete cure. A liquid parting film should be sprayed over the gel coat area. This film is easily removed after gel coat is cured.

17. Sand patch with 220-grit wet sandpaper on sanding block. Then change to 600-grit for finish sanding. Buff with polishing compound for final finish. It may be necessary to repeat steps Nos. 14 and 15, sanding between applications to assure a smooth, even gel coat surface.

When the damage is below the floor surface or deck so that the work must be done from outside, the following procedure should be followed:

1. Cut away the edges of the hole, enough to allow a hand to reach inside. Sand inside with rough paper on sanding block, feathering hole 2 to 3 inches from edge.

2. Prepare patch of a layer of glass mat and cloth on a piece of corrugated cardboard slightly larger than patch. Don't cover cardboard with cellophane. "Wet out" with catalyzed resin, with mat on top to bond to hull. (See steps Nos. 5, 6, and 7 in previous instructions.) Cut wood strips to bridge outside of hole and prepare piano wire in a "U" shape.

3. Insert wires through patch and cardboard backing, with both ends of wire outside. Place wires as close to edge of hole as possible.

4. Insert wired patch into hole and tighten wires around sticks to pull patch into contact with inside of hull. Pull as tightly as possible and tie around sticks. Allow patch to cure completely before proceeding.

5. Cut wires at surface of patch and proceed with the repairs, beginning at step No. 9 in previous instructions. The cardboard backing will remain in the hole, but will be bonded to the patch.

General Inspection. When going over the hull, examine all deck hardware such as chocks, bitts, cleats, winches, ring bolts, sheet travelers, stanchions, and fair-leads; tighten all fastenings; free all scuppers and other water drains; check hatches; clean all brightwork and protect with polish or varnish applied as directed by the manufacturer; make sure all portholes and doors are in good condition; check ventilators; replace hardware as necessary; and clean all metal and protect with polish. Before yachts were equipped with the various electronic devices found aboard many modern sailboats, little difficulty was experienced with electrolytic action on propellers, shafts, struts, and hull fittings. Therefore, after hauling out your boat, check for any signs of electrolysis. If you don't find any, I wouldn't do anything other than to replace zinc plates that may have been eaten away. When replacing these plates, be sure that they are bonded to the strut or other underwater fitting which they are installed to protect, with a copper strap or mounted on the fitting itself. On the other hand, should your boat show that she is affected by electrolytic action, then by all means have an expert at the boatyard attempt to find the trouble and take care of it. If neglected, electrolysis can cause great damage to underwater fittings and fastenings.

Speaking of electronic equipment: tune, fix, and fit it out on your boat, by all means, but don't tinker and experiment beyond your technical proficiency or the capability of your tools. It is rather silly to play around with gear you know little about and then pay a professional to repair your own damage. Therefore, if you lack experience in electronic work, stick to simple service operations cited in the technical or owner's manual. All other work should be done by professionals.

It is most important to check the steering tiller or wheel, cables, sheaves, and worm or quadrant. Examine pintles, gudgeons, linkage, and steering gear fittings, and lubricate where necessary. Inspect rudder stock for wear and rudder blade for warpage. Connect up the plumbing, flush out the tanks, and fill them sufficiently to check your basin pumps and other fixtures. If you have the yard do this, give the order early in the spring so that the job can be completed before you give the interior the final touches and cleaning. Clean the galley, head, bunks, and lockers. Refinish any interior surfaces that need it. Restock galley, and return all gear that you took off when laying her up.

Tips for Plexiglas Maintenance. Because acrylics, such as Plexiglas, are being used more and more to replace glass on boats, because these materials have a tough body but a tender skin, and because most yachtsmen have had little experience with it, I think it is a good idea to detail its maintenance. To clean, use a mild soap or detergent and water. To avoid sediment smears, stains, or streaks, be sure to use as much water as possible. Apply to large areas with the type of bristle mop used in window-washing and to smaller areas with a clean soft cloth, sponge, or chamois. If it is necessary to dry the washed surface, use a clean damp chamois. Be sure not to use chemical cleaners because many of them can cause checkering, crazing, cracking, and annoying softening.

After cleaning, a coating of a good grade of commercial wax will protect the Plexiglas surfaces and maintain the highest degree of polish. The wax should be applied in a thin even coat and brought to a high polish by rubbing with a dry, soft cloth, such as cotton flannel.

Minor scratches in Plexiglas can be removed or reduced by hand polishing. Polishes can be most satisfactorily applied with a small soft cotton flannel pad dampened with water. Several applications may be necessary but most minor scratches can be reduced and the clarity improved in a relatively short time. Deeply scratched parts can be restored by buffing consecutively on an abrasive wheel, tallow wheel, and finish wheel. At the start of each buffing operation, the Plexiglas should be clean and dry. In buffing, sanding, or polishing, the Plexiglas should be kept constantly in motion relative to the wheel. Pressure against the wheel should be kept to a minimum and the direction of the buffing should be changed often. The friction of buffing, sanding, or polishing too long or too vigorously in any spot can generate heat enough to soften or "burn" the surface. Scratches too deep to be removed by light buffing may be removed by sanding. The finest sandpaper that will remove the imperfections should be used. Usually 320-A will be satisfactory, followed—after washing—by 400-A or finer paper. Use plenty of water while sanding. A wide area should be sanded to avoid objectionable distortions. After sanding, buff with fine abrasive, apply a tallow or wax, and then bring the surface to a high gloss with a final buffing or polishing.

Plexiglas should always be protected from nearby painting, plastering, or similar operations by covering it with kraft paper or dropcloths. If splashed, Plexiglas should be wiped while still wet with a clean soft cloth. To remove paint, soak Plexiglas surface in a 10 to 20 percent solution of caustic soda or trisodium phosphate and subsequently rinse with water. If part cannot be soaked, caustic soda or trisodium phosphate solution can be applied as a paste made by adding wallpaper paste to the solution. *Caution:* Caustic soda or trisodium phosphate attack the skin quickly. Hands should be shielded by rubber or other protective gloves. To remove tar, glazing compounds, grease, oil, and masking paper adhesive, use a soft cloth wet with naphtha, kerosene, or white (unleaded) gasoline, followed immediately with soap and water. Never use razor blades or other sharp instruments, such as a putty knife, to remove spots.

Alterations and Attachments. Preparations for a new season often involve the installation of new equipment or perhaps some rearrangement in the interior. How do you go about the installation of a deck-mounted cleat? Perhaps you want to add curtain rods above cabin windows, or a custom bracket that will hold your binoculars within easy reach of the helm. Or you may want to add deck hardware or add a cabinet or shelves in the cabin. The ordinary techniques for making such changes don't necessarily apply when dealing with fiberglass.

Cleats, chocks, etc., should be bolted in place. Use a twist drill close to the size of the bolt. An electric power drill is much faster than a hand-operated type. Always use generous-sized flat washers between the fiberglass and the nut. Lock washers are recommended. If the laminate is thin and unusually great loads are involved, as in the case of a mooring or towing cleat, bolt or fasten through into a wooden plate which will distribute stresses over a greater area. Factory-installed chain plates, stem plates, towing eyes, etc., are generally bolted into a "beefed-up" laminate section, but the owner usually does not have to go to this trouble. On larger boats, such as auxiliaries, a tight, leakproof fit of such hardware is important. Use a flexible sealing compound or rubber gasket.

Because of the hard, noncompressible nature of a fiberglass laminate, wood screws can't be installed properly. For the same reasons, driving a nail is a hopeless proposition. However, special types of screws can be used. While bolting is generally preferred, there are instances when a nut and washer cannot be applied. In these cases, machine and self-tapping screws (thread forming or thread cutting) will work satisfactorily. As a rule, such fasteners are employed where mild horizontal loads are involved—small chocks, tracks, metal coaming strip, etc. In any case, the installation should be made with care. As another rule-of-thumb, don't try to tap into a laminate that is, say, less than $5/32$ inch thick; the screw needs sufficient thickness penetration for dependable holding power. Select a pilot drill the exact size of the screw barrel and then carefully turn the fastener home. Such screws will "self-tap" themselves pretty well in the material, although the preparatory tapping procedure used in metals is better. If you should wind up with a hole that's out of place or too large, or if you are replacing a fitting where you do have an enlarged hole, the best thing to do is to grind the hole out to about an inch in diameter and rebuild it with fiberglass and resin. Build up the patch on the inside of the hole to keep the outer surface flush.

While most deck fittings have holes for screws or bolts, there may be times when you want to attach metal to fiberglass without metal fasteners. In such a case, you can bond these brackets to the fiberglass with one of the new epoxy glues. The resulting bond is both strong and permanent. Here's how to go about it: Mark the location of the object on the fiberglass. Scrape off any paint or other finish on the glass, and leave a slightly rough surface. Then spread enough glue—mixed as directed by the manufacturer on the container—on the metal to cover it completely, but not so much that big gobs will squeeze out when the bracket is pressed against the fiberglass. Also spread a thin layer of glue on the fiberglass, and work it into the roughened surface. Where a fitting is bonded to a vertical surface such as a bulkhead, it is necessary to hold the fitting in position until the epoxy is set. Use clamps, masking tape, or anything else that will keep the fitting from moving. An infrared heat lamp placed near the epoxy will help to speed the curing process, which usually takes about 24 hours without heat. This same epoxy glue can be used in bonding most other materials to fiberglass, or to each other. But if you want a flexible bond between components, you can use one of the silicon-base compounds. These are offered to the yachtsman primarily as seam caulking, but can be used in a wide variety of ways. Good examples would be as a waterproof gasket between metal fittings and the deck, and over electrical connections for both insulation and waterproofing. When using a silicon-base compound between a deck fitting and a fiberglass deck, remember that it has tremendous adhesion, and that it's not going to be an easy task to remove that fitting at some future date.

When you want to add a cabinet or shelves against a bulkhead, you'll want to distribute the weight of the installation over as much bulkhead area as possible. To do this, use a board, glued with epoxy to the bulkhead, to support shelves, cabinet, or bracket. The size of the mounting board is determined by the shape of the object it will support and the amount of space available on the bulkhead. It should be at least as long and as high as the unit to be installed. Be sure to paint or varnish the board—or cover it with a layer of fiberglass and finish to match the rest of the bulkhead. A mounting board is used, of plywood at least ½ inch thick. It is usually 3 or 4 inches longer and wider than the tank it will support. Mounting holes are located on the board and drilled. Bolts are inserted from behind the board, with wide washers—up to 3 inches in diameter—between boltheads and the wood. The area to which the board will be fixed is cleaned of paint or other coating, and a mixture of chopped fiberglass and resin is applied to a depth of about ½ inch. The mounting board is set down in this. For additional support, two or three layers of fiberglass cloth strips are run up from the floor over the edges of the wood.

Preparing the Engine. The engine work should also be completed as soon as possible. This is usually a dirty job; and the sooner it is finished, the better. Final checking and tuning-up, of course, should not be done until after the boat is in the water. If you've stored the boat in a good boatyard, have the mechanic there check over your engine and let him decide what should be done to put the engine into top running condition. If you place limitations on the engine work to be done, those are all the mechanic will do, and you'll have no grounds for complaint if your engine gives trouble during the season because other necessary work was not done. The following is the typical spring service for a typical auxiliary engine in a sailboat:

1. Close all drain cocks. Tighten all nuts and bolts.

2. Manifold. Replace drain plug. Check manifold bolts for tightness because some gaskets shrink more than others.

3. Water pump. Close drain cock and replace drain plug. Lubricate pump by grease cups. Replace packing if required.

4. Lubrication system. Remove all oil from oil pan and reverse gear housing. Refill with quantity specified by the manufacturer.

5. Cylinders. Remove spark plugs. Pour 1 or 2 ounces of oil in cylinders to lubricate walls, rings, etc.; turn engine over without spark plugs in place.

6. Valves and tappets. Check and lubricate if required. Remove seal over breather tube end.

7. Distributor. Clean and lubricate as required. Remove any moisture seals. Clean and set distributor points.

8. Spark plugs. Clean spark plugs and reset gap to .025 inches. Replace burned or broken plugs.

9. Ignition wires. Replace damaged or brittle ignition wires. High-tension electrical leakage prevents good operation of an engine.

10. Starting motor. See that the starter pinion is clean and lubricated with light oil. Remove any moisture seals. Lubricate bearings. Clean commutator and brushes with sandpaper. *Do not use emery cloth.*

11. Generator. Remove any moisture seals. Clean commutator and brushes with sandpaper. *Do not use emery cloth.* Lubricate as required.

12. Battery. Reinstall fully charged battery. Clean the cable terminals and fasten securely to clean battery terminals. Coat terminals with vaseline to reduce corrosion.

13. Fuel system. See that fuel system is clean and free from scale,

sludge, or obstructions. Drain out any water that has accumulated in tanks or fuel lines. Check over for loose connections, tightening any found. Remove cover from carburetor air intake. Oil carburetor choke and throttle shafts. Check for easy operation. Clean flame arrestor.

14. Exhaust system. Remove moisture seal.

15. Propeller. Examine propeller for nicks and dents; repair or replace as indicated. Examine lock nut and cotter pins.

16. Shaft. Inspect shaft for wear or damage and have repaired or replaced. Examine shaft coupling and replace coupling bolts if necessary. Also look at shaft log and strut and take any necessary action.

17. Turn engine over by hand with the spark plugs out to see that all bearings are free.

18. With boat in water, check freedom of propeller shaft in bearings and alignment of propeller shaft with engine.

19. Tighten stuffing box just enough to stop leakage along shaft. Excessive tightening will cause power loss and burned stuffing material.

20. Clean motor thoroughly and repaint.

Before starting your engine, ventilate the engine compartment by opening hatches and starting blower fans (if you have them). Check the fuel supply and make sure fuel lines are tight. Any fuel seepage or leaks *should be corrected* before you attempt to start the engine. Check the oil level—use SAE 30 detergent oil. Check all electrical connections. Ground is negative. The ground terminal should be attached to engine block. Don't allow flames or sparks near battery openings. Gases produced during normal charging are explosive. Make sure water pump is lubricated with water pump grease.

To start the engine follow the same procedure you do when starting a new engine for the first time, which is:

1. Clutch lever should be in neutral position.

2. Fill fuel pump bowl, using the hand primer on the fuel pump.

3. Place throttle lever at one-quarter open position.

4. Pull out choke rod.

5. Turn on ignition switch and press starting button.

6. As soon as engine starts, gradually push in choke lever until choke valve is completely open.

7. Run engine at idling speed of 800 to 1000 rpm.

8. Check oil pressure; it should be 30 to 35 pounds when engine is cold. Check oil after about 10 minutes of running. Add oil to bring level to full mark if needed.

9. Check cooling system and make sure water pump is operating by checking water out of exhaust pipe. Temperature indicated on gauge should gradually go up to 140 to 150 degrees Fahrenheit.

10. If oil pressure or water flow (or operating temperature) isn't normal, stop engine at once and check installation to correct problem.

11. Cast off and place clutch lever into engaged position. You are now under way. When shifting into forward or reverse position, the engine should be running at about 1000 rpm.

Electrical System. Since the batteries were probably removed from the boat during winter lay-up, they should be checked with a hydrometer before being placed aboard. The hydrometer should indicate a fully charged condition of each cell. If any cell has a low reading have your battery service station determine the source of trouble. Don't start the season with a poor battery. Storage batteries are expensive, but if given reasonable care during the period of use as well as during winter lay-up they should last for several years. This is particularly true of standard brands that are designed for marine service.

Inspect main switch panel, and clean all terminals. Examine all wiring for worn insulation and replace if worn. Check all navigating lights, cabin lights, and all other electrical equipment, and if they don't operate properly, take the necessary action to make sure that they do.

Tuning the Rigging. Getting aluminum booms and masts ready to go is a lot easier than preparing wooden booms and masts, but they should get some attention. Aluminum is subject to oxidation and eventual pitting. To prevent this, scrub the mast down with bronze or copper wool until it's shiny. Then bring it up to a high luster with rubbing compound. Finally, give it a liberal coat of a good commercial automobile wax. But, if you have an anodized mast or boom, just wash it, wax it, and forget it. Heavy buffing with wire wool will just wear away the anodized finish. Any splits or dents should be very carefully checked, and if found unsound, should be replaced. It usually isn't a good idea to start the sailing season with defective masts or booms. Wooden masts and booms should be very carefully inspected and painted or varnished as necessary. Apply either of these finishing materials as directed by the manufacturer.

After checking and refinishing of the spars is completed, inspect all rigging hardware to make sure that it is secure. Also look at sheaves and clevis pins for wear and replace if they show an appreciable amount of wear. Another piece of hardware that needs attention —and one that is rapidly fading into oblivion—is the sail track. Besides seeing that it is solidly fastened, make sure all the joints are properly aligned and the whole track lubricated. A simple test is to

Figure 11-2: Before stepping the mast, make certain all the rigging and light connects are made (left). The male portion of the electrical connection is shown in the center illustration, while the female portion is shown at the right.

shove a single slide from end to end. On masts up to thirty-odd feet, it should make it with one shove. If it does, you can be sure of getting the sail down in a hurry when you really need to. When making any hardware replacements, never put bronze fittings on an aluminum spar. Use stainless steel or plastic.

If the rigging was marked when it was removed from the spar as previously suggested, or if you're thoroughly familiar with the rigging, it will be an easy task to put it back on. Be sure you haven't overlooked any cotter pins in the rigging, and make certain that the ends of the cotter pins are properly turned back to prevent tearing the sails. (Where pins come into direct contact with the sails, it is wise to cover them with tape.) Vertical clevis pins should have their heads on top so that if the cotter pin does work loose the pin will stay in by gravity. Screw pin shackles aloft should be avoided. Inspect shrouds, lazy jacks, struts, stays, chain plates, spreaders, and topping lifts. All swaged fittings should be examined with the greatest of care, preferably with a magnifying glass. Any visible longitudinal fracture in the sleeve is cause to discard the shroud or stay. This may sound drastic, but wide experience has shown that once the sleeve has fractured, it is useless and the wire may pull out at any time. A good way to prevent splitting is to put a little epoxy glue around the neck of the sleeve so that water can't run down inside and cause rust to split the fitting. The wire itself should be locked over and replaced if wear is found. The running rigging also deserves equal attention. Here the deficiencies are usually pretty obvious. Any line that appears in poor condition should be retired to a position of less responsibility, such as fender lines.

It's a good idea to do all this work before the mast is stepped. Also check the electric wiring to the spreader and masthead lights to be sure connections are tight and the bulbs are good. Make certain that the wind pennant and anemometer are installed before the mast is stepped. Check the turnbuckles to be sure they work freely. Actually, anything else that you can do to have everything in good shape and ready for the riggers will save them time, and will reduce the cost to you of stepping the spar. For example, once the spar is stepped and the shrouds are in place, make sure that the standing rigging is properly adjusted. In some boatyards, you can leave the problem of adjustment to the riggers, but I always prefer to do it myself, because I feel that I am more familiar with the amount of tension the shrouds should have. Whether you or the rigger makes the final adjustments, a general rule to follow is that the uppers and intermediates should be fairly taut, and the lowers just tight enough to leave a little sag in the wire. The forestay should be quite taut so that headsails won't sag off to leeward. While adjusting the rigging, sight up along the sail track to be sure the mast is straight and set the shrouds accordingly. It's wise to tape over all cotter pins in the turnbuckles. Also, when putting in the mast wedges, don't drive them in hard; just a few taps of the mallet is sufficient. It's best to place as even a strain as possible on them all around the spar. Before setting the sails, check them for wear and needed repairs. Also make sure the battens are in good order—no splinters.

The finer points of tuning the rigging can only be discovered by working with your own individual boat. It can easily take a couple of seasons' experimenting to find out the fine points of adjusting the rigging to get the most from your particular boat; perhaps you'll find out the ultimate if your perceptions are keen enough. This is the lure of the never-ending art of sailing.

Before you set sail, make sure all safety gear is on board (see Chapter 1) and is in good or operative condition. Check your ground tackle carefully; and examine your mooring, including anchor, chain, buoy, and pendant, before setting it in place. This should mark the finish of your labor, and the beginning of your fun. But one final word: after a shakedown cruise the chances are that the rigging will need retuning or readjustment. In fact, after sailing in any heavy blow, some checkup is necessary, even in well-stretched riggings. Actually the most important thing to remember about tuning your rigging, in order to get the most out of your boat, is that tuning rigging, as tuning a Stradivarius violin, is a process that never ends. The framework that presents your sails to the breeze is just as critical as how you trim your sheets—perhaps more so.

Sail Care

Too many sailors have the erroneous opinion that the advent of nylon and dacron has eliminated almost all need for the care of sails. However, the care is certainly different than that given cotton sails. For instance, all "breaking-in" traditions and theories developed for cotton sails are eliminated with dacron. There is no need to reach around for hours in moderate winds and to gradually work out the foot and luff day by day. Stretch dacrons until the sail takes proper shape and sail on the wind as soon as you like. Most sailmakers suggest that new sails be set first on a reasonably dry day in moderate air, so you can look them over carefully and make various adjustments to luff and foot. It is still good practice to help the mainsail leech by holding up the after end of the boom when hoisting and lowering. Dacron won't stretch much, but just a little can have a big effect—often bad. Also keep in mind that dacron, being a much firmer material than cotton, is more easily distorted by improper tension and poor spar fittings. The tack and clew pins must allow the luff and foot to lie in a straight line. The halyard sheave also must let the halyard lead "fair" to the headboard. The softer cotton would absorb some of these problems, but with dacron, which has far less give, any distortions at the corners cause serious hard spots and creases that will affect a large area of the sail.

All large racing boats now have wire halyards on all sails except the spinnaker staysail and mizzen staysail. These sails can be set on rope halyards, as a small amount of stretch is of no consequence. However, just a small amount of stretch will ruin the set of a small boat's main or jib when the breeze pipes up. A rope halyard is poor if it stretches when you want the luff taut, so I highly recommend a switch to wire if you still have rope halyards.

Chafe is a problem common to everyone who uses sails. The stitching of a dacron sail remains exposed and is susceptible to damage from any contact. How nice it was with cotton, where the thread could find protection in the soft fabric! The small-boat racers who have gone to grooved spars must continually check the headboard and clew for chafe. (The use of wax on the luff rope will probably help somewhat with this problem.) The shrouds take a toll on seam stitching every time the main is eased for a run. When track slides are used, the seizings normally do not last more than a season or two at most, and many sailmakers are now using small shackles. Headsails, especially the overlapping variety, show signs of chafe around the clew and lower leech after surprisingly few heavy-weather races because of contact with shrouds and mast on every tack.

The cruising-boat owner has all the chafe problems of the one-design racer and many more of his own. He does have the advantage of rigging rollers on his shrouds (too much windage for the little boat) to help his headsails around, but spinnaker pole fittings and winches on the mast offset this help. He must also continually watch his jib hanks, especially the lowest one, as tremendous strain is exerted along the foot of big genoas. Chafing patches should be installed by your sailmaker where the genoa foot breaks over the life lines, where it meets the shrouds, and also aloft on the leech where the spreader makes contact. Usually it is best to set the genoa and mark the areas that need to be protected before placing patches.

The fact that an ocean racer or coastwise cruiser might run before the wind for days rather than hours emphasizes the need to guard against chafe. A mainsail wearing on a spreader, lee shroud, or running backstay, or a slatting topping lift for this length of time, is bound to be damaged. A boom vang will help to quiet the main and keep it off the spreader. The lift should be made of vinyl-covered wire. A number of systems are used for controlling the lift; one system is a combination double wheel that goes up the permanent backstay as the boom is eased. The use of a long piece of shock cord running from the lift to the tack area of the main is another. With the latter it is necessary to change the shock cord to the windward side each time you tack, but the extra effort pays dividends in the long run. No boatowner can afford to wait until the end of the season to inspect his sails for chafe—it should be a constant routine.

It does sails no good to allow them to slat unnecessarily. Not only does slatting wear the stitching but it also weakens the cloth itself by causing the threads of which it is made to rub one against the other. Moreover, excessive slatting is likely to tear batten pockets which, in turn, may result in battens being lost or broken. If you must dry sails on a windy day, don't hoist them. Instead, spread them out on deck, loosely bunched so the air and sunshine can do their work. Two things you should avoid, however, with dacron sails are extreme heat (like lighted cigarettes) and sharp creases.

All skippers in salt-water areas should keep in mind that salt is harmful to nylon and definitely stiffens dacron. Sails on small boats will often not set properly if caked with salt and will lose much of their efficiency. A soaking in fresh water or a rinsing by hose while hung loosely outdoors on a quiet day will help immediately. If they become really bad or are too big to handle they should go to the sailmaker for a complete washing. Not only can a sail's shape be improved but also its life can be extended. While clean sails may make the boat go a little faster and last a little longer, the psychological advantage of a new-looking sail is also worth something. Before you set a main or jib be sure the mast and boom and rigging have had a thorough going-over. Aluminum spars especially seem to pick up an oily dirt that is almost impossible to remove from dacron. As previously stated, bronze wool and warm water do a good job if you can get to the rig before it is stepped. Wipe down shrouds and stays as well as the mast during the season and you will be astounded at the filth you take off. Also, if you always wash down decks as soon as you get aboard, your sails will stay whiter. Remember that oil and grease spots can be removed with carbon tetrachloride cleaning fluids.

Two-, three- and four-ounce dacron as well as spinnaker nylon can be temporarily mended with spinnaker repair tape or white rigging tape. Pressed with the fingers on both sides of a tear or open seam, the tape in most cases will hold until the sail can be taken to be repaired. It is usually better to leave the sewing to an experienced machine operator or sailmaker so that no puckers or hard spots are sewn in. The cruising-boat owner cannot rely on repair tape except for spinnakers and other sails of spinnaker cloth. There are three basic sewing repairs that can be easily learned and applied with needles, a palm, dacron thread, and some scraps of dacron. The first is the overhand or round stitch for closing seams, darning very small holes, and repairing tears of about an inch. For a longer tear, but one not at a point of great tension, the herringbone stitch is excellent. The third possible repair is the patch.

Battens can be a special headache to the offshore racing man, because dacron is rougher than cotton. The stiffer material not only helps break wooden battens but it then lets the rough edges chafe through in short order. One method of overcoming this problem is to run white rigging or medical tape down both edges and then wrap the entire batten from one end to the other. The tape, besides keeping the batten from splintering, will act as a guard against chafe. Whether you tape your battens or not it is a good idea to give them a couple of coats of varnish so that they will not pick up moisture and encourage mildew in the batten pockets. Most mildew found on dacron sails has been in and around batten pockets, and was very likely caused when sails were furled without being dried after a sail in wet weather.

Before leaving the subject of sails, it may be a good idea to say a word or two about sail bags and covers. As a rule, it's best to have them made of the same type of material as the sails. There are fabrics coated with impervious plastic or rubberlike coatings which look fine and are supposed to be—and doubtless are—waterproof. But these don't permit the air to circulate freely about a sail, with the result that mildew frequently appears. (Although mildew does modern sail-cloth no harm, as previously stated, it makes them look bad.) The best bags and covers are those that are slightly porous so that the sails can breathe. Sail covers that don't fit too tightly are best. The closure used at the bottom should permit air to get in and circulate around the sail.

First Aid for Your Yacht

First aid for humans was discussed in Chapter 7, and now I would like to go into some first-aid problems that boats may face. If you take good care of your boat and check her parts carefully each time you go out, chances of a breakdown are slight. But, for example, if you fail to replace a defective stay before you go out, there is always the distinct possibility of its failing and causing you to lose the mast.

As in the case with human first aid, yacht first aid needs a kit of tools and equipment with which to accomplish the best results. Because the amount of spare equipment, tools, and repair material will depend on the size of your boat and the nature of her voyage, I have not made a list of items you should have aboard. Instead, look around your boat and imagine what different accidents might happen; then visualize what might be done about them. See that you have the necessary gear in your "yacht's own first-aid kit" to make all repairs.

Rigging Repairs. A broken spar can be very adequately repaired by "fishing" with strips of wood or metal (called "fish") and wire or rope. When making such a jury rig to reinforce a broken spar, remember that the repair depends upon the strength of the material used as a fish, the strength of the lashing, and the firmness of their union. Items used for a fish include boat hooks, oars, the boom crutch, and spinnaker poles. Sometimes two or more fish are used around the damaged spar to hold it tightly together like splints on a broken leg. When using more than one fish, it's usually wise to employ separate lines to hold each piece. Light line or wire, generously and tightly wrapped, is better than a few turns of a heavy one.

If a spreader or shroud fails, the first task is to take the strain off the mast as quickly as possible by jibing or tacking. (If the jib or forestay fails, fall off and run before the wind, while if the backstay goes, luff up.) Then make a temporary repair until a new spreader can be rigged. For instance, a spinnaker pole squared well aft with the shroud attached at the outboard end, and with the pole guyed down forward and aft, will do the job nicely. Similarly, the main halyard might be used with the pole to replace a parted shroud. Thimbles and wire clamps can be employed to replace a broken true-lock splice or fitting.

If the mast should go over the side, the first task is to get it clear of the boat before it can punch a hole in her hull. If the standing rigging pins can be removed quickly, do so, because this will allow you to save the wire and turnbuckles and leave just that much more equipment to rig a temporary or jury mast with. If you can't remove the pins, the wire can be cut with wire cutters at the ends. But, always try to save the mast. It and its rigging will make a most effective sea anchor which can be used until the weather moderates. While doing this, it is a good idea to rig fenders or cushions over the side to prevent damage to the hull. When conditions permit, it may be possible to salvage the mast or at least some of the fittings.

Loss or Disablement of a Rudder. If you should lose the use of your boat's rudder, a substitute "blade" can be found by employing a door, hatch cover, oar, table leaf, or a combination of these nailed together. This blade is then lashed to the transom and used like the steering sweep installations employed on lifeboats at sea.

Another possible way to steer a small boat that has lost her rudder is to use a drag at the stern; for instance, by towing a bucket. When the drag is located in the center of the stern, the craft will go straight ahead. When you wish to make her turn, haul the drag to the side to which you desire to turn.

Hull Repair. As stated earlier, the foresighted skipper going far from shore should always provide his boat with a stock of spare parts and the necessary materials for emergency repairs and this includes repairs to the hull. The fiberglass-boat owner should, therefore, avail himself of a repair kit of glass and resin. These kits can be purchased from a marine hardware store or plastics supply house. Here is what I suggest in the way of essential contents:

Fiberglass cloth—several square yards.
Fiberglass tape 6 inches wide—10 yards.
Polyester resin—at least a quart in pint cans.
Fiberglass mat—1 square yard.
Epoxy cement—several tubes.

The cloth and mat would be largely useful for taking care of a fracture or hole (see page 278). The tape can be enormously useful—perhaps for restoring a fractured spar or temporarily stopping a leak in a pipe or the cold end of the exhaust tube. Polyester resin would be easiest to handle under field conditions because it will wet the glass rapidly and cure more quickly than epoxy. The epoxy cement can be considered as a "super" glue or solder and has many obvious applications.

Quite obviously, accidents don't always occur in such a convenient way that this recommended repair kit can be immediately employed. That is to say, you can't apply a patch to the hull when you are rolling around in a sea or when it's raining and cold. You may have to apply some ingenuity and special techniques to protect the watertight integrity of the boat until you can get into a sheltered spot and then use the fiberglass repair materials. Impromptu techniques have been employed by seamen for generations—stuffing the hole with a rag, pillow, or mattress is one example; a collision mat is another. It would even be possible in certain circumstances to drill through the fiberglass hull and bolt in place a makeshift dam constructed from any available wooden member in the boat.

Within the limitations expressed above, emergency repairs are easy to do on a fiberglass boat. Last summer I talked to a fiberglass auxiliary owner who, while on a cruise, had been rammed by another boat. The break was amidships, above the waterline, about 2 inches wide by a foot long. He made a temporary but effective repair with fiberglass materials. The job was unsightly, but it was strong and kept the water out. He lost only a few hours' time on his vacation cruise and as a matter of fact sailed the boat the rest of the summer in this condition, leaving the finishing touches on the repair to be done after hauling for the winter.

When a Boat Goes Aground. There are several types of grounding situations; the several variables include the amount of current, the type of bottom, the direction and velocity of wind, the type of bottom, and state of tide. Perhaps your boat was forced ashore by wind or current; or perhaps, through faulty piloting on your part, she went upon a shoal. I could go on for hours as to the causes of grounding. It is enough to say that each situation requires different handling depending on the position of the craft, the extent of damage, the kind of assistance anticipated, and gear available on board.

Going aground in tidal waters, for example, may offer no serious problem if the tide is on the flood. An anchor promptly put out in the direction of deep water, with all available scope, will prevent the craft's being carried into shallower water as the tide rises. Then as the tide rises, you may use the pull on the anchor to break the boat free, or use the spinnaker pole or an oar to give a "poling" push. Sometimes a man overboard can shove the boat off a shoal as the tide floods.

For the small-boat yachtsman, another possible way of freeing a grounded craft is to run a line to the anchor at one side, tie it to the halyard, and pull on the other end of the halyard. As the mast tilts, the boat will heel over, shifting away from the anchor. (All crew members should be on the heeling side.) If the keel breaks free, push or pole the boat into deep water before she hangs up again.

If you have an auxiliary aboard, it's often possible, in both tidal and inland waters, to employ the engine's propeller in a freeing operation if it's clear of the bottom, clear of any obstruction immediately astern, and if it's undamaged. Although the propeller thrust is lessened in reverse, it can still be effective if you time it with a shove from the shoal, a poling push, or a pull on the anchor line set in deep water. (In the latter case, watch the line so it doesn't foul the propeller.) Employing the rudder, swing the stern slightly from side to side. This frequently gets faster results than a straight reverse pull. It is also often possible to get free by waiting for the wake of a passing vessel to give sufficient lift to break the suction and allow the grounded craft to back off under her own power.

There are times when all these methods will fail and towing by another boat, or boats, will be necessary. Unfortunately, few sailboats are equipped with deck fittings capable of withstanding the towing strain that is sometimes required to break free a keel-bottom boat. While a towing hawser secured to the main bow cleats would most likely hold, it wouldn't permit the towing strain to be applied astern in the proper direction. Since it's usually desirable to have the stern towed off first, the most desirable method of attaching a towing hawser is a bridle. In most cases, the bridle can be rigged by carrying the heaviest available line (doubled if length permits) completely around the hull from bow to stern just below the level of the deck level, suspended in position by lines led across the deck and deckhouse spaced a few feet apart. (Don't forget chafing gear to protect the topsides.) The two ends of the bridle should be secured to each other, outboard of the stern where the hawser will be attached. The pull of the hawser, even under strain, will tend downward, hence the bridle must be particularly well supported in position across the deck aft. Also some provision must be taken for letting the towing hawser go instantly if the applied strain begins to cause damage. One method of doing this is to take three full turns of the hawser around the bridle with a single half hitch on itself in the form of half a bowknot, leaving enough end to bring back on board. A yank on the end will release the half hitch, which frees the hawser.

The actual towing effort itself should await optimum conditions; all preparations should be properly completed and the tide should be at its highest stage. The auxiliary engine, if one is aboard, shouldn't be started until just before the towing effort, to prevent sucking mud or sand into the water intakes. When the pulling strain from the towing vessel is applied, not before, try full throttle in reverse. If the sailboat isn't moved the rescuing craft should maintain the strain while reversing an arc from the port quarter to the starboard quarter of the stranded vessel. This maneuver, accomplished by rudder alone, will usually succeed in breaking the suction. Breaking suction can be expedited if the stranded boat is small enough to be rocked by her crew.

Capsizing. Capsizing is probably the most common *small-boat* sailing accident. (It is rather difficult to capsize a keel-bottomed racer-cruiser–type boat.) Usually it occurs when least expected. But if you will consider a capsize as a part of the fun of sailing, you will be completely safe. That is, of course, if you know what to do. Actually, many of the really top-notch racing skippers practice capsizing and then righting their boats. But, in normal sailing for fun there is no excuse for tipping over or capsizing. However, there are numerous reasons why it occurs. For example, it can be caused by having too much wind for the amount of sail carried, by the improper balance of the crew, by jibing in a strong wind with the centerboard up too far, by not keeping the boat under full control at all times, and by being caught in the shifting winds of a squall.

If your craft should capsize and throw you into the water, swim to the boat and stay with it. (Most modern sailboats are equipped with flotation chambers so that even a heavy-keel craft won't sink.) To make this task easier, take off your deck shoes and all excess clothing. If not already on, get life preservers on. Even if you and your crew are all good swimmers, the life preservers prevent persons in the water from tiring quickly and will help keep them relatively warm. Even more important, a life preserver allows you to work around the boat without fear. Speaking of your crew, be sure that they all are accounted for and are able to take care of themselves. Occasionally someone may get caught under the sail, become entangled with lines, or get hit on the head with the boom and require assistance.

Under most conditions it's possible to uncapsize or right the boat. But before attempting this, the sails almost always should be brought down and tied to the boom. Start by releasing the main halyard and pulling the mainsail down the mast toward the boat. Then furl it as best you can and secure it with an extra piece of line or the mainsheet. Follow the same procedure for the jib and then make all sheets and halyards fast. Take your time during this operation, since it's a fairly difficult job, especially when your sails are flat in the water. Don't tire yourself out while in the water.

Once the sails are down and secured, make sure the centerboard (if she has one) is down as far as possible. Now stand on the far end of the centerboard or keel and take a secure hold of the gunwale or the coaming. While pulling backward, push down with your legs on the centerboard or keel, and the craft should slowly right itself. One of the crew members can help by going to the opposite side of the boat, treading water, and giving the shrouds or mast an initial push upward. Then carefully help one member of the crew to climb into the hull over the stern while the others help to balance the boat and keep it from rolling. The person on board should stay in the center of the craft and bail out the hull as quickly as he can. When the hull is buoyant enough to hold the remaining members of the crew, they should get on board and all should again begin to bail it out completely.

Fire Afloat. Despite a yachtsman's best efforts, fires are always a possibility and do occur. For this reason, you should be foresighted in this regard. Having your fire-fighting gear handy and in good condition is the first step in successfully combating fire. Although this equipment might be limited to only one fire extinguisher and a bailer, their availability and proper operating condition could mean the difference between prompt extinguishment and disaster. In addition to having equipment ready in advance, you should think about the action that you would take in case of fire. More can be done in the first minutes than in the following few hours.

Fires are mainly extinguished by one of two methods or a combination of both, namely cooling, smothering, and both cooling and smothering. A fire requires heat as well as oxygen to support combustion. Extinguishing agents such as dry chemical, carbon dioxide, and foam smother and to some extent cool. They are most effective on oil or grease fires when the extinguishing agent is directed at the base of the flames. The fire, if possible, should be approached from upwind so that the breeze will carry the extinguishing agent into the fire. Burning items such as wood, mattresses, and rags are best extinguished by water. For this reason a bailer or bucket can be a most valuable piece of equipment. You'll have an unlimited supply of water available on all sides. If the burning object is movable, try to throw it over the side (unless there is risk of burning your hands or clothing). If a fire occurs in a relatively confined space, the closing of hatches, doors, vents, and ports will tend to keep oxygen from fanning the flames. In addition, should the fire be in the engine compartment, shut off the fuel supply.

The maneuvering of your boat will also assist in extinguishing fires. When under way, wind caused by the boat's motion fans the flames. Also, it would make sense to keep the fire downwind—that is, if the fire is aft, head the bow of the boat into the wind; if the fire is forward, put the stern of your boat into the wind. Such action helps to reduce any tendency of the fire to spread to other parts of the boat, and may reduce the hazard of smoke enveloping persons on board.

Since most pleasure boat fires are caused by, or can be traced to, improper fueling procedures, it may be wise to give the safety rules that every auxiliary owner should follow when this task must be done:

Before Fueling:

1. Moor securely to the dock.
2. Close ports, windows, doors and hatches.
3. Stop engines and turn off all electrical devices.
4. Put out lights and galley fires.

While Fueling:

1. Don't smoke, strike matches, or throw switches.
2. Keep nozzle in contact with fill pipe.
3. Don't let fuel spill into hull or bilges.
4. Complete fueling before dark.

After Fueling:

1. Close fill opening, wipe up *all* spills.
2. Let boat ventilate for five minutes before starting machinery, lighting fires, or cigarettes.
3. Check for gasoline odor in engine compartment.
4. Be ready to cast off as soon as engine starts.

Troubleshooting an Engine. A gasoline engine depends upon three main factors for proper operation: an unfailing fuel supply, uninterrupted ignition, and good compression. When any one of these is not present, or present only intermittently, engine failure will result. The following "troubleshooting" information is designed to help the operator locate and overcome some of the most probable causes of engine failure or improper operation. Probable causes are listed in the most likely order of occurrence. Only one correction should be attempted at a time and that possibility eliminated before going on to the next.

Trouble	Probable Cause	Correction
Starter will not crank engine	Discharged battery	Charge or replace battery
	Corroded battery terminals	Clean terminals
	Loose connection in starting circuit	Check and tighten all connections
	Defective starting switch	Replace switch
	Starter motor brushes dirty	Clean or replace brushes
	Jammed Bendix gear	Loosen starter motor to free gear
	Defective starter motor	Replace motor
Starter motor turns but does not crank engine	Partially discharged battery	Charge or replace battery

Trouble	Probable Cause	Correction
	Defective wiring or wiring of too-low capacity	Check wiring for worn acid spots
	Broken Bendix drive	Remove starter motor and repair drive
Engine will not start	Empty fuel tank	Fill tank with proper fuel
	Flooded engine	Remove spark plugs and crank engine several times. Replace plugs
	Water in fuel system	If water is found, clean tank, fuel lines, and carburetor. Refill with proper fuel
	Inoperative or sticking choke valve	Check valve, linkage, and choke rod or cable for proper operation
	Improperly adjusted carburetor	Adjust carburetor
	Clogged fuel lines or defective fuel pump	Disconnect fuel line at carburetor. If fuel does not flow freely when engine is cranked, clean fuel line and sediment bowl. If fuel still does not flow freely after cleaning, repair or replace pump.
Engine will not start (poor compression and other causes)	Air leak around intake manifold	Check for leak by squirting oil around intake connections. If leak is found, tighten manifold and if necessary replace gaskets
	Loose spark plugs	Check all plugs for proper seating, gasket, and tightness. Replace all damaged plugs and gaskets
	Loosely seating valves	Check for broken or weak valve springs, warped stems, carbon and gum deposits, and insufficient tappet clearance
	Damaged cylinder head gasket	Check for leaks around gasket when engine is cranked. If a leak is found replace gasket
	Worn or broken piston rings	Replace broken and worn rings. Check cylinders for "out of round" and "taper"

Trouble	Probable Cause	Correction
Excessive engine temperature	No water circulation	Check for clogged water lines and restricted inlets. Check for broken or stuck thermostat. Look for worn or damaged water pump or water pump drive
Engine temperature too low	Broken or stuck thermostat	Replace thermostat
Engine will not start (ignition system)	Ignition switch "off" or defective	Turn on switch or replace
	Fouled or broken spark plugs	Remove plugs and inspect for cracked porcelain, dirty points, or improper gap
	Improperly set, worn, or pitted distributor points. Defective ignition coil	Remove center wire from distributor cap and hold within ⅜ inch of motor block. Crank engine. Clean sharp spark should jump between wire and block when points open. Clean and adjust points. If spark is weak or yellow after adjustment of points, replace condenser. If spark still is weak or not present replace ignition coil
	Wet, cracked, or broken distributor	Wipe inside surfaces of distributor dry with clean cloth. Inspect for cracked or broken parts. Replace necessary parts
	Improperly set, worn, or pitted magneto breaker points (magneto models only)	Remove spark plug wire and hold within ⅜ inch of engine block. Clean sharp spark should jump between wire and block when engine is cranked. If spark is weak or not present clean and adjust breaker points
	Improperly set, worn, or pitted timer points. Defective coil or defective condenser	Remove spark plug wire and hold within ⅛ inch of engine block. A clean sharp spark should jump between wire and block when engine is cranked. Clean and set timer points. If spark still is not present when engine is cranked, replace coil
	Improper timing	Set timing

Trouble	Probable Cause	Correction
No oil pressure	Defective gauge or tube	Replace gauge or tube
	No oil in engine	Refill with the proper grade oil
	Dirt in pressure relief valve	Clean valve
	Defective oil pump, leak in oil lines, or broken oil pump drive	Check oil pump and oil pump drive for worn or broken parts. Tighten all oil line connections
Loss of rpm (boat or associated equipment)	Damaged propeller	Repair propeller
	Bent rudder	Repair
	Misalignment	Realign engine to shaft
	Too-tight stuffing box packing gland	Adjust
	Dirty boat bottom	
Vibration	Misfiring or preignition	See correction under misfiring and preignition
	Loose foundation or foundation bolts	
	Propeller shaft out of line or bent	
	Propeller bent or pitch out of true	
Preignition	Defective spark plugs	Check all spark plugs for broken porcelain, burned electrodes, or electrodes out of adjustment. Replace all defective plugs or clean and reset
	Improper timing	Readjust timing
	Engine carbon	Remove cylinder head and clean out carbon
	Engine overheating	See correction under "Engine will not start" portion of this table
Backfiring	Insufficient fuel reaching engine due to dirty lines or strainer, or blocked fuel tank vent. Water in fuel tank	See correction under "Engine will not start" portion of this table
	Poorly adjusted distributor	See correction under "Engine will not start" portion of this table

Trouble	Probable Cause	Correction
Low oil pressure	Too-light body oil	Replace with proper weight oil
	Oil leak in pressure line	Inspect all oil lines Tighten all connections
	Weak or broken pressure relief valve spring	Replace spring
	Worn oil pump	Replace pump
	Worn or loose bearings	Replace bearings
Oil pressure too high	Too-heavy body oil	Drain oil and replace with oil of proper weight
	Stuck pressure relief valve	Clean or replace valve
	Dirt or obstruction in lines	Drain and clean oil system. Check for bent or flattened oil lines and replace where necessary
Sludge in oil	Infrequent oil changes	Drain and refill with proper weight oil
	Water in oil	Drain and refill. If trouble persists check for cracked block, defective head gasket, and cracked head
	Dirty oil filter	Replace filter

Abandoning Ship. Most boats involved in casualties will continue to remain afloat indefinitely. If it becomes necessary to abandon your boat due to fire, swamping, capsizing, or other emergencies, don't leave the area. Generally a damaged boat can be sighted more readily than a person in the water, and it may help to keep you afloat.

Keep in mind that distance over water is deceptive. Usually the estimated distance is much shorter than the actual distance. Keep your head and restrain your initial impulse to swim ashore. Calmly weigh the facts of the situation, such as injuries to passengers, the proximity of shore, and your swimming abilities, before deciding your course of action. But remember that in 999 cases out of 1000 it's best to stay with your boat.

If there is time before abandoning ship, don your life preserver and give distress signals. Don't foolishly waste signaling devices when a small likelihood of assistance exists. Wait until you sight

someone or something. If your boat is equipped with a radiotelephone, a distress message should be sent.

Midseason Care

Sailboat maintenance is a year-round job. Most of us give our
boats the needed time in the fall to haul them up properly and
during the winter and spring to fit them out in the best possible
way. This is all good. However, all too many of us think that the
summer is for sailing only and drop all maintenance work. For
instance, you should check all rope and wire splices, spinnaker halyard, spinnaker guys, main and jib sheets. All wire rigging should be
examined for broken strands and fatigue, especially where the wire
passes over sheaves. If the strands fly out when the wire is bent, the
wire probably needs replacing. If it looks rusty, it may not require
replacing at once but should be inspected frequently. The rigging
and the wire halyards should be run through a greasy rag occasionally, but not too much grease should be used for the grease will
be transferred to the sails. Wire rope can also be protected by finishing it with aluminum paint that has been thinned with turpentine
and linseed oil. The linseed oil penetrates to lubricate the rope
internally. Oil all blocks occasionally to insure that the sheets run
freely. Much of the material covered earlier in the chapter deals with
points that must be constantly checked. For care and maintenance
during the sailing season itself is just as important as that given
during the fall lay-up and spring fitting-out.

Glossary

To the person who has never sailed before or been around boats the language of the sea is very strange and unusual. But to the sailor the terms of sailing are usual and meaningful. Many nautical words and terms in this book are explained in the text. To provide a handy reference, however, this glossary lists and defines those most frequently used.

Aback. The set of a boat's sails with the wind on the leeward instead of windward side.

Abaft. Astern of, toward the stern; at the rear of, with reference to a boat or any part of it. opposite to forward of.

Abeam. At right angles to the keel.

Aboard. On board, or in a boat.

About. To change direction in sailing. When the wind fills the sails from the other side. To come about; change course.

Adrift. Loose from the moorings or dragging the anchor.

Afloat. A boat or other object buoyant enough to be resting on the surface of the water.

Afore. Opposite of abaft, forward.

Aft. At, toward, or near the stern.

Aground. Touching the bottom.

Ahead. Toward the bow of a boat, or in front of a boat.

Aid to navigation. A charted mark to assist in navigation, such as a buoy, beacon, light, radio beacon, etc. Generally, any information published for the assistance of mariners.

Alee. To the leeward side; often referring to the helm, or tiller, when it is positioned away from the direction of the wind.

All in the wind. A boat pointing too high causing all sails to shake.

Aloft. Up above; up the mast or in the rigging.

Amidships. In the center of the boat, with reference either to length or breadth.

Anchor. A device shaped so as to grip the sea bottom. From it a line is fastened to a craft to hold her in a desired position.

Anchorage. A sheltered place or area where boats can anchor or moor without interfering with habor traffic.

Anchor light. A white light visible all around the horizon, displayed from the forward part of a boat at anchor.

Anemometer. An instrument to measure the velocity of the wind.

Astern. To the rear of a boat or behind a boat.

Athwartships. Across the keel of a boat.

Auxiliary. A boat propelled by both sail and power.

Aweather. To windward, toward the weather side.

Aweigh. To raise or trip the anchor; to raise the anchor up from the bottom.

Back. To back a sail is to throw it aback (to throw it to the windward side). To back and fill is to alternately back and fill the sails.

Backstay. A wire brace from masthead to stern.

Backwind. When the wind that has passed over one sail hits the back (leeward side, away from the wind) of another sail.

Bail. To bail a boat is to throw water out of her.

Ballast. Weight inside or outside a hull to counterbalance the weight of the gear aloft in a sailboat or to make a boat sit lower in the water.

Balloon jib. A large headsail with considerable draft, generally used in light weather.

Bare poles. The condition of a boat when she has no sail set.

Barometer. An instrument used to register or measure the atmosphere's pressure.

Batten. A thin wooden, metal, or plastic strip placed in a pocket in the leach of a sail to help hold its form.

Batten down. To secure or to make watertight; said of hatches and cargo.

Beacon. A navigational aid or mark, usually placed on land, to warn boats of danger.

Beam. The greatest breadth of a boat, usually amidships.

Beam sea. Wind at right angles to the boat's keel, as on a beam reach.

Beam wind. A wind which blows athwart a boat's fore-and-aft line.

Bear. To *bear down* is to approach from windward. To *bear off* is to up-helm and run more to leeward.

Bearing. The direction of one object from the position of the observer, expressed in terms of compass points or degrees.

Beat. To sail to windward.

Beaufort scale. A table used for describing the velocity of the wind.

Becalm. To intercept the wind. A boat to windward is said to becalm another, so one sail becalms another. Also, a boat is becalmed if there is no wind.

Becket. An eye or a loop made with rope.

Before the wind. Sailing in the same direction toward which the wind is blowing (with the wind from astern).

Belay. To make fast to a cleat or pin. Also, to change an order.

Below. Under the deck.

Bend. To fasten a sail to the boom and mast. Also, to fasten one rope to another.

Berth. The dock or anchorage occupied by a boat. Also, the place where a person sleeps.

Bilge. That part of the inside hull above and around the keel where water will collect.

Binnacle. A stand with receptacle containing compass and compensating magnets.

Bitt. A vertical post extending above the deck to which mooring lines are made fast.

Blanket. To take the wind from the sails of a boat that is to leeward of yours.

Block. Pulley consisting of a frame in which is set one or more sheaves (shivs) or rollers. Lines are run over these rollers.

Board. A tack or leg to windward when beating.

Bos'n's-chair. A piece of canvas or wood on which a man working aloft is swung.

Bolt-rope. The rope surrounding a sail and to which the material is sewed.

Boom. A spar at the foot of a fore-and-aft sail. Also, a pole used to hold spinnakers outboard.

Boom cradle (Crotch). A prop that lifts the boom off the deck and secures it when not in use.

Boomkin. A short spar projecting from the stern to which the mizzen or jigger sheet is secured.

Boom-vang. A tackle secured to the boom to prevent it from lifting on a reach or run, and to flatten the sail.

Boot-top. The strip of paint at the waterline, usually of a different color than the side or bottom.

Bow. The forward part of a boat. Also, the curve of the stem.

Bowline. A knot used to form an eye or loop in the end of a line.

Bow line. A docking or mooring line led forward through a bow chock.

Bowsprit. A spar extending forward from the bow to which jibs and stays are made fast.

Brightwork. Varnished wood or polished brass.

Bring to. The act of stopping a boat by bringing her head up into the wind.

Broach. To swing around toward the wind in a dangerous manner when running free, generally due to heavy seas or poor steering.

Bulkhead. A partition or wall below decks.

Bunk. A sleeping berth.

Buoy. Any floating object anchored in one place to show position.

Buoyage. A system of buoys or marks to aid navigation.

Burdened vessel. A craft required to keep clear of a vessel holding the right of way.

Burgee. A small swallow-tailed or triangular flag identifying the owner or the yacht club to which he belongs.

By the lee. Running with the wind on the same side as the boom.

By the wind. Sailing close-hauled.

Cast off. To let go a line.

Catamaran. A twin-hulled boat.

Centerboard. A keel-like device that can be hoisted or lowered in a well or trunk to act as a keel in shoal draft boats.

Chafing gear. Canvas or other similar material secured about a line or sheet to protect it from abrasion and wear.

Chain plates. Metal plates bolted to the side of a boat to which stays are attached to support rigging.

Chart. The proper term for a nautical map.

Chock. A metal fitting which serves as a lead for lines that go over the side.

Chronometer. A highly accurate clock used by navigators.

Cleat. A wood or metal fitting for securing a line without a hitch.

Clew. The aftermost corner of the sail.

Close-hauled. Sailing as close to the wind as possible.

Close-winded. A craft capable of sailing very close to the wind.

Coaming. The raised protection around a cockpit.

Cockpit. The space at a lower level from the deck in which the tiller or wheel is located.

Coil. To lay down a line in circular turns.

Colors. The ceremony of hoisting the national flag at 8 A.M. The lowering at sunset is called *making colors.*

Come up into the wind. Steer toward the direction from which the wind is coming.

Coming about. To bring the boat from one tack to the other when sailing into the wind.

Companionway. A staircase to a cabin or below.

Compass. Magnetized needles attached to a circular compass card that tends to point to the magnetic north.

Compass card. A calibrated card which has the points of the compass.

Compass point. One-thirty-second part of a full circle or $11\frac{1}{4}$ degrees.

Compass rose. A graduated circle printed on a chart that has the points of the compass.

Compensate. Correcting a compass from local magnetic attraction so that it will point as nearly as possible to the magnetic north.

Corinthian. An amateur sailor interested only in the sport without any thought of compensation for services rendered during a cruise or race.

Course. Direction sailed as measured by the compass.

Cradle. A frame used to hold a boat when she is hauled out of the water.

Cringle. A ring sewn into the sail through which a line can be passed.

Cuddy. A small cabin or protective cover over the fore part of the cockpit.

Dead ahead. Directly ahead of a boat's course.

Dead reckoning. Determining a boat's position at sea by noting the course sailed and the distance covered.

Deviation. An error of compass caused by the proximity of magnetic materials.

Dew point. The point at which a given amount of air becomes saturated, condensation forms and fog begins.

Dinghy. A small rowing boat that sometimes is rigged with a sail. Also called *tender* or *dink*.

Dip. A position of a flag when hoisted part way of the hoist. Also, to lower a flag part way and then hoist it again, as a salute.

Displacement. The weight of water displaced by a boat.

Douse. To take in or lower a sail. Also to put out a light. Same as *dowse*.

Downhaul. A tackle or single line by which a sail is hauled down.

Down helm. To bring a boat up into the wind. Same as *up helm*.

Downwind. To leeward.

Draft. The depth of water required to float a boat.

Draw. A sail draws when filled with wind, while a boat draws enough water to float her.

Drift. The leeway of a boat.

Ease. To let out the sheet so as to relieve the pressure on the sail and perhaps spill some wind.

Ensign. A national flag flown on a boat.

Even keel. Floating level.

Eye of the wind. The exact direction from which the wind is coming.

Fairlead. An eyelet fitting which changes the direction of a sheet or halyard led through it.

Fairway. A navigable channel.

Fair wind. A favorable wind.

Fast. To secure.

Fathom. A nautical measurement for the depth of water. One fathom is equal to six feet.

Fend. To push off.

Fender. Made in various shapes of rope, canvas, and rubber to keep anything alongside a boat from scarring the sides and topsides.

Fetch. When a craft sailing to windward can make her objective without another tack.

Fid. A pointed stick or pin used in making rope splices.

Fill away. A sailboat gathering headway on a new tack or the sails filling out as the bow goes past the eye of the wind.

Fit out. Preparing a boat for launching or an extended trip.

Fix. To find a boat's position by celestial or land observations.

Flotation. Air tanks or other similar devices or materials which help to prevent a swamped boat from sinking.

Flow. Spilling the wind by easing the sheets.

Foot. The lower edge of a sail.

Fore. In or toward the bow of a boat.

Fore-and-aft. In the direction of the keel, from front to back. Also, a sailboat's sailing rig.

Fore mast. Forward mast of a sailing vessel having two or more masts.

Fore peak. The part of a boat below decks at the stem.

Fore reach. The movement or shooting ahead a sailboat makes when going about or luffing into the eye of the wind.

Foul. To become entangled or clogged. Not clean.

Free. Sailing with the wind anywhere from abeam to due aft. Also means to cast off, untangle, permit to run easily.

Freeboard. The distance from the top of the hull to the water.

Full and by. Sailing as close to the wind as possible with all sails full.

Furl. To roll up a sail snugly on a boom and to secure it.

Gaff. Spar hoisted on the aft side of the mast to support the head of a sail, hence *gaff-rigged*.

Galley. A nautical kitchen.

Gasket. A piece of rope or canvas used to secure a furled sail.

Gear. A general term embracing all rigging or boat equipment.

Genoa. A large, overlapping jib.

Ghosting. A boat making headway when there is no apparent wind.

Go about. To change tack to windward.

Gooseneck. A metal device that secures the boom to the mast.

Goose wing. A sailboat sailing wing-and-wing.

Gripe. To tend to come into the wind, to carry a hard-weather helm.

Grommet. A metal ring sewed into a sail. Also, a ring made of rope.

Grounding. Running ashore.

Ground tackle. Anchor, cable, etc., used to secure a boat to her moorings.

Gudgeon. An eye fitting into which the rudder's pintles are inserted.

Gunkholing. Shallow water sailing.

Gunwale. The rail of the boat at deck level.

Guy. A rope or wire used to steady or support.

Hail. To speak or call to someone aboard your craft or another vessel.

Halyard. A line used to hoist sails. Same as *halliard* or *haliard*.

Hand. A member of the crew.

Hard-a-lee. A command to come about.

Hard-a-weather. To put the tiller up as in changing course from close-hauled to a reach or broad reach without changing tack.

Hard down. To put the tiller as far to leeward as possible.

Hard over. The order to put the tiller as far over as possible to the side designated.

Hatch. An opening in a deck with a cover.

Haul your wind. To sail closer to the wind.

Haul to windward. When sailing free, to bring a sailboat up into the wind.

Hawser. A heavy line used for towing a boat or for mooring.

Head. The upper corner of a sail. Also, a boat's toilet.

Header. A sudden wind shift toward the bow.

Headboard. The fitting at the head of a sail with holes to receive the shackle of the halyard.

Headsails. All sails forward of the mast.

Head sheets. The sheets of the headsails.

Headstay. Wire from the bow supporting the mast.

Head-to-wind. With the bow headed into the wind and sails shaking.

Head up. To luff.

Headway. Moving ahead.

Heel. The tilt, tip, listing, or laying-over of a boat, usually due to the wind.

Helm. The tiller or wheel by which the rudder is controlled.

Helm down. When the tiller is pushed away from the wind. Same as *helm alee*.

Helmsman. The person who steers.

Hike. To climb or to lean out to windward to counteract excessive heeling.

Hoist. The vertical edge of a sail. *To hoist* is to haul aloft.

Hull. The main body of a boat as distinct from spars, sails, and gear.

Inboard. Inside a hull.

In irons. A boat is in irons when she is in the wind's eye and, having lost all headway, will not go off on either tack.

Inshore. Toward the shore.

In stays. When a boat is in the wind's eye while going from one tack to another.

In the wind. Pointing too high into the wind resulting in some wind being spilled from the sails.

Irish pennant. An untidy loose end of a rope.

Jib. A triangular sail set forward of the mast.

Jib boom. A boom or spar extension beyond the bowsprit used for setting of additional headsails.

Jibe. When running, to bring the wind on the other quarter so that the boom swings over. Same as *gybe.*

Jib-heated. A sailing rig that has all sails triangular. Same as *Marconi* and *Bermudian.*

Jib sheet. The line that leads from the lower aft end of the jib to the cockpit. It controls the angle at which the sail is set.

Jibstay. Forward stay on which the jib is hoisted.

Jigger. Another name for the mizzen on a ketch or yawl.

Jumper stay. A truss-like stay on the upper forward side of the mast. Same as jumper strut.

Jury. A term used for making a temporary or makeshift rig. For example, a jury rig is any kind of a temporary rig that can be used to take a dismasted sailboat back to port.

Kedge. A small anchor.

Kedging. To move a boat by hauling on a kedge anchor.

Keel. The backbone of a boat running fore-and-aft.

Keel boat. A craft with a fixed keel that extends below the hull.

Keep her full. An order to keep the sails filled.

Keep her so. An order to steady on the course.

Knot. Nautical measure of distance; 6,080 feet = 1 nautical mile. Speed: one nautical mile per hour.

Lacing. A line used to secure a sail to its spar.

Lanyard. A short line used for making anything fast.

Lash. To secure by binding with a thin line.

Launch. To set afloat.

Lazarette. A stowage compartment in the stern.

Leach. The after edge of a sail. Same as *leech*.

Leach line. A line which is used for hauling up the leach of a sail.

Leading edge. Forward part of a sail.

Lee. The side away from the wind on a boat is called the lee side.

Lee helm. Condition of a sailboat out of balance which will not point into the wind if rudder and sheets are dropped when sailing close-hauled.

Leeward. Direction away from the wind.

Leeway. The amount a boat is carried to leeward by the force of the wind.

Leg. A tack. The course from one mark to another.

Light sails. Spinnakers and other sails of light materials used to increase boat's speed off the wind.

Line. Nautical term for rope used for riggings, anchoring, tying up, etc.

Locker. A chest or cabinet for storing gear.

Log. Device by which speed of a boat is estimated.

Log book. A book which contains the daily record of a vessel's courses, distances, winds, weather, boat activities, and everything else of importance.

Loose-footed. A fore-and-aft sail that is not secured along the foot of a boom.

Lubber line. A mark on the compass bowl that is used to indicate the fore-and-aft line of a boat.

Luff. The leading edge of a sail. Also, to turn the boat's head into the wind causing the luff of the sail to flutter.

Luff her. An order to bring a sailboat into the wind by putting the tiller down.

Lying-to. Keeping a boat stationary with her head in the wind, usually by means of a sea anchor.

Mainsail. The large sail set abaft the mast.

Mainsheet. The line that controls the angle of the mainsail in its relation to the wind.

Make. To set a sail is to make a sail.

Make fast. To belay or secure a line.

Mast. The vertical pole or spar supporting the booms, sails, etc.

Masthead. The top of the mast.

Mast step. A frame or slot into which the lower end of a mast is shipped.

Mend. To refurl an improperly furled sail; to rebend a sail to a boom.

Midships. The broadest part of the boat.

Miter. A type of sail cut. Same as *mitre*.

Mizzenmast. The shorter mast aft on a yawl or ketch.

Mizzensail. A sail set from the mizzenmast.

Moor. To secure a boat to an object such as a dock, buoy, post, etc.

Mooring. A place where a boat is permanently anchored. Usually consists of a chain, buoy, pennant, and an anchor.

Motor sailer. A vessel combining the features of both a sailboat and motorboat.

Off the wind. Sailing downwind or before the wind.

On a wind. To sail close-hauled.

One-design class. A number of sailboats that are built exactly alike.

Outboard. Beyond a boat's side or hull.

Outhaul. A line used to haul the clew of a sail out to the end of the boom.

Out point. To sail closer to the wind than another sailboat.

Overall. The extreme fore-and-aft measurement of a boat.

Overhaul. To gain on another boat.

Overlap. A sailboat is overlapped when an overtaking sailboat is clearly within two overall lengths of the longer boat.

Overstand. To sail beyond an object, such as a buoy.

Owner's flag. The private signal of a boat owner; usually of his own design.

Painter. Bow line by which a small boat is towed or made fast to a mooring.

Parachute. A spinnaker cut so as to resemble a parachute.

Part. To break. Also, the hauling, standing, or running part of a line.

Pay-off. To turn the bow away from the wind.

Pay-out. To slacken a sheet or line.

Peak. Highest point of a sail.

Pelorus. A compass card fitted with sighting vanes and used for taking bearings.

Pennant. A length of line. Also, a small, narrow flag.

Pinch. To sail a boat so close to the wind that her sails shake or her progress slows.

Pintle. Metal braces or hooks upon which the rudder of a boat swings.

Point. To sail as close as possible to the wind. Also, one-thirty-second of a circle.

Port. The left side of a boat, looking toward the bow.

Port tack. A sailboat is on the port tack when the wind is coming over the port side.

Privileged vessel. One which has the right-of-way.

Purchase. A system of ropes and blocks to increase the hauling power.

Quarter. The after part of a boat's side; that part of a craft which lies within 45 degrees from the stern, known as the port quarter or starboard quarter.

Rail. The outer edge of the deck.

Rake. The inclination of a mast from the vertical.

Reach. All sailing points between running and close-hauled. *Close reach,* sailing nearly close-hauled with sheets just eased. *Beam reach,* sailing with the wind abeam. *Broad reach,* sailing with the wind abaft the beam and with sails well out on the quarter.

Reef. To reduce sail area by partly lowering sail and securing the surplus material to the boom.

Reef points. Short lengths of rope which are on each side of the reefband of some sails and are secured to the foot of the sail when it is reefed.

Reeve. To pass lines through blocks or fairleads.

Ride. To lie at anchor.

Ride out. To weather out a storm safely, whether at anchor or under way.

Rig. Arrangement of a boat's sails, masts, and rigging.

Rigging. A general term applying to all lines, shrouds, and stays necessary to spars and sails.

Roach. Outward curve of the leech of a sail.

Rode. An anchor line.

Roller reefing. A method of reducing the area of a sail by winding it up on a revolving boom or stay.

Rudder. A flat member attached to the stern of a boat which controls the course of the boat.

Rules of the road. The international regulations for preventing collisions at sea.

Running. Sailing before the wind.

Running by the lee. Sailing before the wind with the wind coming over the same quarter as the boom.

Running lights. Lights carried by a vessel under way; they are required by law.

Running rigging. The lines, such as halyards and sheets, that are used in the setting and trimming of sails.

Scope. The length of mooring or anchor line out.

Scud. To run before the wind in a storm.

Sea. Refers in this book to all sailing waters.

Sea anchor. A drag device, usually canvas, used to keep a boat headed into the wind during very heavy weather.

Secure. To make fast.

Set. The shape of a sail.

Sextant. An instrument used in navigation by determining altitude of sun and stars.

Shackle. A U-shaped piece of metal with a pin across the open end

Shake. Sails shake when wind is spilled such as when pointing too high and luffing.

Shake out. Let out a reef. Also, hoist the sails.

Sheave. The wheel in a block.

Sheet. A line used to trim a sail.

Shroud. Standing rigging, usually of wire, running from the mast to the sides of a boat to support the mast.

Spar. Term for masts, booms, spinnaker poles, etc.

Spinnaker. A large, light sail used when a boat is sailing before the wind or on a reach.

Splice. To join rope by tucking the strands together, such as short, long, eye and back splice, etc.

Spreader. A horizontal strut to which shrouds or stays are attached, to support the mast and spread rigging.

Standing rigging. The shrouds and stays as well as other rigging which are not moved in working a boat.

Starboard. The right side of a boat, looking toward the bow.

Starboard tack. Sailing with wind coming over the starboard side.

Stay. A piece of rigging (usually of wire) used to support a spar. Also, a change of tack.

Staysail. A fore-and-aft triangular sail set upon a stay.

Step. To step a mast is to set it in position.

Stern. The after part of a boat.

Stop. A narrow band of canvas or piece of rope used in furling a sail.

Storm jib. A small triangular sail at the bow of the boat, used in very heavy weather.

Stow. To put away.

Tack. The lower forward corner of a sail. Also, to proceed to windward by sailing on alternate courses so that the wind is first on one side of the boat and then on the other.

Tackle. A system of blocks and ropes arranged for hauling.

Taut. Stretched or drawn tight. Also, neat and tidy.

Tell-tale. A short piece of ribbon or string tied to a shroud to indicate the direction of the wind.

Tiller. A bar connected with the rudder head. By this bar the rudder is moved as desired.

Topping lift. A line that takes the weight of the boom while the sail is being set.

Topside. Usually the side of the boat lying between waterline and rail. In a broad sense, topsides is any above-water part of the hull.

Transom. The stern facing of the hull.

Traveler. A metal rod for sheets to slide athwartships rather than having a sheet block coming to a cleat; if rope is substituted for a metal rod it becomes a *bridle*.

Trim. To trim sails—to put them in correct relation to the wind by means of sheets. Also, the way a boat floats on the water—on an even keel, heeled over, or down by the bow or stern.

True course. A course steered by a boat's compass that has been corrected for deviation and variation.

Turnbuckle. A device used to maintain correct tension on standing rigging.

Unbend. To cast adrift or untie.

Under way. A vessel when not aground, made fast to the shore, or at anchor.

Unfurl. To unfold a sail.

Vang. A line to steady the boom when off the wind.

Variation. The difference in degrees between true and magnetic north.

Veer. A change of direction, as in the wind.

Wake. The foamy path of disturbed water left behind a moving boat.

Warp. To move a boat into a desired position by manipulating lines extended to shore, dock, etc.

Watch. Working shifts aboard a vessel.

Waterline. A line which is painted on a boat's side indicating the proper trim.

Way. Movement through the water.

Wear. To turn away from the wind, jibe.

Weather. Windward side of a sailboat.

Weather helm. A sailboat wanting to come up into the wind.

Wedge. A device used to steady a mast.

Weigh. To raise an anchor.

Wheel. Steering device used on larger sailboats in place of the tiller.

Whip. To whip a line is to bind the strands of its end with yard or cord.

Whisker-pole. A light pole or stick extending from the mast and used to hold the jib out when off the wind.

Winch. A mechanical device to give increased hauling power on a line.

Windlass. A winch for hauling in cable, etc.

Wind's eye. Exact direction from which the wind is blowing.

Windward. Toward the wind.

Wing-and-wing. Sailing before the wind with the jib on one side and the mainsail on the other.

Working sails. Sails used in ordinary weather.

Yacht. General term for a boat used solely for the personal pleasure of the owner.

Yaw. To swing off course (usually due to heavy seas) without regard for the position of the rudder.

Index

Abandoning ship, 304–305
Absentee flag, 254, 255
Accidental jibe, 60
Aerodynamics of sailing, 33–37, 39
Aground, freeing from, 129, 175, 295–297, 307
Aids to navigation, 24, 26, 131, 135, 139, 140, 142, 145–151, 159, 307
Air conditioning, 183
Airfoil, 36, 42, 54
Airman's Guide, 157
Alberg, Carl A., 7, 227
Alcohol, stove, 164, 171–172, 173
Alterations, 281–283
America, 12
America's Cup, 8, 213
Anchor
    knot, 95
    light, 81, 159, 193, 308
    lines, 15, 16–18, 22, 101, 127
    scope, 16–17, 78, 79–80, 81, 295–296, 317
    trip line, 82
    weighting of, 81–82
Anchorage, 29, 70, 73, 78–79, 80–81, 135, 175, 250, 256, 308
    leaving an, 70, 73
Anchoring technique, 78–82, 127
Anchors, 15–18, 19, 22, 74, 85, 87, 95, 129, 176, 185, 199, 250, 251, 289, 295, 308
    CQR plow, 16
    Danforth, 15, 16
    mushroom, 15, 16, 18–19
    patent, 15, 16
    sea, 127–128, 294, 318
    stockless, 15, 16
    wishbone, 16
    yachtsman's, 15, 16
Anemometer, 47, 118, 288, 308

Application of numbers, 31–32
Aquaplanes, 179
Association, class, 4–5, 227–230
Auxiliary power, 13–14, 73, 74, 77, 78, 81, 84–85, 88, 89, 126, 128, 129, 137, 166, 175, 187, 193, 296, 297, 299–300, 308

Backstay, 44, 308
Backwinding, 221
Bad weather sailing, 124–131
Barometer, 26, 103, 114–118, 308
Battens, 52–53, 90, 291, 292, 308
Batteries, 193, 286, 300
Beacons
    day, 148, 154, 215, 308
    radio, 149, 150, 155–157
Beam reaching, 67–68
Bearings, 62–63, 81, 139, 140, 141, 151–158
    bow-and-beam, 152–153
    cross, 151–152
    danger, 153–154
    electronic, 155–158
    seven-tenths rule of, 153, 154
Beating, 48, 308
Beaufort scale, 106, 108, 118, 121–123, 308
Bedding, 179
Bell, ship's, 15, 130, 261–262
Bending sail, 50, 309
Bermudian sail, 39
Bilge pump, 20
Binoculars, 26, 281
Blanketing, 221, 225
Blankets, 124, 179, 180, 269
Boarding ladder, 201
Boat
    aground, 129, 175, 295–297, 307
    hauling out, 180, 267–268
    heater, 182, 183

Boat (*cont.*)
  leaving, 89–92
  maintenance, 8, 9, 265–305
  midseason check, 305
  numbers, 31–32
  spring fitting out, 273–289, 305
  trailers, 266
  winter lay-up, 265–273, 305
Boating regulations, 14–15, 19–21, 31–32, 75–78, 129–130, 197, 210–211
Boatkeeping, 175, 186, 187, 192–193
Boatkeeping gear, 26, 175
Boatyard, 27, 29, 265–267, 271, 273, 280, 284, 288
Bonner Bill, 31–32
Boom, 39, 46, 47, 50, 51, 54, 57, 61, 64, 66, 68, 70, 83, 84, 89, 119, 120, 124, 163, 286, 309
  crotch, 70, 89, 309
  tent, 163, 164
  vang, 223, 224, 291, 309
Bowline, 17, 18, 93, 94, 309
Bow pulpit, 20
Broaching to, 60
Broad reaching, 62, 64, 126, 223
Brown University, 37
Bunks, 163, 179, 195, 198, 280, 310
Buoyage system, 145–148
Buoys
  mooring, 73, 82, 83, 84
  navigational, 26, 131, 134, 139, 142, 145–148, 150, 151, 161, 200, 215–216, 250
Burgee, 47, 55, 62, 253–254, 256, 257, 260, 310
Burgoo, 233, 247

Cabin, 6, 11, 92, 163, 165, 182, 193, 281
Capsizing, 297–298, 304
Care of
  electrical system, 193–194, 286
  engine, 270–271, 273, 283–286, 300–304
  fiberglass, 267, 268–269, 271, 272–279
  hull, 268–269
  line, 100–101, 270
  mast, 286–287
  Plexiglas, 280–281
  plumbing, 270, 280
  rigging, 267–268, 270, 286–289
  sailboat, 8, 9, 265–305
  sails, 89–90, 269, 289–293
  toilet, 196–197, 269
Catboat, 3, 4
Celestial navigation, 24, 135, 157, 160
Centerboard, 35, 36, 60, 61, 62, 64, 70, 84, 91, 267, 298, 310
Chafing gear, 17–18, 41, 100, 128, 310

Charts, navigational, 20, 23–24, 25, 78, 135–136, 137, 138, 143, 151, 153, 155, 156, 160, 161, 166, 200, 269, 310
Chlorinating device, 197–198
Chronometer, 24, 262, 310
Civil Aeronautics Administration, 103
Class
  association, 4–5, 227–230
  boat, 4–6, 183, 233–234
  boat racing, 212
Close
  hauled, 48, 54–59, 62, 77, 80, 126, 144, 310
  reaching, 62, 126, 223
Clothing
  cruising, 168–170, 181–183, 269
  yachting, 262–264
Clouds, 105, 109–113, 200
  altocumulus, 105, 110, 111, 113
  altostratus, 110–112, 113
  cirrocumulus, 109, 110, 112, 113
  cirrostratus, 109, 110, 113
  cirrus, 109, 110, 113
  cumulonimbus, 113
  cumulus, 111, 112, 113
  fractonimbus, 112
  fractostratus, 112
  nimbostratus, 110, 112, 113
  stratocumulus, 110, 111, 112, 113
  stratus, 110, 111, 112, 113
Clove hitch, 17, 94, 95
Coastal Warning Facilities Charts, 103
Coast Guard, *see* U. S. Coast Guard
Coastwise navigation, 134, 151–158
Cockpit, 6, 11, 12, 46, 64, 92, 162, 163, 181, 199, 204, 242, 310
  cover, 92
  self-bailing, 12, 242
  tent, 163, 164
Coiling line, 91, 98–100
Collision mat, 295
Coming about, 57–58
Compass, 20, 62, 101, 135, 136–139, 142, 156, 158, 159, 160–161, 311
  course, 139, 143, 144, 244
  error, 137–138, 141
  rose, 137, 138, 139, 141, 155, 311
  steering by, 139
Consolan, 157–158
Construction, hull, 8–12
Converters, 193–194
Cooke, Carleton S., 248
Corinthians, 247–248, 311
Course, compass, 139, 143, 144, 244
  correcting, 143–145
  plotting, 141–145, 187, 188, 225–226
  steering, 139, 149

Crew, 167–168, 179, 181, 187, 191, 243–246, 298
Crew's meal flag, 255
Cruise, planning, 165–168, 188, 198
Cruiser-racer, 4, 5, 6–7, 8, 10, 13, 14, 23, 41, 42, 45, 67, 78, 89, 120, 127, 163–165, 232, 234, 265, 290–291, 297
Cruising, 7, 27, 67, 70, 90, 161, 162–185, 186–193, 198–206
  activities, 201–206
  auxiliary, *see* Cruiser-racer
  boat, 7, 67, 143, 162, 163, 176, 188, 197, 290, 292
  clothing, 168–170, 181–183, 269
  Club of America, 20, 231, 234–239, 254
  companions, 167
  crew, 167–168, 179, 187
  day, 162, 183
  fall, 180–183
  gear, 168–179
  group, 183–185
  records, 187–188
  routine, 186–187, 200
  with children, 179, 187, 198–201
Cuddy cabin, 6, 162–163, 311
Current, 50, 71, 79, 119, 132, 133, 136, 140, 141, 144–145, 161, 176, 220, 223, 224–225
Curtains, 177–179, 269
Cushions, 167, 179, 195, 269, 294
Cutter, 3, 4, 212

Danger bearing, 153–154
Day beacons, 148, 154, 215, 308
  cruising, 162, 183
  sailer, 4, 5, 6, 28, 75, 162–163, 188, 265, 266
Dead reckoning, 158, 311
Deck, 11, 39, 198, 291
Delano, Frederick M., 248
Depreciation of powerboat, 6
  sailboat, 5–6
Depth finder, 25, 131, 157, 193, 267, 269
Deviation, compass, 135, 137–138, 139, 141, 156, 311
Dinghy, 20, 22, 32, 44, 70, 75, 127, 175–177, 178, 188, 200, 201, 270, 311
  loading, 177
  sailing, 75, 200
  storage, 176, 178
  towing, 176–177, 178
Direction finder, 25, 155–157, 158, 161, 269, 305
Distance racing, *see* Ocean racing
Distress signal gear, 22, 209
Distress signals, 209–211, 250, 304–305
Dock, sailing from, 73–74

Docking gear, 74
  lines, 74, 87–89
  procedure, 86–89
Downhauls, 46, 311
Dutton, Benjamin, 135

Eating afloat, 188–192
Electra Day Sailer, 227
Electrical system, 193–194, 286, 287, 288, 300, 301
  care of, 193–194, 286
Electrolysis, 279
Electronic bearings, 155–158
  equipment, 25–26, 131, 134, 155–158, 269, 279–280
  navigation, 25–26, 134, 155–158
Emergency procedures, 206–211, 293–305
Engine, 6, 13–14, 73, 74, 78, 81, 85, 89, 92, 126, 193, 265, 270–271, 273, 283–286, 300–304
  care of, 270–271, 273, 283–286, 300–304
  selection of, 14
  spring tune-up, 283–286
  trouble shooting, 300–304
  winterizing, 265, 270–271
Ensign Class Association, 227–230
Ensign Class boat, 4, 6
Ensign, national, 252, 253, 255, 256, 257, 311
  yachting, 252, 255, 256, 311
Estimating speed, 143, 144
Etiquette, flag, 252–261
  yachting, 249–252
Eye splice, 97, 98

Fall cruising, 180–183
Federal Boating Act, 31–32
Federal Communications Commission, 25
Fenders, 73, 74, 85, 86, 87, 92, 294, 312
Fiberglass, care of, 267, 268–269, 271, 272–279
  construction, 6, 7, 8–12
  painting, 273–275
  repair of, 8, 10, 275–279, 294–295
Figure eight knot, 93, 94, 95
Fire afloat, 298–300, 304
Fire extinguisher, 15, 22, 298, 299
First aid, 206
  kit, 20, 206
Fisherman's bend, 17, 18, 95
Fishing, 25, 175, 179, 200, 202
Flag
  absentee, 254, 255
  crew's meal, 255
  etiquette, 252–261
  flag officer's, 254, 256
  fleet officer's, 254

Flag (*cont.*)
  guest, 254
  halyard, 45
  International code, 20, 211, 256, 257–261
  owner's meal, 255
  owner's private, 252–253, 256, 257, 316
  routine, 252–261
  skin diving, 202, 250, 255
  U.S. Power Squadron, 255, 256
Flaking, 89, 90
Flame arrestors, 15
Flares, 22, 211
Flotation, 12, 242, 270, 297, 312
Fog, 106, 113, 129–131, 141, 151, 155, 188
Foghorn, 20, 129, 130, 134, 210
Fog signals, 129–130, 131, 149, 151, 161
Food menu, 191–192
  supplies, 124–125, 187, 189–192
Foul-weather gear, 125, 169–170
Fresh-water supply, 174
Fueling procedure, 299–300

Gaff-headed sail, 39
Gale warning, 104
Galley, 163, 164, 199, 280, 312
  gear, 26, 171–175, 187
Generator, 194
Genoa jib, 13, 38, 39–41, 42, 43, 52, 58, 68,
  290, 312
  sheet, 52, 58
Gold Cup course, 213
Government Printing Office, 132
Great Lakes, 20–21, 150, 155, 159
  rules, 210–211
Ground tackle, 15–19, 270, 289, 313
Group cruising, 183–185
  racing, 185, 233
Guest flag, 254
Guys, 41, 46, 47, 64–65, 68, 313

Half-hitches, *see* Two half-hitches
Halyards, 45, 47, 53, 64, 66, 67, 68, 91, 120,
  204, 290, 294, 296, 298, 305, 313
Handicap racing, 212–213, 233
  system, 4, 7, 212, 233–239
Hauling out boat, 180, 267–268
Hawk Class, 266
Head, 12, 163–164, 194–198, 280, 314
Headsails, 3, 38–41, 313
Headstay, 44, 313
Heater, 182, 183
Heeling, 36, 55–56, 204, 224, 313
  error, 139
Helmsman, 74–75, 244, 313
Herreshoff, Captain Nat, 8
Herreshoff "S" Class, 69
Hiking, 36, 204, 314

Hill, John C., 135
History of sailing, 1–2
Hoisting sails, 45, 51, 53–54, 64–68, 71, 73,
  90
Homing, 156–157
Horn, 15, 161
Hull, 8–12, 35, 36–37, 267, 268–269, 294–
  295, 313
  care of, 268–269
  construction, 8–12
  repair of, 294–295
Hurricane warning, 104–105

Icebox, 163, 164, 172–174, 189, 190, 269
Identification numbers, 31–32
Inflatable raft, 20, 242
In irons, 58, 87, 314
Inland
  rules, 21, 129, 130, 210–211
  waterways, 24
Insect control, 194
Insurance, marine, 30–31
International
  Code signal flags, 20, 211, 256, 257–261
  rules, 20, 21, 129, 130, 210–211
  Yacht Racing Union, 216
Intracoastal Waterway, 146, 150
Inverters, 193–194
Invicta Class, 231–233

Jib, 1, 3, 13, 37, 40, 41, 43, 51, 52, 53–54,
  55, 56, 59, 60, 61, 66, 68, 71, 72, 82, 84,
  90, 120, 124, 126, 127, 290, 314
  halyard, 45, 82
  -headed sails, 38
  -sheet, 39, 46, 52, 54, 56, 57, 59, 61, 70,
    72, 73, 75, 125, 305, 314
  -stay, 39, 41, 44, 87, 314
  storm, 23
Jibe, 60–61, 208, 217, 314
  accidental, 60
  controlled, 60–61
Jumper stays, 45, 314
Jumper strut, 45

Keel, 8, 20, 24, 35, 36, 55, 75, 79, 138, 152,
  267, 297, 298, 314
Ketch, 3, 4, 212
Knickerbocker Yacht Club, 242
Knots, 92–95

Lake Huron Lightship, 149
Laundromat, 168, 170
Laying to, 82, 127, 315
Lay-up time, winter, 265–273, 305
Lead line, soundings, 24–25, 131, 158

Leaving an anchorage, 70, 73
  boat, 89–92
  dock, 73–74
  mooring, 70–73, 86
Lee helm, 35, 74, 315
Leeway, allowance for, 143–144
Life belt, 125
  jackets, 22, 23, 32, 125, 163, 199
  lines, 20
  preserver, 15, 22, 127, 199, 269, 298
  raft, 20, 242
  rings, 22, 32
Lighted buoys, 147–148, 160
Lighthouses, 131, 134, 149, 150, 154, 200, 215
Lighting fixtures, 193, 194
Light Lists, 150, 151, 155
Lightships, 149, 150, 151, 215
Lights, 19–20, 21, 101, 131, 149, 150, 159–160, 193, 261, 287, 288
  anchor, 81, 159, 193, 308
  Inland rule, 19, 21, 159–160
  International rule, 19–20, 21, 159–160
  navigation, 19–20, 21, 159–160, 193
  range, 149
  running, 101, 131, 317
Line, anchor, 15, 16–18, 22, 101, 127
  anchor trip, 82
  care of, 100–101, 270
  coiling, 91, 98–100
  dock, 74, 87–89
  life, 20
  lubber's, 137, 140, 315
  mooring, 19, 70, 71, 73, 92, 101, 270
  splicing, 95–97, 98, 318
  using, 100–101
  whipping, 98, 320
Lipton, Sir Thomas, 1
Lloyd's Register of American Yachts, 247, 253
Logbook, 2, 25, 187–188, 315
Long splice, 96–97
Loose-footed sail, 39
Loran, 157
Luffing, 56, 125–126, 223, 224, 315
Lure of sailing, *see* Sailing, lure of

Mail port, 166–167
Main halyard, 45, 293–294
  sail, 37, 39, 42, 46, 50, 51, 53, 54, 55, 59, 66, 67, 70, 71, 72, 73, 74, 119, 126, 127, 290, 298, 315
  sheet, 45–46, 51, 54, 61, 75, 83, 124, 125, 305, 315
Maintenance, sailboat, 8, 9, 265–305
Making fast, 91, 95, 101
Man overboard, 208–209

Marconi sail, 39
Marina, 27, 29, 30, 166
Marine insurance, 30–31
Marlinspike seamanship, 92–101
Mast, 3–4, 11–12, 20, 37, 44, 47, 64, 65, 66, 120, 163, 204, 253, 254, 255, 267, 286, 290, 294, 298, 315
  care of, 286–287
  repair of, 294
  stepping a, 11–12
Mattresses, 179, 195, 269, 295, 299
Measurement rule, 233–239
Megaphone, 161
Melville, Herman, 1
Menu, food, 191–192
Midget Ocean Racing Club, 7, 242–243
Midseason care, 305
Mixter, George W., 135
Mizzenmast, 3, 72, 127, 254, 255, 316
Moby Dick, 1
Mooring, 18–19, 27, 29–30, 70–73, 82–85, 86, 90, 92, 101, 270, 289, 316
  buoys, 73, 82, 83, 84
  leaving, 70–73, 86
  line, 19, 70, 71, 73, 92, 101, 270
  permanent, 18–19
  picking up, 82–85
  offshore, 27, 29–30

National ensign, 252, 253, 255, 256, 257, 311
Navigating department, 187
Navigation aids, 24, 26, 131, 135, 139, 140, 142, 145–151, 159, 307
  books on, 135, 179
  celestial, 24, 135, 157, 160
  charts, 20, 23–24, 25, 78, 135–136, 137, 138, 143, 151, 153, 155, 156, 160, 161, 166, 200, 269, 310
  coastwise, 134, 151–158
  electronic, 25–26, 134, 155–158
  equipment, 20, 24–26, 141, 168, 269
  lights, 19–20, 21, 159–160, 193
  night, 158–161
  offshore, 134–135
Navigation and Piloting, 135
Navigator, 243, 244, 262
Newport-Annapolis Race, 70
Newport-Bermuda Race, 7, 70, 157, 231, 233, 242, 247
Newton, Sir Isaac, 33 34
New York Yacht Club, 235, 252, 255–256
Night navigation, 158–161
North American Yacht Racing Union, 216, 234, 235, 241
Notices to Mariners, 135
Numbers, identification, 31–32

Ocean racing, 7, 20, 69–70, 90, 135, 157, 231–248
  crew, 243, 244–246, 247–248
  skipper, 119, 243, 244–247
  techniques, 243–247
Offshore mooring, 27, 29–30
Offshore racing, 233, 243, 245
Off Sounding Club, 234
Olympic Games, 213–214, 230
One-design boats, 2, 4–6, 8, 38, 213, 233, 316
Outboard motor, 5, 14, 175
Overhand knot, 94
Overnight race, 233, 243
Owner's meal flag, 255
Owner's private flag, 252–253, 256, 257, 316

Painting fiberglass, 273–275
Pelorus, 139–140, 155, 316
Permanent moorings, 18–19
Pets on board, 167
Photography, 179, 201, 202–206
Piloting, *see* Coastwise navigation
Pilot Rules, 14
Pinching, 54–55
Plexiglas, care of, 280–281
Plumbing system, 269–270, 280
Pointing, 36, 54
Points of sailing, 47–50
Potter, Thomas A., 7
Pram, 164
Primer of Navigation, 135
Private signal flag, 252, 253, 256, 257, 316

Race committee, 213, 216, 217, 234, 255
Racer day-sailer, 4, 5, 6, 12, 14
Racing, 2, 4, 6, 7, 27, 67, 90, 179, 204, 212–227, 231–248
  boats, 42, 45, 47
  classes, 4, 5, 42, 212, 213–227
  courses, 213–215
  handicap, 212–213, 233
  instructions, 215–216
  rules, 4, 27, 216–217, 255
  techniques, 218–227, 243–247
Radar, 157, 158, 210
  reflector, 20, 131, 158, 210
Radio directional finder, 25, 155–157, 158, 161, 269, 305
  beacons, 149, 150, 155–157
  receiver, 26, 102, 103, 157
  telephone, 25, 193, 209–211, 269
  weather reports, 102–103
Radio Navigational Aids—Consolan, 157
Raft, inflatable, 20, 242
Rafting, 85–86

Range lights, 149
Ranges, 134, 149, 154–155, 156
Ratsey, Ernest, 51
Reaching, 48, 56, 61–64, 67–68, 217, 223–225, 317
Ready about, 57
Rectifiers, 193
Reefing, 119–124, 126, 317
  roller, 119, 120, 317
Reef knot, 93–94, 120
Reef points, 119, 120, 317
Refrigerator, *see* Icebox
Rendezvous race, 233, 240–242
Repair of fiberglass, 8, 10, 275–279, 294–295
  hull, 294–295
  mast, 294
  rigging, 293–294
Rhodes 41 Class, 239
Rigging, 12, 16, 20, 41, 44–47, 54, 181, 192, 267, 270, 286–289, 293–294, 305, 317
  fittings, 46–47, 288
  repairs, 293–294
  running, 44, 45–46, 47, 70, 268, 270, 317
  standing, 44–45, 267, 268, 270, 318
  tuning, 12, 286–289
Right-of-way rules, *see* Rules of the Road
Routine, cruising, 186–187, 200
  flag, 252–261
  yachting, 252–262
Rudder, 35, 36, 57, 71, 83, 91, 92, 280, 294, 296, 317
Rules of the Road, 75–78, 129, 160, 200, 217, 249–250
Running, 48, 56, 59–61, 77, 80, 126–127, 129, 217, 223, 225, 226, 317
  lights, 101, 131, 317

Safety
  belt, 22
  equipment, 14–26, 168
Sail bag, 68, 89, 90, 292
Sailboat depreciation, 6
Sailcloth, 12–13
Sailing club, 183
  before the wind, *see* Running
  dinghy, 75, 200
  history of, 1–2
  instructions, *see* Racing, instructions
  lure of, 1–3
  to windward, *see* Close, hauled
  wing-to-wing, 59
Sailmaker, 12, 13, 41, 51, 89, 272, 290
Sails
  care of, 89–90, 289–293
  cotton, 12–13, 41, 42, 90, 289–290, 292
  cover, 70, 90, 292–293

Sails (*cont.*)
  cut of, 42–44
  dacron, 13, 42, 90, 289–290, 291, 292
  gaff-headed, 39
  Genoa jib, 13, 38, 39–41, 42, 43, 52, 58
  headsails, 3, 38–41, 313
  history of, 1, 12–13
  hoisting, 45, 51, 53–54, 64–68, 71
  jib-headed, 38
  jib, storm, 23
  locker, 68, 90
  loose-footed sail, 39
  nylon, 13, 42, 90, 291, 292
  racing, 13
  weight of, 41–42
  working, 13, 38, 42, 320
  See also Setting sails, spinnaker
San Diego to Acapulco Race, 231
San Pedro to Diamond Head Race, 231
Schooner, 3–4, 212
Scuba diving, 200, 201–202, 255
Scuppers, 11, 23, 279
Sea anchor, 127–128, 294, 318
  bags, 72, 170
Seacocks, 23, 196, 269
Seasickness, 206–208, 245–246
Self-bailing cockpit, 12, 242
Setting sails, 45
  spinnaker, 64–68
Sheepshank, 93, 94
Sheet bend, 93, 94
Sheets, 45–46, 47, 54, 56, 58, 61, 62, 65, 66, 71, 82, 298
Ship-to-shore radio, *see* Radio, telephone
Ship's
  bell, 15, 130, 261–262
  mail, 166–167, 187
  office, 179
Short splice, 95–96
Shrouds, 41, 44, 71, 288, 290, 291, 293–294, 298, 318
Side splice, 97
Signal halyard, 45, 305
  horn, 77
  whistle, 77
Sink, galley, 163, 164, 180
Skin diving, 200, 201–202, 250
Sleeping bag, 163, 179
Sloops, 2, 3, 37, 39, 127, 212
Slot effect, 37, 38
Small craft warning, 103–104, 136
Sounding lead, 24–25, 131, 158
  pole, 24–25
Soundings, 24–25, 131, 158
Spars, 1, 8, 44, 59, 90, 95, 267–268, 287, 290, 291, 293, 318

Speed, 143, 187
  estimating, 143
Splice, eye, 97, 98
  long, 96–97
  short, 95–96
  side, 97
Splicing line, 95–97, 98, 318
  wire rope, 97–98, 99
Spinnaker, 13, 38, 39, 40, 41, 42, 43, 59, 89, 90, 223, 224, 225, 292, 318
  boom, 41, 46, 64–65, 67, 68
  downhaul, 46
  guy, 47, 305
  handling, 46–47, 64–68
  pole, 41, 46, 64–65, 67, 68, 224, 290, 293, 296
  setting, 64–68
  sheet, 41
  staysail, 290
Spreaders, 44, 53, 267, 268, 270, 318
Spring fitting-out, 273–289, 305
Squall, 111, 126, 181
Square knot, 93–94
Standing rigging, 44–45, 267, 268, 270, 318
Stays, 44, 71, 288
Staysail, 13, 39, 290, 318
Steering, 35–36, 50, 139
  by compass, 139
Stepping a mast, 11–12
Steward's department, 187
Storage of sailboat, 265, 267–269, 271–273
  space, 163, 180, 192, 195
  wet, 272–273
Storm jib-sail, 23
  trysail, 23, 127
  warning signals, 103–105, 136
Storm Trysail Club, 234, 240
Stove, galley, 164, 171–172, 178, 187, 192
Sun, protection against, 170, 177
Superintendent of Documents, 103
Swimming, 179, 200, 201

Tacking, 48, 56–59, 61, 70–71, 77, 81, 86, 129, 139, 208–209, 217, 218–219, 220–223, 318
Taffrail log, 143
Telltales, 48, 50, 55, 62, 319
Tender, *see* Dinghy
Tide Table and Current Tables, 24, 79, 132, 144, 145
Tides, 50, 119, 131–133, 135, 136, 225
Tiller, 1, 3, 22, 35, 50, 55, 56, 57, 58, 61, 70, 71, 73, 74–75, 82, 84, 87, 91, 124, 125, 126, 127, 189, 280, 319
Timber hitch, 95
Time allowance, 212, 233–239

Toilet, 194–198
    care of, 196–197
    electric, 197
Topping lifts, 46, 50, 70, 288, 291, 319
Towing, 130, 176–177, 178, 296–297
Trans-Pac Race, 242
Trimming sails, 45, 61, 62, 65, 75, 82, 126, 204
Triton Class, 7, 8, 230, 239
Trysail, storm, 23, 127
Tuning the rigging, 12, 286–289
Two half-hitches, 17, 94, 95

United States
    Army Corps of Engineers, 24
    Coast and Geodetic Survey, 23–24, 78, 132, 135, 136, 138, 158
    Coast Guard, 14, 23, 25, 31, 102, 135, 150, 155, 250, 256
    Hydrographic Office, 157
    International Sailing Association, 230
    Naval Oceanographic Office, 135
    Navy, 256
    Olympic sailing team, 230
    Power Squadron flag, 255, 256
    Weather Bureau, 103, 108, 116, 117

Vanguard Class, 10
Variation, compass, 135, 137–138, 141, 319
Ventilators, 11, 15, 92, 279

Watches aboard ship, 244, 246, 261–262, 319
Water supply, 174
Wearing, 61
Weather, 26, 102–131, 181, 188, 225, 233
    forecasting, 102, 108–119

Weather (*cont.*)
    helm, 35, 74–75, 127, 319
    instruments, 114–119
    map, 102, 105–108
Weaver's knot, 94
Western Rivers rules, 210–211
Wet storage of boat, 272–273
Wheel, 22, 35–36, 50, 126, 127, 280, 319
Whipping a line, 98, 320
Whisker pole, 59, 320
Whistle, 15, 22, 129, 161, 211, 257
White Cap Class, 69
Whole gale warning, 104
Wind
    apparent, 48–50, 118
    pennant, 47, 50, 62, 288
Winter cover for boat, 271–272, 273
Winter lay-up, 265–273, 305
Wire rope, 97–98, 305
    splicing of, 47, 97–98, 99
Wood construction, 7, 8, 10
Working
    jib, 39, 40, 41, 43, 58
    sails, 13, 38, 42, 320

Yacht club burgee, 47, 55, 62, 253–254, 256, 257, 260, 310
Yacht clubs, 27–29, 30, 129, 166, 183, 185, 233, 242, 248, 251, 254, 256, 261
Yacht ensign, 252, 255, 256, 311
Yacht Racing Association of Long Island Sound, 212, 240
Yachting
    etiquette, 249–252
    routine, 252–262
Yachtsman's clothing, 262–264
Yawl, 2, 3, 4, 72, 127, 212, 255